The Craft of College Teaching

The Craft of College Teaching

A Practical Guide

Robert DiYanni and Anton Borst

Princeton University Press

PRINCETON AND OXFORD

Published by Princeton University Press
41 William Street, Princeton, New Jersey 08540
6 Oxford Street, Woodstock, Oxfordshire OX20 1TR

press.princeton.edu

Library of Congress Cataloging-in-Publication Data

Names: DiYanni, Robert, author. | Borst, Anton, author.
Title: The craft of college teaching : a practical guide / Robert DiYanni and Anton Borst.
Description: Princeton : Princeton University Press, [2020] | Includes bibliographical references and index.
Identifiers: LCCN 2019035391 (print) | LCCN 2019035392 (ebook) | ISBN 9780691183794 (hardback) | ISBN 9780691183800 (paperback) | ISBN 9780691202006 (ebook)
Subjects: LCSH: College teachers—Training of. | College teaching. | Teacher effectiveness. | Active learning.
Classification: LCC LB1738 .D59 2020 (print) | LCC LB1738 (ebook) | DDC 378.1/25—dc23
LC record available at https://lccn.loc.gov/2019035391
LC ebook record available at https://lccn.loc.gov/2019035392

British Library Cataloging-in-Publication Data is available

Editorial: Peter Dougherty and Alena Chekanov
Production Editorial: Mark Bellis
Text and Cover Design: Pamela Schnitter
Production: Brigid Ackerman
Publicity: Alyssa Sanford
Copyeditor: Cynthia Buck

This book has been composed in Verdigris MVB Pro Text and Berthold Akzidenz Grotesk

Printed on acid-free paper. ∞

Printed in the United States of America

10 9 8 7 6 5 4 3 2 1

For Debra Szybinski, whose visionary educational leadership inspires all who know her.

Contents

Illustrations

Preface

Teaching is more than a job or a career, though it certainly embraces both; it is a profession, a vocation, and a summons to the mysteries of learning. Teaching is also a craft that can be mastered over time with practice, persistence, and patience.

As a vocation, teaching involves devotion—devotion to our students, to our profession, and to the craft of teaching. Thinking of teaching in terms of vocation suggests an important relationship we have with students: the "encounter" with an "other" (each student) in a reciprocal, mutually respectful, and authentic human engagement.

We encounter our students authentically when we are receptive to them and open to their questions, their needs, and their sense of possibility. In teaching with devotion, we remain open to our students' hearts and minds, to their feelings as well as their thinking.

Successful teaching and learning result from this kind of receptivity. Being receptive opens us up to surprises about what we are able to do as teachers. It allows our students to surprise themselves as they learn, to discover something they didn't know they could do. Our job as teachers is to create the conditions in which they can make those discoveries and do those remarkable things. And if we succeed, we will become, for our students, influential teachers—like those special teachers who have had a lasting impact on us.

We wrote *The Craft of College Teaching* to become the best possible versions of our pedagogical selves. We wrote it to both discover and share what we have learned through reflecting on a half-century of classroom practice and to contribute to an ongoing conversation about what successful college teaching can be.

Our book's title, *The Craft of College Teaching*, highlights our belief that teaching can be learned, improved, even mastered. Its subtitle, *A Practical Guide*, points to teaching's practical, applied nature. Our chapter titles reflect the topics of our New York University workshops—from

"Motivating Student Learning" and "Making Learning Last" through "Teaching and Technology" and "Assessment and Grading."

The first half of the book (chapters 1–6) explores the topics expected in a book about teaching, from motivating students and teaching via lecture and discussion to using a variety of pedagogical strategies and techniques. The second half of the book (chapters 7–11) explores other aspects of teaching and learning, including experiential learning and technology, critical thinking, and writing and learning. The concluding chapter discusses the challenges of assessment and grading.

The brief "interludes" that appear between our chapters offer short takes on basic pedagogical elements and challenges—such as what to do on the first day of class and how to manage group work—as well as less familiar topics, including "Metaphors of Teaching," "Scientific Teaching," and "Embarrassment and Learning." The interludes raise questions about the theory and practice of teaching, while offering specific suggestions for effective classroom protocols.

The teaching practices we recommend are anchored in learning science research. Along with our pedagogical recommendations, we provide context and rationale for *what* to teach, *how* to teach, and *why*. What do we teach? Concepts and ideas rather than facts; frameworks and relationships between and among facts and ideas. How do we teach? Using active learning strategies that engage students through problems, cases, scenarios, and deliberate practice accompanied by constructive feedback. Why do we teach this way? Because with this approach students learn more and learn better. With this approach, their learning lasts.

Acknowledgments

We would like to thank, first, our colleague to whom we have dedicated this book, Debra Szybinski, who values good teaching and who for decades created opportunities for teachers to improve their pedagogical practice. Debra has supported, encouraged, and validated our work at the NYU teaching center and at the Faculty Resource Network, where we have explored the principles and practices we advocate in *The Craft of College Teaching*. We also wish to acknowledge another teaching center colleague, Anne Lydia Ward, with whom we have had many productive conversations about teaching and learning.

We wish to thank, next, our editor, Peter Dougherty, who signed us to write this book and who supported us wholeheartedly from start to finish. This book simply would not exist without him. Peter entrusted our book to his talented Princeton University Press colleagues, who, along with Peter, helped us brainstorm prospective titles and whose probing questions nudged us to clarify the book's key concepts and distinctive features.

Thanks to Mark Bellis, our production manager, who steered the project through its multiple phases with grace and skill.

Thanks to Cynthia Buck, our copyeditor, who saved us from any number of mistakes that we ourselves overlooked.

Thanks to David Campbell and Chris Lapinski for their respective domains of expertise in providing engaging copy text and coordinating the book's design. Thanks to Pamela Schnitter for creating an attractive text and cover design.

Thanks to Barbara Tonetti and Julie Haenisch for their guidance in bringing the book to the attention of prospective readers, reviewers, and course adopters. We have been fortunate indeed in having this first-class team behind our book.

At each stage of our work, we benefited from the comments and suggestions of colleagues. Foremost among these were those of Robert Lapiner, who read the entire manuscript and offered ideas for improvement both local and global. Another NYU colleague, Marla Wolf, offered astute comments and suggestions on an intermediate draft of the book. And a third, Trace Jordan, has offered us the gift of his professional expertise and interest in improving college and university teaching. We thank Trace, too, for leading us to our interlude on scientific teaching.

We received advice from colleagues beyond our immediate NYU environment. We thank each of the following for their careful reading and thoughtful response to portions of our manuscript at various stages of its development: Todd Cherches, William Costanzo, Joan DelFattore, Michael Hogan, Virginia Maurer, Ethan Miller, Joseph M. Pastore Jr., Adelia Williams, and Eric Wimmers.

And we wish to thank, finally, the professional educators who reviewed our manuscript and made helpful suggestions for its improvement, many of which we incorporated into this published version.

The Craft
of College
Teaching

Introduction

It is no secret that higher education in the United States is, if not in a state of crisis, certainly experiencing serious and wide-ranging challenges. Aside from escalating costs, one major challenge is the uneven quality of undergraduate classroom instruction, which impedes and limits student learning. A second, related challenge is the inadequate attention being paid to the craft of teaching by faculty hired and promoted for their research, grants, and publications. In some cases lack of support for teaching is a function of college and university culture; in others it results from insufficient resources directed toward the university's teaching mission.

The nature and quality of a student's experience in higher education has a dramatic impact on his or her future—and not just future earnings and job opportunities. Students' potential for personal and professional growth, development, and happiness are also affected. We work from the premise that higher education—higher learning—can alter students' perception of themselves, and especially their perception of their talents and capabilities. Quality education, grounded in effective teaching and resulting in productive, transformative learning, is the ultimate life-changer. We wrote *The Craft of College Teaching* to provide guidance for instructors looking for ways to improve their students' ability not only to achieve academic success, but also to engage in meaningful, authentic, long-lasting learning.

A number of recent and important books have noted the serious challenges faced today by higher education in the United States. In *The Struggle to Reform Our Colleges* (2017), Derek Bok poses key questions about the quality of higher education with respect to pedagogical concerns, asking "how responsive is the curriculum to the evolving needs of students and society" and "how effective are the methods instructors use to help their students learn" (p. 21). Bok questions the extent to which students are acquiring useful kinds of knowledge and mastering the skills necessary for success in subsequent learning, especially for professional study and work (p. 28). Some of his recommendations for improving student learning, such as aligning learning goals with curriculum and assignments (p. 37) and adopting active learning instructional methods (p. 39), are among those we take up in some detail.

Steven Brint echoes Bok's concerns and adds others in *Two Cheers for Higher Education* (2018), where he identifies a number of problems that hinder student learning. These include students' declining commitment to study along with a consumerist mentality driven by the high cost of higher education and the demands of the marketplace (pp. 289, 303). Brint highlights three pathologies of learning that interfere with student learning, when they don't inhibit it outright: amnesia, fantasia, and inertia (p. 305). His prescription for curing these ailments are those we advocate: providing motivation for student learning, teaching for deep understanding, and requiring students to apply their knowledge in presentations, performances, and the creation of written products (p. 306). Bok and Brint both advocate for an increased emphasis on learning science and on the "scholarship of teaching." This term was coined by Ernest Boyer in his influential *Scholarship Reconsidered* (1990), in which he includes teaching as one of four domains of scholarship—the others being discovery, integration, and application. Boyer argues that higher education administration and faculty need to move beyond the "tired old teaching versus research debate and define, in more creative ways, what it means to be a scholar" (Boyer, p. xii, quoted in Brint, p. 298).

One way of thinking about the relationship between scholarship and teaching is to look at teaching as a form of scholarship—or "scholarship in action," as Ann E. Berthoff (1981) has suggested (p. 115). The integration of scholarship and teaching is echoed in another Carnegie Foundation publication, "Stewards of the Discipline," in which Chris Golde and George Walker suggest that academic disciplines require stewardship, which is accomplished when scholars apply the new knowledge they generate and conserve through their writing and their teaching (Levenson 2018, p. 52).

Leon Botstein (2018), in a recent issue of *Liberal Education*, argues that "the dichotomy between research and teaching is false." Botstein suggests that new discipline-specialist scholars need training to enable them to connect with their students. We suggest that the kind of training needed is a grounding in pedagogy, part of which comes from research in learning science, part of which derives from reflection on classroom teaching practices, and part of which emerges from sustained discussion of pedagogy with teaching colleagues.

As Derek Bok (2017) points out, the problems associated with student learning are compounded by the challenges of providing all students with opportunities to enroll regardless of their race and income (p. 20). A related challenge is to match students with the higher education institution that best enables them to fulfill their academic and general human potential. Former longtime NYU president John Sexton (2019) notes that students from the bottom economic quartile who do attend college tend to be "undermatched" (p. 138)—that is, they enroll in schools with less advanced and demanding programs than these students can handle and benefit from. Another problem is that faculty instructors, full- and part-time, tenured and nontenured, do not receive the help they need to teach effectively the diverse student populations they meet in their classrooms.

We aim to extend and apply the significant research about teaching practices that leads to deeper and more enduring student learning. The best of this research has been captured in a dozen recent and recently revised books; though valuable resources, these books go only part of the way toward providing college instructors, especially those lacking experience, with what they need to become effective teachers. Our book complements and supplements these resources, especially the briefer ones. A number of these books cover every imaginable teaching topic, making them useful as encyclopedic references but less than ideal as an introduction to the essentials of college teaching. Drawing on the best learning science research, we offer a compact, readable, user-friendly book that provides instructors with a basic practical guide to teaching and learning across the spectrum of challenges that teachers and students confront together in the classroom.

As Maryellen Weimer (1999) pointed out more than twenty years ago, research "debunks the myth that nobody knows what makes teaching effective" (p. 7). We have drawn on both earlier research that Weimer cites and on more recent research in learning science. Like Weimer, we believe that some teaching practices yield more effective student learning than others. We also concur with Weimer that beyond particular pedagogical strategies and teaching techniques, we can improve our teaching by demonstrating knowledge and love of our subject, sharing an enthusiasm for teaching and learning, and carefully preparing and organizing our classes and courses (p. 7). These general qualities are necessary, but not sufficient; we also need to develop an ability to stimulate our students' curiosity, to provoke their thinking, and to explain ideas and concepts clearly and effectively. We address these and other related pedagogical challenges throughout this book.

For *The Craft of College Teaching* to be of real use and value to instructors, however, it needs to speak to the needs of the students who populate their courses. Just who are the students attending college and university programs today? Many of them are first-generation higher education attendees. Some are veterans, and many have jobs and support families. We now see among our students more of those with disabilities and mental health challenges, more LGBTQ students, more women, more Latinx students, and more students for whom English is not their native language. They include commuters, transfers, and international students. The new normal in college and university classrooms is now a wide range of students representing a broad and diverse population.

We are long past the time when students made up a homogeneous group of any kind in our classrooms. A significant challenge for teachers, therefore, is maximizing the benefits of a diverse student population while addressing their pedagogical needs. The first thing to note is that diversity as a concept is itself diverse. We need to think about the diversity of diversity—the many ways in which our students differ among themselves in gender, race, and ethnicity; in their social and cultural backgrounds; in their academic experience and preparation; and in the ways in which their varied prior learning experiences accentuate these and other differences when they enter our classrooms.

These kinds of diversity suggest that we need to know our students—to learn who they are and how they learn—so that we can motivate them and use productive teaching strategies with them. We need to figure out how to welcome their range of differences and create a space where diverse perspectives, ideas, and values can be accommodated and validated.

This openness speaks to a fundamental principle of teaching: the importance of creating an environment in which all students feel included and are confident in presenting their ideas and conveying their feelings, and in which all voices can be heard.

To accommodate this diverse array of students we need to do a number of things. We need to provide special support for non-native speakers and include course materials that reflect the diversity of students' linguistic and cultural backgrounds. We need to introduce forms of community engagement, including service learning. We need to lecture less and use techniques of active, engaged learning more. We need to get to know students' needs and concerns and to establish clear classroom policies that support student learning. And we need to carefully model and explain what quality academic work looks like and how to produce it.

We can use case studies and other kinds of scenarios to generate discussion. We can have small-group discussions and then come together as an entire class to hear what was said in the small groups. We can use theater to engage students with issues of diversity. We can provide faculty colleagues with coaching and guidance in facilitating discussions of diversity. We can include and reference research on diversity and include a statement about diversity on the syllabus. We have to think seriously and practically, individually and collaboratively, about how to meet our students where they are and how to help them achieve the academic success of which, with our help, they are capable.

In a book about reading literature with autistic individuals, *See It Feelingly*, Ralph James Savarese explains how and why providing an enabling environment, with support, accommodation, and routine, increases students' chances for academic success. Savarese urges those who work with students on the broad spectrum of autism to understand that autistic individuals are heterogenous, just like other learners. And as with other kinds of challenges teaching presents for our students' learning, we need to see difference and not dysfunction in their academic abilities (p. 94).

The Craft of College Teaching was developed from the workshops we conduct at New York University for full- and part-time faculty and for graduate students and postdocs on a wide range of classroom teaching practices. We offer these workshops a dozen times a year and attract participants from the university's eleven schools and three institutes. One of the special features of our workshops is that instructors and graduate students from liberal arts disciplines join those from business and engineering, nursing and dentistry, social work and social policy, education, the performing arts, and professional studies in exploring pedagogical challenges they face, whatever the level of their students or the size of their classes.

Our workshops are interactive and inquiry-based. They require reflection and writing. And they alternate small-group conversations with large-group, full-room discussion. Our role as facilitators of these pedagogical inquiries has enabled us to listen and learn from experienced colleagues as they share their teaching practices, as well as to provide suggestions from our own combined sixty-plus years of teaching across a dozen secondary and higher education institutions.

We typically begin our two-hour workshop sessions with a fundamental question that pertains to that day's topic. For example, for our workshop on syllabus and course design we ask: "What is a syllabus?" "What is your concept of a syllabus; how do you conceive of it?" "What does a syllabus do?" These questions provoke thoughtful reflection among participants, which they then share briefly with one or two others. During the full-room discussion (usually of thirty or more participants) that follows these small-group conversations, we explore the ramifications and implications of the various syllabus metaphors that participants give us. You will find some of the fruits of that discussion in chapter 2, "Course, Syllabus, and Lesson Design," and in interlude 2, "Metaphors of Teaching." Our goal in generating discussion with fundamental questions about pedagogy is to make instructors more deliberate about their teaching concepts, principles, and practices. We then provide suggestions for how they might modify their practice to improve their students' learning.

The learning science research that underlies our suggestions for improving undergraduate teaching in this book represents the conjunction of theory and practice—practice grounded in theory and theory tested in classroom practice. Splitting theory from practice results in a dysfunctional pitting of academic theorists against clinical practitioners, to the benefit of neither and the detriment of both. By finding its fulfillment in the art of teaching practice, learning theory can enable a fruitful dialectic between art and science, with teaching the testing ground of theory.

At many colleges and universities nationwide and beyond, centers for teaching and learning perform the service of bridging theory and practice. We have benefited from meeting colleagues from a number of these centers, and from perusing the useful resources and advice they provide online. Among those we find ourselves revisiting are those associated with Assumption College, Brown University, Columbia University, Harvard University, Princeton University, Purdue University, Stanford University, the University of Kansas, the University of Michigan, Washington State University, Washington University in St. Louis, and a number of others. These and other teaching and learning centers are at the forefront in providing support for new and experienced faculty across a wide range of pedagogical challenges that instructors confront in their classrooms and in their professional lives more generally every day. The trick is making academic departments aware of their services and then getting instructors to use them.

The pedagogy we advocate derives from our work during the past six years at the New York University Center for the Advancement of

Teaching. Our pedagogy derives, as well, from our epistemology. As Berthoff (1981) suggests, "Pedagogy always echoes epistemology: the way we teach reflects the conception we have of what knowledge is and does," how knowledge is acquired and deepened, and "how we think about thinking" (p. 11). The pedagogy we present in *The Craft of College Teaching* reflects a view of teaching as an organic rather than a mechanical activity, a point that we regularly highlight and advocate in our teaching workshops.

Our teaching recommendations arise from our understanding of how learning actually occurs in the classroom and out. The practices we encourage reflect our beliefs about what education is for. They also testify to our conviction that true learning arises from intrinsic motivation; that it is animated by desire and fostered by active engagement; that it is best nurtured in community, in collaboration with others; and finally, that if it is to matter, learning must become for students a long-lasting habit.

We hope that you find our reflections and recommendations regarding the art and science of teaching and learning of use and value. We know from long experience that teaching and learning are inextricably intertwined, and that successful teaching and learning require sustained, deliberate effort over the course of a lifelong career. They require, as Henry David Thoreau once wrote about the skill of reading well, "a training such as the athletes underwent, the steady intention almost of the whole life" (Thoreau 1854/1989, p. 403).

Chapter One

Motivating Student Learning

Motivation is critical for all learning. Without a real need or desire to learn something, whether acquiring information or developing a skill, learning does not last—if it takes place at all. Motiveless learning is shallow learning and does not take root as enduring knowledge in our students' minds.

As teachers, we assume that all students will be interested in what we have to teach. To us, the appeal and value of our subject may be self-evident, but this is not the case for every student we teach, especially those new to our field. There are ways, however, we can bolster our students' motivation to learn and help them succeed in our classrooms and beyond.

What Motivates Learning?

Before we consider how to motivate students to learn, we need to ask ourselves what motivates our own learning. What motivates us to take on tasks and put forth effort, to set and pursue learning goals, to do the work and make the commitment to learn?

One answer, in part, is rewards—external rewards. Perhaps money—such as the attraction of a job that pays well—is a motivating force. Perhaps it is status and prestige, which also come with particular kinds of employment. Perhaps we are motivated by a desire to compete with others not only for money or prestige but for recognition, acknowledgment, fame. Such extrinsic rewards are undeniably powerful, but they are not all that motivates us. Extrinsic motivators might very well matter less to us, in fact, than internal, intrinsic forms of motivation.

We are motivated intrinsically when we do something for its own sake; intrinsic motivation is self-generated and self-sustained. We might be motivated to learn (and to practice) guitar, piano, or drums less to achieve fame and glory, less to impress others, than for our own sense of accomplishment, for our own satisfaction and enjoyment.

Extrinsic and intrinsic motivation each have their place in learning. Extrinsic motivation may provide an initial incentive for learning, but research has shown that intrinsic motivation anchors learning more securely and sustains it longer. When difficulties emerge in the process of learning, extrinsic motivational factors are more easily swept aside than intrinsic ones. Providing external rewards as a way to motivate better performance has been shown to be ineffective (Kohn 2018). Student learning sinks in deeper and lasts longer when the motivation for learning comes from within (Lang 2016; Pink 2011).

Studies have shown that the primary motivator for people to continue working at a job is not, as we might expect, money. Instead, it is autonomy: having latitude to make decisions about our work, especially about how we do it. The freedom we generally seek in the workplace is a freedom within limits, a latitude within boundaries. We don't expect that we'll be able to do anything we want at work. Our superiors decide what needs to be done. However, we tend to accept more readily being told by superiors what we need to accomplish when we have some say in how we will accomplish those things. "Tell me what to do," we might say, "but let me decide how to do it."

Along with autonomy, another major motivating influence is mastery—the opportunity to get better at what we do—to improve, make progress, and develop our skills and talents. We are motivated to work hard and to work well when we can see ourselves getting better; making such progress motivates us.

Both autonomy and mastery are self-directed goals: they come from within, and are each their own reward. These intrinsic rewards can also be used to motivate students. It is important for us, then, to find ways to provide our students with occasions to exercise autonomy in their learning and to create opportunities for them to develop and recognize their mastery.

Autonomy and mastery contribute to the pleasures associated with learning, with having choices and experiencing improvement while learning. In the best of situations, our students, too, can learn for the pleasures learning brings, pleasures that derive from learning's intrinsic rewards. We can create conditions for students to experience these pleasures and rewards by giving them latitude in their assignments and projects. Allowing them to choose their own topics for papers, presentations, experiments, and reports is one way to do this. Another is to provide regular coaching feedback that recognizes their progress in achieving the learning goals we set for them (or they set for themselves).

A third form of intrinsic motivation is having a meaning or purpose for what we do. Meaning is essential for intensifying and strengthening motivation. The young entrepreneurs described in Tony Wagner's *Creating Innovators* (2012) cite this kind of motivation as personally fulfilling and as a driving force in their work. We seek work that we believe is important, work that makes a difference, work that matters to us. In addition, the kind of meaning that matters most may have some significant value beyond ourselves, such as doing something for others.

In reviewing research into motivation that induces people to work hard, Daniel Pink explores these three motivating factors—autonomy, mastery, and meaning—in his book *Drive* (2011). Pink finds that the expected motivators—money and fame, for example—are far less important to most people most of the time than autonomy, mastery, and meaning. These three motivational forces work together. Give us a project and turn us loose to figure out how to accomplish it our way, and we are ready to work. Allow us to grow and develop our skills and talents in the process, and we deepen our commitment to the work. Help us also to see the work's value, purpose, and meaning for ourselves and how it can serve and help others, and we commit ourselves to it completely.

Wagner presents a set of three motivating factors analogous to Pink's. Wagner wanted to understand what drives innovators, what motivates them to create new businesses and new products and to work extraordinarily hard at making those products and businesses successful. Like Pink, Wagner discovers that though money is important, it is not the dominant or motivating force. He learns from the innovators he interviewed that they are motivated by passion, play, and purpose.

These innovators love what they are doing. It matters to them as much as anything in their lives; hence they are passionate about it. Second, the young innovators see the challenges they confront in developing their businesses as opportunities, and they have fun engaging with those challenges. They see their work overall as play, and thus revel in exploring ideas and experimenting with different approaches to solving problems. And last, like the people Pink interviewed, Wagner's innovators have a sense of purpose in what they are trying to do. It is work that, though it benefits them, also benefits others—an equal if not more important motivating factor for most of them.

Autonomy, mastery, meaning; passion, play, and purpose. How might we use these powerful forms of motivation in our teaching and for our students' learning?

How can we make these motivators relevant as we design our courses and lessons, activities and projects, quizzes and exams? How can we help our students experience these intrinsic aspects of learning? These are essential questions for all teachers.

Though precisely how we choose to marshal intrinsic motivation will vary according to who we are teaching, what we are teaching, and at what level, a number of strategies can be applied across the board. From the research and from our own work with faculty and students, we have distilled eight approaches to motivating student learning:

- Demonstrating care
- Providing feedback
- Identifying purpose
- Emphasizing possibilities and progress
- Using emotion
- Employing active learning
- Arousing curiosity
- Embracing uncertainty and failure

Demonstrating Care

Students crave attention, and they appreciate it when we give them our full attention. One way to begin the process of demonstrating care is to learn their names as early as possible. Let them know that you care about them enough to know their names, first and last, and something more about them that they might care to reveal. Learning the names of students can be a challenge, especially in diverse classrooms where students' names reflect a variety of cultures, ethnicities, and countries of origin. You can ask students to pronounce their names, and you can invite them to correct you when you mispronounce them. You can also respect their diversity by asking them not only how they prefer to be addressed—by a nickname, for example—but also giving them the opportunity, if they wish, to share which pronouns should be used to refer to them.

In laying out your course goals for them, let your students know that it's not just learning that matters in the course, but *their* learning, the learning of each one of them individually. Make sure they understand that the goal is not just writing improvement, acquisition of lab skills, or exercise in critical thinking in general that you value, but *their* writing, *their* lab skills, *their* critical thinking—the writing, lab, and thinking skills of each student. Be clear that you will attend to and assist with the progress of each toward their individual learning objectives as well as to the learning goals for the class as a whole.

We can demonstrate this care and build this trust by showing our students that we want them to succeed for the same reasons they want to succeed. Some of these reasons will be extrinsic motivations—grades, for example, to help them gain admission to graduate school, or professional skills that will increase their likelihood of success in the workplace. These are reasonable and realistic motivations that will increase student effort. But we also want them to take their learning beyond successful completion of a course, beyond passing or even acing exams. We want their learning to last, to have an impact on their self-development and understanding of the world, to shape their sense of who they are.

We can also show our students that we want to see them making progress toward acquiring knowledge and mastering skills. We can do this by carefully scaffolding assignments and providing them with regular, targeted feedback. Sometimes such support will require nudging and encouragement on our part. Sometimes it will require that we be cheerleaders rather than critics of their work. And other times we will need to offer constructive criticism, letting them know just where they are falling short and what they can do to improve.

Our greatest aspiration as teachers is to see our students experiencing the intrinsic value of learning and its associated pleasures, an experience that leads to the most enduring, most deeply rooted learning (Lang 2016; Kohn 2018). And so we need to show our students that we care about this deeper learning for them, that we care about their intellectual development beyond their grades and beyond our courses. We need to persuade them through our pedagogical practices that the learning they experience in our classroom matters for the long haul and in the long run—that it matters for their lives and not just for their grades.

In doing this, we are demonstrating how our own work with them is meaningful for us. And if we (and they) are lucky, they will come to see their learning as purposeful and meaningful.

Providing Feedback

Students want to know how they are performing—what's working and what's not in their learning. They want to know where they stand—how they are doing with respect to their classmates and with respect to a standard against which they are being measured. Timely and specific feedback—both positive and critical—motivates students. Positive feedback encourages them; critical feedback, when clear and constructive, shows them what to improve and how.

Some types of positive feedback are more useful and effective than others. The research of Carol Dweck (2007) has shown that students work harder, learn better, persist through difficulties, and more, when they are not praised for how intelligent or gifted they are, but for how hard they work at their assignments and how persistent they are in meeting challenges. Analogously, Peter Johnston in *Opening Minds* (2012) suggests that we provide process-oriented feedback rather than person-oriented feedback. He advises praising the work rather than the student. Instead of saying, "You are good at this," say, "You tried hard," or "You found an interesting and useful solution."

Johnston suggests that we praise students primarily for how they figure things out—for the strategies they use in approaching assignments. Praising strategies, even more than praising effort, benefits students because it provides them with specific ways of working that they can use again on another assignment or project (see chapter 11).

Identifying Purpose

The value of work is rooted in purpose, which often derives from interest. We can establish the value of what our students are learning by finding ways to link course topics and materials to students' interests. This requires much more than finding out what music our students enjoy, what social media they use, or what they do in their spare time. To make a deeper kind of connection we must get a sense of what matters most to students, finding out what they truly care about and understanding their hopes and ambitions, along with their struggles and challenges. Knowing at least a few things about their contemporary frames of reference is useful of course, and applying academic rigor to pop culture topics can indeed spark student engagement. But we need to go deeper with them and find the fundamental links between learning and life, no matter the subject.

To that end we need to clarify the purpose of the work we ask students to do, and especially to find ways to align that coursework with what students value, what matters to them. Having a clear purpose helps persuade your students of the value you place on assignments, exercises, and exams, as well as on the class activities you devise for them. Explain why you are doing what you are doing in the course—both on your syllabus and on individual assignments. Take opportunities to explain the purpose of exercises, assignments, activities, group work—all the things you do—repeatedly. Write up these purposes on the board and in a blog both at the beginning and end of the course and at the beginning and end of each class. Keep before your students your large-scale goals for them and your more immediate learning objectives. You cannot remind them too often of what matters in your course.

One way to establish such connections is to give students authentic assignments that have real-world applications or that serve a public purpose. You can have them write a letter to a local newspaper, create a website to share their research online, present a proposal for improving a job, or design a strategy for cleaning a nearby river—whatever is relevant to your course and its learning goals. Even if the project's impact is hypothetical (for example, the waterway cleanup plan will not actually be taken up by the city authorities), students will understand the relevance of what they're learning to their community and for themselves.

As teachers, we can also identify what we ourselves value in our teaching and in our students' learning—and explain why. Not only the skills, concepts, dispositions, and outlooks essential for a particular course or discipline, but the means we use to teach these things—discussion, group work, lab activities—why are we adopting these concepts and methods as opposed to others? How do our methods extend and deepen students' learning? We should be clear about priorities, about what's more and less important, and why. These concerns are especially important for students from educationally and culturally diverse backgrounds and experiences.

Lastly, we can also reveal our own passion and enthusiasm for our subject, discipline, or profession. Why did we decide to pursue this field in the first place? What compelled us? What sparked our imagination? Teaching gives us the opportunity to become reacquainted with our own sources of inspiration. We should find ways to share this inspiration with our students, both in our classes and in our individual encounters with them. Our goal, as always, should be authentic engagement.

Emphasizing Possibility and Progress

A sense of possibility and progress is essential for student motivation, particularly for more vulnerable students, for the less confident, and for the less academically prepared. As with anything, if the work isn't purposeful or success seems impossible, what's the point?

Our assignments therefore need to be at an appropriate level of difficulty. Students should be challenged, but not overwhelmed; they should be able to succeed, but not without some struggle. We need to create problems and projects within a "Goldilocks zone" of desirable difficulty—at a level of challenge or demand that's not too hard, not too easy, but just right. Research continues to show that students who struggle appropriately with comprehending and applying newly learned concepts remember them much longer and understand them more deeply than students who are not so challenged (Ambrose, Bridges, and DiPietro 2010; Brown, Roediger, and McDaniel 2014). If the challenge level is too high, however, students give up. We need also to offer support and encouragement (and intervention) as students struggle with the academic and intellectual challenges we present them with.

Susan Ambrose and her coauthors recommend supporting students by providing them with effective study strategies. Not all students know how to study effectively. Many of them believe, falsely and counterproductively, that highlighting textbook and journal article material, and then rereading it, adequately prepares them for course exams. Recent research, however, shows that it is far better to try to recall, or retrieve, the key points of a textbook chapter than simply rereading it in whole or in part. Searching the memory engages students' brains and their thinking powers far more effectively than simple review—even if what they retrieve is incorrect—as long as they are corrected or check themselves against their notes or textbook afterwards (Brown, Roediger, and McDaniel 2014). Providing students with study strategies that work and with assignments that yield clear learning benefits sends the message that they can be successful learners (see chapter 4).

Our students do not all start from the same place; it's never an even playing field for them. And though we have particular standards and markers for student achievement, it is extremely helpful and valuable for students to see their learning and skill development even when—especially when—they are not yet meeting our benchmark standards. Evaluating students' progress is critical for keeping them motivated. It helps them see where they are and where they need to go, and it provides them with some assurance that they are indeed learning, even though important milestones remain. Helping students set realistic targets and benchmarks to measure their progress reinforces other forms of motivation.

There's no better validation of effort than success. Too often the first opportunity for students to see their progress is the midterm exam. We should find opportunities early in the semester for our students to experience success, however modest it may be. And when they submit reports, papers, essays, projects, presentations, problem sets, and prototypes throughout the semester, we should provide feedback that includes affirmation as well as constructive criticism, in a timely and helpful manner.

Using Emotion

Emotion can be a powerful force for learning. Engaging students on an emotional level, while not something to do all the time, reminds them that education need not be merely an "academic" experience. Our students' learning involves them as complete human beings who have feelings as well as thoughts, emotions as well as ideas. Tapping into emotion sends a message that in our teaching we intend to reach our students as full human beings, not just as machines for absorbing information. It also shows that we are interested in their learning more than facts and figures, concepts and connections. Bringing emotion into the learning process makes learning a more complete human experience. It makes the educational experience real for both students and teachers.

Whether we intend it or not, our classrooms will have an emotional atmosphere, which is mostly under our control. What kind of environment will we create? And how will we create that emotional atmosphere? Group work of various kinds, for instance, can help us create a productive and positive emotional classroom environment (see interlude 5).

Inviting emotional responses in the classroom, of course, can create problems. Depending on the degree of emotional engagement we solicit, and depending on the inherently emotional nature of highly charged topics we might be discussing with students, we may find it challenging to manage students' responses, and perhaps our own as well. If we can negotiate the challenges, however, students will value their learning not only as an intellectual accomplishment but also as an emotional experience.

Employing Active Learning

Many of the previously identified strategies for motivating students can be applied through active learning techniques. Active learning teaching strategies motivate students by engaging them in doing rather than simply in listening and absorbing information. They require students to respond, to engage, to think. Since these techniques are discussed more fully in chapter 3, we will only touch on a few elements of active learning here.

One way you can implement active learning is to provide your students with opportunities to make connections and predictions based on the lectures, discussions, readings, and problems. You can require them to describe these connections and express their predictions both orally and in writing, however briefly. This gives them a chance to check their own understanding, and it gives you a chance to see what they understand—and what they don't or, more likely, what they only partly understand. This feedback enables you to adjust and calibrate your teaching preparation to address students' difficulties.

Equally important is to give your students time to apply the skills you are teaching. Try to make time for in-class practice. If you are teaching analysis of texts—in a humanities or social science course, for example—have students do some textual analysis in class. They can annotate a passage, paraphrase or summarize it, ask questions about it, consider its implications, connect it with other passages, predict what might come after it, and the like. Students need to express what they notice—to show you in writing what they take from a text and what they make of it. You can identify the strengths and weaknesses of their developing analytical skills, regardless of what they are analyzing.

Have students practice mindfully—and deliberately. Have them reflect on their practice. Explain what's working and not working in their small-scale, low-stakes attempts. Your classroom is the place for them to make mistakes, to stretch themselves analytically, not to remain safe in the confines of their comfort zone, doing only what they already know how to do. Some of this practice, of course, will need to take place outside of class as well. And that practice, too, should be evaluated—even if your evaluation of that work remains relatively low-stakes.

Self-explaining is an active learning technique that requires students to explain not only *what* they are doing, but also *how* they are doing it, and *why*. Self-explaining reinforces their understanding of concepts, frameworks, and processes. As a form of metacognitive practice, self-explaining enables students to better understand how to think, how to approach problems, and how to work through texts so that when they are on their own—without your help or that of a classmate—they can function competently and confidently in doing their academic work.

We can reduce our advice on active learning to three suggestions: (1) require *explanations* of both principles and processes; (2) prompt students to explain the *what*, the *how*, and the *why* of what they are doing; and (3) call for the *application* of concepts and principles. In short, require students to be intentional about what they are doing; require, too, that they put their understanding of theories into *practice*.

Arousing Curiosity

Among the most important strategies for motivating student learning is stimulating their curiosity. Children are innately curious; their curiosity spurs their continued learning. For adults, curiosity continues to spark personal and professional growth. In extending the boundaries of our curiosity, we expand the parameters of our knowledge and broaden our realm of experience.

Curiosity is essential for developing a beautiful mind. It is also essential for innovation and progress because it fosters open-mindedness and provokes creative thinking. But curiosity isn't valuable only for its results. It also possesses intrinsic value, fulfilling us, enlivening us, and making us more interesting to ourselves and to others. Students remain curious throughout their educational careers, and if they don't retain the completely curious natures they possessed as children, they do remain curious about the things that matter to them personally.

One approach is to look for ways to invite students to speculate, to engage in imaginative thinking. We can spark their curiosity with activities, exercises, and assignments that ask "what if?" and "why not?" and "how else?" Curiosity begins with questions like these—open-ended questions that lead to other questions. It is the right questions more than the right answers that stimulate successful critical and creative thinking. We need to avoid questions for which an instructor has a single right answer in mind. As Leon Botstein (2018), president of Bard College, suggests, we can use the counterintuitive and the obscure to generate our students' curiosity, which drives their learning.

Here are a few ways to stimulate your students' curiosity:

- Begin class with a scenario, situation, case, or problem that the class can speculate about individually and discuss in pairs or small groups.
- Show students an image and invite them to speculate about it.
- Start with a story or puzzle or question that will engage them. Ask them to make predictions about it.
- Explain a scenario that allows for different perspectives and interpretations.
- Present them with a case and ask them individually and in groups to address the challenges it presents.

In *Small Teaching* (2016), James Lang, director of Assumption College's teaching and learning center and a regular contributor to the *Chronicle of Higher Education*, advises having students make predictions about cases and scenarios. He also suggests having students make predictions about what they think will be discussed in a subsequent class (p. 60). Predictions, Lang notes, make us curious. We want to know whether our predictions are accurate. Inviting students to predict also increases their attention.

Curiosity and attention work together to intensify student engagement, the kind of engagement necessary for active and long-lasting learning.

We can take advantage of the pleasures of curiosity, including its association with wonder and surprise. In *A Curious Mind* (2016), Brian Grazer suggests that we make curiosity a routine, a discipline, and a habit, and that we do so largely through asking productive questions. He advocates questions because questions create space for ideas, suggest a willingness to listen, and invite stories. Questions develop independence and self-confidence, and they serve as a tool for discovery.

Effective thinking, both critical and creative thinking, involves asking questions. The kinds of questions we ask are important, as are the ways in which our initial questions lead to others. Good questions direct our thinking, encourage exploration, and open our minds to varied possibilities. Productive questioning enlivens curiosity, provokes thinking, and excites the imagination.

Asking our students stimulating, open-ended questions is one way to arouse curiosity. However, we also want our students to develop the ability to ask their own questions—a skill and, at best, a habit that will help them learn throughout their lives. In *Developing More Curious Minds* (2003), John Barell offers a set of questions that can help students form their own. He uses the abbreviation KWHLAQ.

These are Barell's questions:

- What do we *Know* or think we know?
- What do we *Want* to know or find out?
- *How* are we going to get that information or knowledge?
- What have we *Learned* from our efforts?
- How can we *Apply* what we have learned?
- What additional *Questions* do we have? (pp. 137–38)

Notice how this set of questions ends with a question that leads to further questions. Questioning, like learning, and like thinking, never ends.

Embracing Uncertainty and Failure

One of the great virtues of uncertainty is that it stimulates discussion. Certainty, on the other hand, forecloses dialogue. When answers are known, nothing remains to be discussed. Letting students in on what's unknown, what's unclear or not entirely settled in your discipline, can motivate them to become part of the conversation and active contributors to the search for knowledge. We can do this in part by acknowledging our own uncertainty, by making clear to our students that we don't know everything ourselves. And though uncertainty will certainly be unsettling for some students (and teachers), we think that both teachers and students need to become comfortable with it. Uncertainty provides a foundation for research, a basis of inquiry, and a spur to investigation and discovery.

In *Failure* (2015), Stuart Firestein, a neurobiologist researcher and a professor at Columbia University, develops these ideas with specific application to science and scientific research. He suggests that in teaching any scientific concept or discovery, we can motivate students by telling the story of how it came about, including the blind alleys, false leads, errors, and misconceptions that had to be overcome along the way. He advocates telling the stories of how scientific puzzles originated, how they were modified, and how they were eventually solved—often through addressing new puzzles that arose in the process of solving the original puzzle.

Here are some of Firestein's suggestions for using failure and uncertainty to motivate student research, discovery, and learning:

- Get rid of coverage; go deep rather than wide.
- Provide context and story.
- Focus on the pleasures of intellectual activity.
- Teach failed ideas and their history and what was learned from them.

Firestein adds what we might call a set of principles for scientific learning in particular. They form a framework for understanding not just how science works, but how learning occurs across academic disciplines. Questions are more important than facts. Answers are temporary. Data, models, and hypotheses are provisional. Failure happens a lot. Patience is essential, a necessary requirement. Science and discovery stumble along, without a smooth arc of discovery.

Although errors can be annoying, disconcerting, even painful, they can also be amusing, serendipitous, and productive. Errors and mistakes are something we can smile about and laugh at en route to seeing and accepting ourselves as fallible beings.

What are the implications for the classroom? How can we harness uncertainty, ignorance, error, and failure as pedagogical motivators? One thing we can do is to explain to students how errors can lead to discoveries that would not have been made without them. We can share stories about scientific discoveries that resulted from accident and error, such as the discovery of penicillin and the invention of Post-it notes. We can tell students about our own failures and errors, and how they led us to accomplish something productive from them. We can even design experiments and assignments with no directions and no clear-cut answers so that students become accustomed to dealing with uncertainty and its cousins, ambiguity and complexity. Our course lectures and readings can include activities and assignments, projects and assessments, that allow for multiple approaches, alternative explanations, various solutions—highlighting, privileging, and otherwise encouraging students to engage regularly and consistently with pedagogical challenges that are rich with uncertainty.

Applications

1. For one of your courses—past, present, or future—what extrinsic and intrinsic learning rewards might you present to students?
2. How do you plan to establish the value of what students will learn in your course?
3. How might you create positive expectations about learning among your students?
4. What strategies do you plan to use to motivate your students to learn?
5. How might you use curiosity, uncertainty, and failure to motivate students?
6. Use the KWHLAQ questions to think about one of the following: a painting, photograph, sculpture, or work of architecture; a poem, short story, novel, play, or movie; a scientific or mathematical formula or discovery; a historical figure or event; a religious or philosophical question or problem; a musical, dance, or theatrical work; a print advertisement or television commercial; a television show of any genre; or a political, social, or economic idea or theory.

First Impressions and the First Day of Class

The first day of class is one of the most important of the entire term. On this day you gain a first impression of your students, and they get their first impression of you as a teacher. What image of yourself do you want to present? How will you create and convey that image?

If you are new to teaching, you very likely have not thought much about your teaching persona. If you have been teaching for a while, you have been adapting your persona to the different kinds of courses and students you teach and the different environments in which you teach them. Either way, it's important to develop a teaching persona that feels right, one that's comfortable and suits your personality.

A Teaching Persona

Early in my career, I (RD) began evolving a particular teaching persona that was both a way of presenting myself to my students and a way of envisioning myself as a teacher in relationship to my students and my subject. What, I wondered, did I want my relationship to be with them? At the beginning, of course, I didn't know. Being my students' friend was not an option; I was too close to them in age, and friendship would undermine my tenuous authority. Being a distant, disembodied voice would not work either, for I was a living, breathing, even joking presence before them. Initially, without realizing what I was doing, I became for them an example of the curious, inquiring mind. I served them as a mentor and model, a guide to the intellectual life. I taught them to analyze and synthesize, to question and challenge. I encouraged them to understand before they offered their opinions and to reflect before they spoke. I taught them to listen to each other. By listening to them, recapitulating what they said, asking whether I had got it right, and following up with my own questions and elaborations, I was modeling how to engage with the work and the pleasures of learning.

I didn't realize it at the time, but I was embodying a style of teaching—in part Socratic, in part didactic, in part improvisational. I decided early on that I wanted students to perceive me as a dedicated searcher, an inquirer after truths, a curious thinker who read widely, a scholar who found learning exciting as well as exacting, and a teacher who enjoyed both teaching and learning and who envisioned teaching as a dialogue, a two-way exchange with students, not as a passing-down of wisdom from on high.

My teaching persona evolved over time; it wasn't fully formed when I first stepped into a classroom. I learned by going where I had to go, to paraphrase Theodore Roethke's "The Waking." It took me a few years to settle into one kind of teaching style and stance. Decades later, my teaching persona evolved again, this time into a more patient avatar of my earlier teaching self. In those early years, I needed to be in control—to monitor and lead, to guide and direct, to convey very clear and specific kinds of information I wanted students to know, and to teach very particular ways into literature.

With more experience, I learned to loosen the reins little by little and give students more leeway and more time to think so as to develop their own responses to works and texts we read and viewed together. I allowed them more freedom to develop their own thinking. I looked for ways to help them release their imaginations. I sought approaches that allowed them to engage one another in small-group conversations, based on their preliminary reflections about texts and scenarios that I created for them.

Then as now, my goal has been to create an environment conducive to learning, one that prompts students to think for themselves and encourages small- and large-group discussion, including cross-talk among them. One essential condition for creating this optimum environment for learning is to know your students by name. Another is to provide opportunities for them to get to know one another—to reduce the anonymity of the university classroom.

Introductions

You should introduce yourself briefly and tell your students a few things about yourself professionally and, if you are comfortable with it, perhaps personally as well. How you provide this information, your manner and style of delivery, will set the tone for the course. And so you need to decide what degree of distance, what level of formality, you wish to establish in the class. Students should learn to pronounce and spell your name, and you their names, at least if your class is not too large.

We like to encourage our students to get acquainted during the initial class meeting, so we pair them up to learn about each other and then to introduce, not themselves, but one another to the class. Doing that requires that they listen (and perhaps take a few notes) so they have something to say about their new classmate acquaintance; they must also talk, so their classmate has something to say about them. One benefit of this exercise is that it simply and effectively breaks the ice and dispels any sense of isolation. An additional benefit is that it introduces students to one form of active learning—a pair exchange—that they will be using throughout the term.

An additional component of this activity can help you memorize student names quickly. Before their interviews, have students fill out four-by-six index cards on which they provide basic information about themselves: their name, previous education, prospective major, hometown, leisure interests, a recommended book or film, and something most people don't know about them, or perhaps a special talent they possess.

As you collect the cards, look each student in the eye and pronounce his or her name. While they are busy conversing, you can begin memorizing at least their first names. Once you commit their names to memory, ask the students to begin their introductions. When they present each other, look through their cards, locking in their names, faces, and a few of the more interesting details.

You can review the index cards on days you don't meet them to see how many you can remember, putting any you can't remember on top. Devote a few minutes at the beginning of the second class meeting to reviewing your students' names and introducing yourself a bit more fully than you might have done in the first class session.

Spending time on this activity sends a message: that you care about your students enough to know their names. Learning your students' names helps build a mutually respectful relationship with them. As an added bonus, it also tends to boost teacher evaluations and teaching reputation (McKinney 2006).

Syllabus

Another important first-day element is reviewing the highlights of your course syllabus. You might bring hard copies to class, even though some students will have downloaded the syllabus and others will have either skimmed or even perused it online. Be clear about your own responsibilities toward your students and their responsibilities in fulfilling the course requirements. Let them know what kinds of assignments and tests are required and how they will be graded. You don't need to go into great detail the first day, but you should give them an overview of the course, including its rationale, its prospective value for them, and the broad goals and more specific objectives you have set for their learning (see chapter 2).

In addition to having students pair up to introduce themselves, have them engage in one form of teaching and learning that will be a regular feature of the course. If group work will be important, engage them in a small-group exercise. If website research will be a regular practice, have students begin that research the first day. It's important that students know that the actual work of the course begins the first day. For as vital as it is to establish a sense of who you are and how you teach, and as critical as it is for you to learn their names, it is equally important for them to get down to the actual work of the course right from the start.

Chapter Two

Course, Syllabus, and Lesson Design

As teachers, we are designers. We design courses, syllabi, and lessons; activities, assignments, and assessments. We design a variety of teaching materials, from handouts to websites. Ultimately we are responsible for designing the kinds of experiences our students will have in our classrooms.

In this chapter, we consider our primary pedagogical design responsibilities: courses, syllabi, units, and lessons; activities, assignments, experiences, and assessments. These design elements encapsulate our purpose in the classroom and reflect our pedagogical goals and how we might best achieve them. The key is to align them coherently with one another and with our course learning goals.

Course Design

In our work with faculty across schools, departments, and disciplines in consultations and workshops, one topic recurs more frequently than any other: goals. And so we ask: What are you trying to accomplish in the classroom? More precisely, what do you want your students to be able to accomplish? What, in short, are your goals for your students?

In talking about goals with faculty, we introduce the concept of "backward design." As its name implies, backward design begins at the end. It prompts us to begin our course design process by asking two key questions: What do I want my students to understand at the end of my course? What do I want them to be able to do? You might also consider how they might be different on the last day of class than they were on the first. Once we answer these questions, we can begin thinking about how to help our students achieve those learning goals.

In *Understanding by Design* (2007), Grant Wiggins and Jay McTighe offer a three-point approach to backward design that can guide our course design thinking. Here's what they suggest:

First, identify course goals based on answers to our two questions. Second, plan the instruction that will lead students toward achieving those goals. And third, identify the means for assessing whether students have met those goals—and at what level of success.

In identifying our course learning goals, we are essentially making decisions about what matters most to us, as well as what is more and what is less important for our students to learn. We need to decide which topics, concepts, skills, and habits of mind to prioritize, and why. We need to decide on a framework that incorporates these elements and structures our course content so that the courses we create are coherent and purposeful.

The following sets of questions should aid you in goal-directed course design:

- What is your purpose in the course? Why are you teaching it? Why does it exist at all, and where does it fit into the larger departmental and school curriculum?
- What is the course's trajectory—its beginning, middle, and end—and its overall structure? What is its "story"?
- Why does the course matter? For whom does it matter? And how?
- What political and pedagogical assumptions and perspectives underlie the course?
- What kinds of learning experiences might students expect to have during the course?
- What are your students' educational capacities and level of knowledge and skill? What do you know of their needs and their expectations?
- How will students be able to contribute their own knowledge, experience, and expertise to the course?

Wiggins and McTighe also provide questions to guide course design. Some of these are variations on our broad questions, while others address more specific pedagogical concerns.

First, the all-important course *goals*:

1. What should your students read and hear, view and explore, or otherwise encounter? What knowledge should they become familiar with?
2. What knowledge and skills should your students master? What is essential for them to know and understand, not just know about? What is critical for them to learn how to do?

3. What big ideas does the course explore? What "enduring understandings"—what concepts are most important for them to remember long after the details of the course have been forgotten?

Second, the *instructional* strategies:

1. How will you use direct instruction, such as lecturing and explaining concepts, ideas, and frameworks?
2. What kinds of collaborative activities can you use to engage students actively in their learning?
3. What applications can you devise for the essential concepts central to the course?

Third, the *evidence* that students are learning what is being taught:

1. What will count as evidence that students are making progress toward your course goals? What forms of production will you accept and how will you evaluate the degree of students' success in what they give you? How will this evidence indicate that your students are "getting it"?
2. More specifically, what assessment methods will you use to measure students' progress in their learning? In-class writing and out-of-class essays, reports, and research papers? Quizzes, tests, and exams? Reports and presentations? Problem sets, lab projects, or homework assignments? What kind of homework assignments?
3. How will you assess students' understanding of what they have learned—their ability to explain not just what they know but how they know what they know? How might you evaluate their meta-understanding? That is, how might you assess their processes of learning?

Your goal in course design should be *alignment*: bringing your instructional strategies in line with your goals; linking your goals with your assessments; connecting your assessments to course content. Your course content and skills—and how you teach them—should equip students to complete the activities, assignments, and projects you design for them. And these products and their design should accurately reflect students' progress toward your course goals. The nature of your instructional strategies and the extent to which you lecture, assign group work, employ digital tools, incorporate videos, use experiential learning, require writing, bring in visiting experts—everything depends on how these elements support students' efforts to achieve the course goals.

Assessment also needs to align with course goals. It is covered in detail in chapter 11, but for now, keep in mind the need to implement both *summative* and *formative* assessments. Summative assessment does just that: it sums up your evaluation of student performance, usually with a grade. Formative assessment evaluates students' work-in-progress, sometimes with grades, sometimes with written feedback, sometimes through discussion-based activities. In developing your courses, you can ask the following questions in considering which forms of assessment are best suited to the course goals:

- How can you determine whether your criteria for assessing student learning measure what you think you are measuring?
- What skills do students need to acquire and/or practice in your course?
- How can you break down complex knowledge and skill goals into manageable parts and steps?
- How can you design assessments based on those smaller elements?
- What kinds of course activities might reflect what students will do in the world of work after college?
- How can you determine what is working toward student learning—and what is not?
- How will you get feedback to and from your students about their learning, about their needs, and about the challenges they face in your course? How often will you obtain this feedback?

These three areas of focus—course goals, instruction, and assessment—require us to reflect on our pedagogical practice, inquire into its rationale, explain that rationale to ourselves, and experiment with different modes of teaching and learning. The backward design process forces us to think strategically not just about *what* we are teaching but about *why* we are teaching it, and then about *how* to teach it effectively. Our overall teaching goal is to support and assess accurately how well our students are learning—to see how much and how deeply they understand what we are teaching and how well they can demonstrate the skills we believe are most important for them to master.

Syllabus Design

A syllabus typically describes the essential elements of a course, providing an overview of who's who and what's what. It includes all the usual suspects—instructor's name and contact information, required readings and assignments with their due dates, exams with their point value, and other practical details. A syllabus also includes departmental, school, and university boilerplate language about plagiarism, attendance and absences, grade point conversions, support services, and other information that individual instructors disseminate but over which they have little if any control. And yet a syllabus is—or can be—much more than a mere checklist of course information.

Putting the mandatory elements of a syllabus aside, let's ask a different and more basic conceptual question: Just what is a syllabus anyway? How do you conceive of this pedagogical genre? What metaphors occur to you in describing it? And then, given a particular syllabus metaphor, what implications for teaching follow from it? What teaching practices does that metaphor imply?

During our workshops, faculty members frequently suggest that a syllabus is a contract, which is perhaps the most commonly recognized syllabus metaphor. And to some extent, of course, a syllabus does include contractual elements: requirements, for example, that students must satisfy to earn course credit and the performance level they need to achieve to earn a particular grade. The syllabus also stipulates the instructor's responsibilities. The syllabus as contract typically identifies rewards and punishments (for late work, incomplete work, absences, and so on). Syllabus contract language is formal, even austere, often highlighting minutiae about students' responsibilities, from using correct grammar and mechanics in written work to following precise formatting procedures, abiding by instructor rules and protocols for lab work, and other directives.

Although these elements are indeed necessary, how they are included in the syllabus, the language in which they are couched, and how they connect with other syllabus elements affect how your students perceive you as their instructor. As your initial contact with your students, your syllabus introduces you as well as your course. It sets the tone for your course and conveys an impression of you as an instructor. One aspect of that impression is the voice with which you present yourself to your students.

Your syllabus reflects your teaching *persona* and the value you place on your course. It's the first link between you and your students. As such, it's important to consider how you want to come across to your students; it's equally important to craft a description of your course that excites your students about its benefits for their intellectual development. Your syllabus is an opportunity to sell your course and its value to them.

The syllabus is thus a rhetorical document as well as a contractual one. It's an advertisement for your course, one that simultaneously conveys information about the course and a first impression of you as a teacher.

Let's imagine some metaphors for a syllabus other than a formal contract. Perhaps a syllabus is a map, or a blueprint. Or it could be a journey, an invitation to a set of conversations, an occasion for intellectual provocation.

What are the implications of these different syllabus metaphors? What does each metaphor suggest about the nature of the course that students will experience? What does each imply about how your course should be organized and how that organization might be presented to students? What does it say about how you will teach and how students will learn?

In considering a syllabus from the standpoint of a map, you might focus on the points of reference for the course, highlighting and explaining them. Will readings and lectures be the main points of reference? Will a series of small-scale assignments lead to a larger project—with stopping points for summative assessment and revision along the way? Will the course map show peaks and valleys that reflect greater and lesser obligations for students? Will there be any literal geographical elements in your course (visits to off-campus sites, for example)? In using the syllabus metaphor of a journey, you might consider why you are beginning the course at a particular point, and where the journey will take students. What is the course's end point, and why does it end where it does? What kind of trajectory does the course journey trace?

These map and journey metaphors, and other syllabus metaphors, are neither exhaustive nor mutually exclusive; they interact and overlap. We mention them as an invitation and a provocation to consider the syllabus from a variety of perspectives.

Among the most important syllabus elements are the course goals, which require you to think about learning first and teaching second. Establishing clear course goals drives your thinking about how you will help students achieve them. What will you do in your teaching—in the assignments you create and the demands you make of students—to enable them to reach the course goals you set?

A syllabus should include not only the basic nuts and bolts of a course, but also a clear course concept, a set of achievable goals, a range of teaching and learning strategies, and particular approaches to guiding and assessing student learning. Our metaphors for a syllabus need to encompass these broader and deeper aspects of pedagogy and to embody our educational philosophy, if only tacitly. They also need to convey something of our passion for the subject we teach, the value we place on it, and its potential benefits for our students.

In using the syllabus to map out the course for our students and explain how they can succeed in it, we need to remember that a syllabus should be a living document, one subject to modification—depending on exigencies and contingencies outside our control, as well as on feedback we receive about student learning.

Assessing Your Syllabus: Round I

In designing your syllabus, you can consider a multitude of possibilities. Far from a humble checklist, a syllabus requires a checklist itself to keep track of its multiple purposes and functions. What else does a syllabus do? We believe that a syllabus accomplishes the following, at the very least:

1. It serves as a course-planning tool, which is what we have been primarily describing so far in this chapter.
2. It provides an overview of your course, a description of its content, and its rationale, including requirements for satisfactory completion.
3. It serves as a reference for logistical and other details, including information about dates, times, and places the course meets, your office hours, examination period information, and course, department, school, and university policies, among many other such details.
4. It introduces you to your students and conveys what's important about the course, and why.
5. It is a rhetorical instrument that explains, exhorts, persuades, describes, and performs other important persuasive functions—promissory, contractual, obligatory, hortatory, admonitory, and more.
6. It provides an opportunity to demonstrate inclusion, through readings and assignments that reflect the diverse population of students you teach.

Harvard's Derek Bok Center for Teaching and Learning has developed a series of questions you can ask in assessing how well your syllabus is doing its work. We reprint their four main questions here, with a few samples of their numerous sub-questions.

1. Do the title and preamble [the course description] clearly state what the course is about, orient and excite students?
    -   Does the preamble clearly identify the theme of the course?
    -   Does it challenge or inspire your students? Is there a problem or puzzle to be solved [in the course]?

2. Does your syllabus establish a clear contract between you and your students?
    -   Does it make clear promises regarding due dates, readings, and office hours [and other important logistical matters]?
    -   Does it establish clear expectations for course blogs, chat rooms, or the course website?
    -   Does it make grading policies explicit?

3. Is your syllabus coherent?
    -   Is the logic or story [of your syllabus] best told in vignettes (one per week or month)? Or is it better divided into three or four acts—and if so, are they manageable chunks?
    -   Does that order or logic follow from your preamble?
    -   Are the sections or elements linked to one another, or [presented as] steps that follow one another logically?

4. Does your syllabus build the appropriate skills or competencies? Does it clearly motivate stages of learning or have learning outcomes?
    -   Is the sequencing of assignments laid out clearly?
    -   Do writing or other assignments coincide with the material they address?

Essential Syllabus Information

So far, we've deferred discussion of the strictly informational and logistical administrative aspect of the syllabus to consider its broader pedagogical potential. Information and logistics, however, also require attention.

Here are some of the things that students simply need to know and your syllabus can provide:

- Your name and title, office location and hours, contact email, and perhaps (but not necessarily) your office phone number
- The URL for the course website (if applicable)
- Prerequisites, if any
- Texts, materials, and supplies
- Course description
- Course goals
- Course policies—attendance, lateness, late work, missed exams, requests for extensions, incompletes, expectations for student conduct and behavior in the classroom, laboratory, or studio
- School policies relating to the course—statements regarding class participation, plagiarism, technical support, students with disabilities, and the like
- Course methods
- Course schedule (of class meetings, assignments, exams, and so on)
- Grading policy (including grading standards, criteria, and scale)
- Assignment and exam information

Even this list does not identify all of the features you may need or wish your syllabus to have. Instructors commonly include some or all of the following additional elements on their syllabi:

- Student resources—writing and learning centers, for example
- Supplementary and recommended material—readings, films, websites, and so on
- Caveats—for example, how the syllabus can change and ways to inform students of revisions to the syllabus
- Teacher assistant information, if applicable

Beyond the content of the syllabus, you should also consider how it looks—its aesthetic dimension. Review the spacing, layout, and typography for ease of reading: its major elements should stand out quickly and clearly. It's a good idea to distribute the syllabus in class, even if students have access to it online. The reason? You want to be sure all students have a copy as you review syllabus highlights on the first day of class.

Assessing Your Syllabus: Round 2

In reviewing your syllabus, check for clarity, coherence, consistency, conciseness, and inclusion. Be sure that you have made things as clear as possible—your goals for the course, your assignment instructions, logistical information, requirements, procedures, policies, and all the rest. For example, if a reading or other type of assignment is listed for a particular date, make sure that students know they are to have read the text or prepared the assignment *by* the due date, and clarify whether students are to bring their written work to class or deliver it electronically (by the time the class meets, or by midnight that day, for example). Be sure, too, that they know when you will be available online and in person, and how they should contact you.

Coherence is key as well. The parts of your syllabus should relate, hang together, connect. A logical organization enhances coherence, as do explanations of your pedagogical philosophy that align with the type of assignments you require and the kinds of performance standards you establish.

There are various ways to make your syllabus consistent. Strive for a consistent design—with fonts and spacing and with your use of capitalization, boldface, italics, and other forms of emphasis. Be consistent, too, with your use of heads and subheads—that is, with how you highlight, subordinate, and coordinate information. And be attentive for consistency in the tone of your writing. If you address your students with a personal voice in the first pages of your syllabus, be sure to maintain that personal tone throughout. "I expect you to attend class faithfully, with not more than two excused absences. Plan on being fully prepared to do our coursework for the day." If later in the syllabus you write something like, "All students must turn in their final portfolios for grading to the instructor, personally, on the last day of class," you have shifted to a more formal tone—one at odds with the less formal, more personal style of your beginning. We have often seen this kind of tonal shift on course syllabi. Sometimes variations in tone result from instructors inheriting a syllabus for a long-standing course that was designed by one or more other instructors.

Conciseness aids clarity and coherence. In reviewing your draft syllabus, look for ways to trim excess verbiage—to cut unnecessary words, sentences, and paragraphs. Being concise does not require that you keep your syllabus brief. In recent years, course syllabi have lengthened considerably—partly because of administrative mandates and partly because of the larger functions and richer opportunities the syllabus provides as a support for student learning. But even long syllabi can benefit from concision.

And finally, consider whether your syllabus is inclusive—whether it reflects the diverse composition of your class. You can do this by making explicit that you welcome student participation and contributions whatever students' prior knowledge and educational background and whatever their particular social, cultural, racial, ethnic, or religious background. And you can stipulate that you welcome and encourage a range of views and perspectives on complex issues and controversial topics.

You should also include information about health and wellness and information for students with disabilities. The bottom line here is to convey a sense of welcome to your students. Let them know that they are entering a new learning community.

A Note on Technology

In "How to Create a Syllabus" (2018), Kevin Gannon suggests that an instructor also address the use of technology in the course and classroom. You need to let students know what kinds of technology they will be using for different facets of their coursework. How will they interact with you and their classmates outside of class? Through email? The content management system? A social media platform? What digital tools will assignments and activities regularly depend on? WordPress? Dropbox? Clickers? Students need to become habituated early in using the technology you have selected. They need to know that it's an essential part of their learning for the semester.

Don't assume that students are proficient in the use of any particular technology the course requires. Nor should you assume that all students have the ability to access the bandwidth needed for fast and consistent uses of technology. The digital divide is real, and the expertise of the "digital native" largely overstated.

Also include on your syllabus the protocols you want to establish covering the use of devices during class time. What etiquette will you establish for using technology in your course? Be sure that students know how you define acceptable technological behavior—what's appropriate and what's not (see also chapter 7).

Lesson Design

In the same way that we design courses and syllabi using the backward design process, we can design lessons for individual class sessions and units of instruction, or for other kinds of class session groupings. Our plans for lessons can be informal, such as the topics or questions we might cover listed in the order we think best contributes to student engagement and learning. Our plans can also be more elaborate, with detailed self-instructions for how to conduct the class sessions, along with the precise timing for each activity. Either way, however, precise lesson goals and a clear structure for the allocation of class time should be included.

Early in our teaching careers, we found that creating a clear-cut lesson outline for each class session was essential not only for organizing individual class meetings but also for indicating how lessons were related. Do not assume, as instructors sometimes do, that students will understand the connections from one lesson to another. Articulating these connections yourself and giving students opportunities to make them as well helps make your course more cohesive and enhances student learning (see chapter 4).

One fairly standard approach is to list the elements of your lesson plan and include notes for how to execute each of those parts. Here are the major parts of a standard lesson plan:

Objectives (or goals): Objectives are typically written in behavioral terms. For example: "Students will explain clearly, while using technical terminology, the major parts of the brain and their corresponding functions." Or: "Students will be able to analyze the claims made in an argument and evaluate the evidence offered in its support."

Hook (or bridge): A hook is a strategy that engages students' attention and interest—for example, you could bring a three-dimensional model of the brain into class and hold it up for students to see, or start class by projecting an image of the brain onto a screen with all (or none) of its parts labeled.

Content: Content, of course, is the information and concepts you will teach that help students understand what is being taught.

Activities: Depending on the length of the class, the nature of the material, and the level of the students' knowledge and preparation, you will engage students in activities, usually broken up into two, three, or more segments. These might include, for example, writing responses to a question, summarizing part of a reading or a lecture, or solving problems.

Assessment: You will evaluate what students are learning during the session, either while they are engaged in that learning or afterwards.

Timeline: Your class lesson plan should include an estimate of how you will "chunk" or otherwise divide the time allotted for your class session. Breaking large chunks of time into smaller pieces introduces variety, forestalls monotony, and has been shown to enhance learning (see chapter 4).

This kind of lesson planning model pushes us to identify the learning outcomes we expect from the class session or set of class sessions. It encourages us to think not only of what we will do, but of what we want students to be doing during the class session. In short, lesson planning is a student-centered, student-directed aspect of pedagogy. It's less about us as teachers and our teaching than about our students and their learning. It's about our teaching in terms of their learning. And this is true for syllabus and course design as well as for lesson design.

Applications

1. For a course you have taught, are currently teaching, or plan to teach, write out two or three clear course goals.
2. Decide on the instructional methods you will use in this course to teach your students.
3. Describe the overall structure of the course—break it down into sections and briefly explain the purpose, function, and structure of each unit.
4. Write out a lesson plan for a single class session, using the template provided in this chapter.
5. For that same lesson, or for a different one, describe how you might engage your students, explore a topic with them, explain a key concept, elaborate the concept and apply it, and then evaluate what you expect students to learn.

Metaphors of Teaching

We don't often realize the influence of internalized metaphors on our pedagogical practice. How we envision teaching—how we conceptualize it—matters greatly to how we go about interacting with students. It matters for how we design our courses and assignments, for how we teach, and for how our students learn, as well as for how we assess our students and evaluate our own teaching.

Different metaphors of teaching carry very different implications for understanding our role and responsibilities as instructors. Is teaching more like wrestling or more like dancing? To what extent is teaching comparable to setting things (such as minds and hearts) on fire? Is teaching more like work or more like play? How is teaching related to performance? To demonstration? To communication? To discovery and invention? To exploration and adventure? To conversation and provocation?

In a scene in the 1992 movie *Sister Act*, Sister Mary Clarence is invited to conduct a small group of nuns in choir practice. She takes the baton from another nun who has been responsible for this work, but who has not had much success with the choir. What Sister Mary Clarence does at this point is instructive, particularly with respect to successful teaching practices. She puts down the baton—the symbol of the conductor's authority. She then asks a few questions of the nuns. Who's a soprano? Who are the altos and basses? With this information, she moves the singers to different positions, placing sopranos with other sopranos, altos with other altos, and basses with other basses.

A patient and careful observer, Sister Mary Clarence singles out one nun who sings too loud and another who sings too softly. She takes each one aside individually and, with a few swift interventions, has them both improving almost instantaneously. She compliments the loud singer but reminds her that she is drowning out the other nuns with her "powerful instrument." She brings the soft-voiced singer up close and pushes a finger into her diaphragm, thereby startling the quiet young nun into a brief loud burst of song. Sister Mary Clarence then instructs the little nun in how to project her voice.

Sister Mary Clarence's teaching is efficient and individualized. She targets individuals while considering how each affects the group. She has the group sing a single note, an A, and then a second note and a third, a C-sharp and an E. When the nuns can sing an A major chord harmoniously and in unison, she compliments them. But only up to a point, since beautifully singing a single chord in unison is only a small, if important, accomplishment.

Finally, Sister Mary Clarence inspires the singing nuns, primarily through metaphor, when she tells them that they are singing to God. Their singing, she implies, is a form of prayer. As is her teaching. We might even say that her teaching is a form of grace.

Consider the following metaphors of teaching. Pick two that strike you as especially interesting, important, or necessary. What are the implications of each of the following metaphors of teaching? What do they require? And what do they yield for both teachers and students?

Ministering	Converting	Performing
Collaborating	Indoctrinating	Exploring
Guiding	Liberating	Discovering
Transmitting	Provoking	Inviting
Conversing	Improvising	Instigating
Subverting	Conserving	Inspiring
Inquiring	Demonstrating	Loving

One teaching metaphor we have heard from colleagues is "provocation," a metaphor that highlights an instructor's role in stimulating students to think by provoking them intellectually to take conceptual risks, to move outside their intellectual comfort zones, and to stretch themselves academically. Another teaching metaphor we ourselves value is that of "invitation"—an invitation to an ongoing conversation. Kenneth Burke uses this metaphor for a slightly different purpose, though it overlaps with ours here. In *The Philosophy of Literary Form* (1968), he describes teaching and learning as a never-ending conversation.

> You come late. When you arrive, others have long preceded you, and they are engaged in a heated discussion. . . . You listen for a while, until you decide that you have caught the tenor of the argument; then you put in your oar. Someone answers; you answer him; another comes to your defense; another aligns himself against you. . . . The hour grows late, you must depart. And you do depart, with the discussion still vigorously in progress. (pp. 110–11)

Burke's description can serve as a model for the process of engaging in academic discussion and debate generally. It's also a metaphor for constructing arguments—arguments that we can respond to in speech or writing. By thinking of argument as an art of conversation, we remind ourselves that what others think often differs from what we think. Considering argument as conversation encourages us to be both respectful of others and receptive to their point of view. It increases the likelihood that others will consider our views thoughtfully. These are essential elements for encouraging and sustaining productive class discussions (see chapter 5).

Through the metaphor of teaching as an ongoing conversation, we can introduce our students to the idea of argument as an inquiry into a complex set of issues, challenges, and problems that resist simple, easy, convenient solutions. In short, teaching and learning can be seen as reciprocal elements of an engaged, open conversation, as exploration, and as a form of inquiry.

Chapter Three

Active Learning

"Active learning" is a broad term for an approach to teaching that requires students to demonstrate their learning through doing things. Active learning provides an alternative to more passive forms of knowledge acquisition, such as listening to lectures. It shifts the focus from teachers to their students. Research confirms that when students take an active role in their learning, they improve their conceptual understanding, critical thinking, and interpersonal skills.

Active learning offers an alternative to the transmission model of teaching and learning, in which the teacher speaks and demonstrates, while students listen and observe. In active learning students ask questions, solve problems, conduct experiments, analyze data and texts, synthesize research, and through it all, make their own observations, connections, inferences, interpretations, and judgments. Discussion-based teaching (see chapter 5) is both a catalyst for and an example of an active learning pedagogical strategy.

With active learning, students use and apply information, principles, and concepts to scenarios, situations, and cases, whether actual or fabricated. Students answer questions, explain concepts and phenomena, sketch flow charts, graph distributions, describe frameworks, plot timelines, solve the first steps of complex problems, predict the outcomes of scenarios, evaluate proposals, design models, troubleshoot malfunctioning systems, brainstorm lists, and much more. In active learning, students process information, apply what they learn, receive feedback, and revise their productions and applications of knowledge. All these activities on the part of students and teachers promote and facilitate effective, enduring learning.

Active learning may require students to create an essay, a report, a project, or other product that demonstrates what they have learned. They may create a website, draft a proposal, produce a 3D model, write a comedy sketch, collaborate on solving a case study, deliver a speech, or perform a skit, to cite a few examples. One common and useful active learning assignment is to have students summarize something they have read, heard, or seen, such as an article, book, lecture, or video. In this chapter, we identify, explain, and explore a number of strategies and techniques for active learning in the classroom.

The Benefits of Active Learning

Students benefit from active learning because they learn more and better, and also because their learning lasts longer. Recent research has amply confirmed these claims (Prince 2004; Weiman 2014; Felder and Brent 2016). When an instructor shifts from lecturing to an active learning technique, the level of energy in a classroom rises dramatically. Students wake up; they come alive; they talk to and listen to each other; they explain and debate, question and challenge one another. Successful active learning exercises have a strong influence on the quality and durability of students' learning because they become physically, mentally, and intellectually engaged.

Active learning also improves students' focus and concentration. They pay attention better and engage more intensely when they participate actively in their learning. This engagement translates into more thoughtful papers, presentations, and projects throughout the course. Active learning techniques typically allow all students to participate. In addition, students get to know each other, and the resulting sense of inclusion contributes to a vibrant classroom learning community. An added bonus is that active learning has also been shown to improve student morale and to increase both course attendance and college retention (Prince 2004).

In shifting their emphasis from teaching to learning, from explaining content to checking students' understanding, instructors gain a much clearer picture of their students' progress. Through a question, problem, scenario, case, or other active learning prompt, they get a chance to hear students' reasoning and better understand why students think what they do. Active learning thus allows instructors to check on the extent of their students' knowledge and on the depth of their understanding. Students and teachers have a chance to check in with one another—to ask additional questions, clarify muddy points, and set straight misunderstandings.

Active learning also increases inclusion of diverse perspectives. When all students are actively responding to an assignment or engaged with an activity, a wider than usual range of viewpoints tends to emerge. That's one form of inclusion. In addition to inviting a range of perspectives, active learning pedagogical strategies lead to more inclusive classrooms. It's not only that more students participate and more viewpoints are expressed, but also that students who struggle in courses where they have a more passive role in their learning perform better in an active learning scenario. Many of these students may be disadvantaged, for example, in lecture courses that assume a level of academic preparation and familiarity with concepts and contexts necessary for understanding that they simply do not possess. Active learning can enable instructors to meet their students where they are academically so they can learn more successfully.

The Challenges of Active Learning

Teachers sometimes assume that students will understand and appreciate the value of active learning, but that is simply not the case. Active learning requires students to do more than they may be accustomed to doing: they must do more than listen, take notes, and regurgitate information on multiple-choice and matching tests. Without understanding and appreciating how active learning increases and deepens their understanding, students are sometimes reluctant to engage in active learning exercises and activities. It's thus important to clarify the purpose and value of an active learning approach. Students need to understand that active learning is the standard for teaching and learning in your course—that it's the default mode, the regular pedagogical approach, not an occasional bit of variety, and certainly not a mere option for students. It's important to introduce active learning techniques into your courses as early as possible, even on the first day of class. In doing that, you send a message that active learning will be a regular part of the students' work.

It's also important to explain why you use active learning teaching strategies and to make it clear to the students how they will benefit from them in both the short and the long run. In the short run, of course, they will meet your requirements and demands for the course. In the longer run, they will be better prepared for what is expected of them in postgraduate study, especially for business and the professions, which are highly skills-based and in which an ability to communicate and collaborate is assumed. Through the skills they develop in an active learning classroom, students will be better prepared to work with people from diverse backgrounds and better able to find their place in a global economy.

Like some students, some parents argue that their children should be listening to professors rather than sharing their ignorance with other students in small- and large-group discussions and other activities. Our challenge, therefore, is to make the case for active learning, which we can do in two ways. First, we need to convince our students (and sometimes their parents) that active learning strengthens and deepens their learning. We need to convince them logically and with evidence from research. Second, we need to have students experience the benefits of active learning. We need to design active learning activities that win students over by allowing them to experience for themselves directly, both individually and collectively, how it enhances their learning and makes learning more enjoyable.

Having highlighted the benefit of active learning, we want to caution that there are times when active learning may not be the best mode of instruction for your students. The purpose of this chapter, of course, is to showcase what active learning can do for students. But it's also the case that other forms of instruction, including lecturing, are also appropriate. It's a matter of deciding which method for delivering instruction is best suited for your students at a particular time, on a particular occasion, and with the particular learning goals you have set for them. Even when active learning seems the right choice for your students' learning, you may face resistance based on their prior and current experience with other instructional models.

Getting Student Buy-in for Active Learning

Students may resist active learning because they are unaccustomed to it, because it requires more work from them, or because they believe that discussion with their classmates is less important than learning directly from their instructor's expertise. The following exercise was developed by a former colleague, Ian Stewart, from the New York University Stern School of Business. He used it on the first or second day of class to gain student buy-in for his active learning approach to teaching. (For more ideas about what to do on the first day of class, see interlude 1.)

The Ends of Education: An Exercise for Students

Ask students the following question to prompt discussion:

Considering what you want to get from your college education overall and from this course in particular, which of the following is most important to you?
1. Acquiring knowledge
2. Learning how to use knowledge in new situations
3. Developing skills to continue learning after college

After giving students a minute to do their own ranking individually, have them discuss their responses in groups of three. Items 2 and 3 are usually the most popular choices. We might infer from this that students value the types of thinking that faculty typically see as primary goals for their students' learning, including applying concepts and principles and knowledge and learning how to learn. But while this may indeed be the case, it doesn't necessarily mean that students understand how to achieve these goals.

And so we might say something like this: "Let's think for a moment how best to accomplish these goals. Learning is not a spectator sport—it takes work—both work you do in the classroom and work you do outside it. Which of these three goals do you think you can make headway on outside of class on your own, through reading and studying? Which do you think can be best achieved in class through working with your classmates and your instructor?"

Most students respond that they can make progress with factual knowledge acquisition on their own and want assistance with the other two goals. Goals 2 and 3 cannot be achieved by reading or listening to lectures; students must actively do things to learn how to apply knowledge and develop their skills, including learning how to continue their learning. And even when the goal is primarily knowledge acquisition, students learn best when they take an active role: when they discuss what they read; when they practice what they are learning; and when they apply concepts and principles, ideas and practices, to new situations.

This activity can motivate students to value the kinds of active learning strategies used in the course and help them recognize that the responsibility for learning rests with both student and instructor as partners. Frequent writing assignments, group projects, and regular in-class activities will be seen for what they are: ways to achieve goals important for success in college and beyond.

Active Learning and Agency

When students are actively engaged in their learning—through discussion, problem-finding and problem-solving, writing and revising, creating a presentation, constructing a model, demonstrating a procedure, and the like—they are agents, doers. They become producers engaged in the act of making something, creating a product that didn't exist before. When students possess agency—when they determine for themselves what they might do, or at least how they might do it—they learn better and their learning lasts longer (see chapter 4).

In *Choice Words* (2004), Peter Johnston argues that students need to think of themselves as agents—as decision-makers involved in the development of their schoolwork. Without this sense of themselves, students lack incentive to do more than the bare minimum, which they do in a perfunctory way. Yet exercising agency can be daunting in the classroom, especially for students who haven't had opportunities before to do so.

You can ask your students the following questions to help them think of themselves as agents:

- Why did you choose this topic or approach or project? Why does it interest you?
- How are you planning to go about your work on it?
- Where would you like to go with it? Why?
- Considering where you are with your project now, what are you sure about and what are you uncertain about?
- How did you figure out what you have so far?
- What problems or challenges remain for you to deal with?

Helping students develop a sense of control over their work, a sense of agency, increases their willingness to work hard at something. Agency helps them focus their attention, persist through struggles, understand themselves as competent, and build their confidence. Students who possess agency plan well, concentrate well, and set challenging tasks for themselves. Agency empowers students. It contributes to their sense of well-being, their sense of themselves as able. Agency, moreover, extends beyond a student's individual sense of accomplishment to his or her ability to work collaboratively and productively with others—an increasingly important skill for the workplace.

Active Learning Techniques

Instructors who teach large classes often express dismay in our workshops because they need to lecture and to cover large amounts of course content in their lectures. Our first response is to suggest that they give up the metaphor of "coverage" and replace it with a metaphor more in line with their teaching and learning goals. Instructors, especially those who teach small classes, consistently say that they want their students to attain not just knowledge but understanding; they want their students to be able to apply their knowledge and understanding productively. And so we invite them to consider how active learning strategies can help them achieve those goals.

What are some active learning techniques, and how do they work? Active learning can be initiated through a number of teaching strategies (Angelo and Cross 2009). Some of the following techniques are more suitable for the beginning or the end of class; others work best at strategic junctures within class periods. Most can work in large lecture courses as well as in smaller classes. All require that students exercise their higher-order thinking powers.

Entrance and Exit Tickets or Questions

Entrance tickets (typically in the form of 3×5 index cards) on which students respond to a question or other prompt can focus their attention on the day's topic. The tickets can be used to recall background knowledge relevant to the day's lesson or to check students' understanding of a reading or other assignment due that day. For example, you might ask: "Based on today's assigned readings, what is your understanding of X?"; "Which of the readings for today resonated the most for you, and why?"; or "Which of the problems gave you the most trouble—and why?" You can collect these tickets and read through all of them after class to get a sense of the overall class response and to discern any patterns in them, especially patterns of misunderstanding. Entrance tickets can also be used in class to initiate discussion.

In a similar way, exit tickets can be used to collect feedback at the end of class. They provide students with an opportunity to reflect on what they have just learned, synthesize their knowledge, and link it to learning from previous class sessions. Exit tickets can also be used to check on students' understanding of key points raised during the lecture or discussion. For example, students might be asked: "What is the most important concept you learned today?"; "What are two takeaways from today's class for you? Why are these important for your learning?"; "What is something you wished or hoped would be discussed in today's class that wasn't?"; or "Why were you hoping for a discussion of this topic?"

As with entrance tickets, exit tickets can be collected and reviewed later. They can also be used for a brief concluding discussion at the end of class.

Minute Paper and Muddiest Point

At any point during a class session, you can check students' understanding of a principle, concept, example, or other key point by asking them to answer a question. A "minute" paper can be stretched to two or three minutes, or more, if desirable. Its purpose is to elicit information about students' comprehension.

One specific type of minute paper is the "muddiest point" response. Ask students: "What is the muddiest point (for you) in the lecture (homework, discussion, assignment)?" Or, "What do you remain confused about after today's lecture (about the homework, at this point in today's class discussion)?" Once you have student responses, you can adapt the next lecture or lecture segment—perhaps repeating something you previously taught from another angle or with different examples. If you give students time to think and write about these questions during class, they will respond more productively than if you simply ask: "Any questions?"

Misconception/Preconception

This technique works well at the start of a class and at the beginning of a course. One approach is to present a list of statements about one or more key concepts students have learned through reading or attending lectures. True/false or multiple-choice questions can test their preconceptions or misconceptions about the principle or concept. Student answers can be used to jump-start class discussion or arouse curiosity about the impending lecture. We have seen instructors in large sections with hundreds of students give them clickers for their responses (see chapter 7). Through such exercises we can assess students' knowledge and calibrate our teaching; later the same or a similar exercise can be used to assess growth in students' learning.

You might have students write a brief one- or two-sentence explanation of a concept, principle, or scientific hypothesis. For example, students might be asked to explain their understanding of HIV from a social or a biochemical standpoint. The instructor might ask: "What is HIV and how, specifically, can it be treated?" Or, "What is the accepted procedure for giving someone artificial respiration, and what constraints or limitations do you have to consider when administering it?" Once students volunteer answers, the instructor can affirm correct responses, adjust semi-correct responses, show why an incorrect response is wrong, and perhaps explain why a particular misconception is prevalent. This technique also presents an opportunity to introduce the day's topic, invite cross-talk among students, or prepare them for an upcoming reading.

Self-Explanation

This technique is popular in elementary and secondary education, but it is also effective in higher education settings. Self-explanation requires that students explain their thinking process as they work through a problem, analyze a text, or follow a laboratory or other kind of protocol. It provides students with an opportunity to engage in meta-cognition by explaining what they are doing and then listening to themselves in the process of thinking. Over time, this technique helps students solidify a particular learning process, strategy, or technique by allowing them to identify the extent of their knowledge and understanding, note where they become stuck in a process or protocol, and think about how to remedy whatever problems they encounter.

A variation on self-explanation is simply to have one student explain his or her thinking to another or to a small group. Saying out loud what students are thinking has benefits similar to those of self-explanation. Additionally, listeners can ask questions that give explainers opportunities to extend and deepen their own understanding—such as clarifying questions, elaborating questions, or application and example questions.

Thinking-Aloud Pair Problem-Solving

The Thinking-Aloud Pair Problem-Solving (TAPPS) technique is especially useful for problem-solving, case analysis, or textual analysis. Pair students, designating one an "explainer" and the other a "questioner." Give the explainers a minute or two to explain the nature of the problem (or the opening paragraph of a case or a text). The questioners then ask about what they find to be incomplete or unclear. After the allotted time, have several students provide their explanations of the problem, case, or text. Once you have a satisfactory explanation (perhaps adding your own further clarification or correction), reverse the roles of the student pairs and continue with the second part of the problem, case, text, or other assigned task.

It's important for students to experience both sides of the explaining and listening process, as each requires different skills they need to develop. It is especially important for students to use these skills when they engage in class discussion (see chapter 5).

Concept Tests

Concept tests involve asking a multiple-choice question about a concept with incorrect answers (distractors) that reflect common student misconceptions. Students can respond individually with clickers or hold up cards with their answers. After assessing the number of votes received by each answer, pair the students up to discuss the question before taking a second vote. Then call on a number of students to explain why one answer is correct and the others are not. You can then elaborate and refine their explanations and underscore key takeaways.

This technique can also be used in the form of pop quizzes. Opening a class with a brief quiz—a few multiple-choice or short-response questions—helps students focus and settle in quickly to the work of the day. Such quizzes can contribute a small amount to a student's overall course grade, or they might be used simply to show both instructors and students what has and has not been learned—even without assigning credit.

Think/Pair/Share

One of our favorite active learning techniques is think/pair/share. We use it often in our classes and in our faculty teaching workshops. We like think/pair/share because it works on three levels—the individual student, students in conversation with one other, and the whole group in discussion with the instructor.

Typically, the activity begins with a question for students to think about. For example, "What is critical thinking, and who would you identify as strong critical thinkers?" Let the students reflect briefly on these questions, and then ask them to write for two or three minutes in response. You are not looking for a lengthy explanation, just for a few quick thoughts—bullet points even.

Following this, have students pair up and compare notes to see how they approached the question. What attributes of critical thinking emerged in their thinking and writing? Was there any overlap in their responses or among the individuals they identified as critical thinkers? Then have students volunteer to comment on their discussion. In small classes, require that all pairs contribute, either randomly or in some systematic way that makes sense for the topic and question.

We like to collect students' responses on a whiteboard while they speak. Initially, we want only brief responses. Once we gather their responses, we identify (or ask them to identify) patterns. For example, some of the critical thinking characteristics identified may relate to creativity and innovation. Others may reflect logical reasoning. We can highlight these themes on the whiteboard and elaborate on students' responses by connecting or contrasting them, by filling in what's missing, and the like. Gathering the responses and making connections between and among them allows students to detect patterns of similarity and difference that will prompt them to engage in further analysis and synthesis. Writing students' responses on a whiteboard or flipchart validates their participation visually and publicly, stimulating further discussion.

Questions and Questioning

Learning to ask useful questions is a skill, even an art. The better the questions we ask students, the better chance we have to develop their capacity for higher-order thinking, since questioning is a key element of all thinking (see chapter 10). Questions not only engage students in learning but deepen and extend that learning. Questioning leads to thinking, and thinking leads to fuller and richer understanding of the concepts and skills we teach.

Our questions also contribute to our students' sense of agency. Asking students, for example, what they are considering doing for an assignment, how they plan to go about it, why they chose a particular topic or approach, and what strategies they have for acquiring the information and resources they might need—all such questions help students develop a sense of agency. Questions that encourage students to see themselves as participants in a cooperative enterprise, a collaborative effort to which they are important contributors, are essential for strengthening their sense of themselves as doers, as agents. Such questions, moreover, make learning last by helping it stick.

Good questions direct thinking, encourage exploration, and open our students' minds to unimagined possibilities. Creating useful and productive questions can enliven students' curiosity, provoke their thinking, and excite their imagination.

What are the characteristics of good questions? Good questions are open-ended; they admit of more than a single answer. Good questions generate other questions; they lead beyond themselves. Good questions produce rich and varied answers; you can judge a question by the kinds of answers it evokes. Good questions jump-start thinking; they stimulate, engage, and provoke. Neil Postman, in *The End of Education*

(1996), suggests that the value of a question is determined by the specificity and richness of the answers it produces and by the quantity and quality of the new questions it provokes (p. 187).

Here are some examples of questions that meet these criteria:

- What do we mean by a fact? Is a biological fact different from a historical fact or a mathematical fact? Can facts change? Can something once established as fact be dethroned and shown to be a fact no longer?
- What is the relationship between fact and truth? How would you begin to answer that question?
- How should science be taught in the high school curriculum? How many sciences? In what order? To what extent should teaching and learning the sciences be integrated with one another? To what extent should science be integrated with technology? With other subjects? Which ones? Why?
- Is history a science? Is dance a language? What is a saint? What counts as an experiment? How would you go about answering these questions?
- How do you know what you know? How can you compensate for the limitations of reason, the inaccuracies of perception, or the unreliability of much of what you read and hear?

It is important to drill down with these questions, particularly with "why" questions. A sequence of "why" questions allows us to uncover chains of causal links that identify the stages or processes through which things have come to be as they are. We like to layer our "why" questions in threes—the triple "why." We respond to answers provided to a preliminary "why" question with two more "why" questions. "Why" questions are also valuable because they lead naturally to "why not" and "what if" questions, which move students' thinking from description to disruption, from explanation to innovation.

Questioning Routines

Project Zero at Harvard University, a wide-ranging initiative to improve teaching and learning with an emphasis on critical and creative thinking, incorporates "thinking routines." "See, Think, Wonder" and "Think, Puzzle, Explore" are among those routines illustrated in Ritchhart, Church, and Morrison's *Making Thinking Visible* (2011). "See, Think, Wonder" is particularly useful for thinking about visual art and images. In using this routine, you ask yourself, "What do I *see*?" You take some time looking, trying to notice as much as possible. Then you follow with another question: "What do I *think* about what I see?" Here you consider your perspective, or stance, toward what you are viewing. These initial thoughts are followed with yet another question: "What do I *wonder*?" Here you let your mind wander toward the notions that emerge. In wondering, your grounding is less firm than with the original question, and your direction less clear, but your wondering-wandering mind can often uncover further connections and insights.

"Think, Puzzle, Explore" is designed to deepen thinking. In using this thinking routine, you first consider what you think you know about an object, issue, topic, or problem. You take stock. You then ask yourself what is puzzling about it. What questions do you have about it? What don't you understand? What might be confusing? And finally, you consider how to explore the object, issue, topic, or problem further. You consider what might be done to extend and deepen your thinking and understanding.

Suggestions for Using Active Learning

If you are new to active learning, start small—keep the active learning exercises brief and focused. Experiment with them. See how things go, and then make any necessary adjustments. You will also need a signal to call the class back to attention, particularly in large classes, in which the decibel volume can rise dramatically during group activity. One method is to raise your arm in the air. When some students see this signal, they will raise their own arms, and those who are turned away will eventually see the signal spreading across the room and silence themselves. It takes only a few seconds to regain the attention of the group using this strategy.

Consider the following questions when developing an active learning approach:

- How much class time will you allocate for the activity?
- How will you structure the activity—how will you chunk its parts?
- How much planning will the active learning activity require on your part?
- What prior knowledge is necessary for students to benefit from it?
- What prior experience have students had with the active learning technique?

- What prior experience have you had using it?
- What kinds of interaction can you anticipate between your students and yourself?

Here are a few suggestions to consider when using active learning, especially for those new to its techniques.

- Activities need not be long to be effective. When starting out with active learning, or during sessions in which time is at a premium, aim for no more than three to five minutes, ten minutes maximum.
- If you assign multiple exercises during a session, don't require students to report their results to the class after every exercise.
- When an activity is wildly successful, it may take more time than you envisioned. Have a plan B for the class—and for the class that follows.
- Avoid using the same techniques too often. Vary the type of active learning activities you implement, and do not always require that students turn in the results of their work in some form.
- When using pair-share activities, pair students up with different partners—sometimes with a student sitting next to or behind them, other times with a student across the room.
- Develop some longer, more important (and graded) assignments based on one or another in-class active learning exercise. think/pair/share exercises are particularly appropriate for this kind of work.
- Announce how much time is being allotted for the activity, and let students know when a minute or two of class time remains for it.
- Debrief by asking some pairs and small groups to explain what they discussed and learned. In small classes, all pairs or groups can respond; in large lectures, ask for a few volunteers or cold-call a few.

Active Learning and Relevance

We recognize that many students have pragmatic academic aims—they come to college and university primarily, though not exclusively, because they believe that a postsecondary education will lead them to jobs and careers. And so, at least some of the time, we need to connect course objectives and learning goals with what employers want from college graduates. The following activity, also created by our former NYU colleague Ian Stewart, is based on a 2012 study by the National Association of Colleges and Employers; it enables students to see what skills employers value most in college graduates.

Begin by asking your students: "How important is it for you to develop skills in your college courses that will help you land (and keep) a job when you graduate?" Not surprisingly, students regularly agree that this is very important to them. Next ask: "Which items in the following list are the top five most desired characteristics hiring companies want to see in recent college graduates?" Here's the list in alphabetical order:

- Analytical/quantitative skills
- Computer skills
- Creative skills
- Grade point average (GPA) above 3.0
- Leadership skills
- Problem-solving skills
- Teamwork skills
- Oral communication skills
- Written communication skills

Students then work in groups of three to five to identify what they think are the top five characteristics most valued by employers. Each group must establish a consensus among its members. After perhaps five minutes, reveal the actual employer survey results, according to the National Association of Colleges and Employers:

1. Leadership skills (81 percent)
2. Problem-solving skills (75 percent)
3. Written communication skills (75 percent)
4. Teamwork skills (74 percent)
5. Analytical/quantitative skills (73 percent)

Students are usually surprised that GPA doesn't appear in the top five. Teachers, too, may be surprised that creativity isn't among the leading contenders, given how important innovation is in the business world. What's interesting is that, quantitatively, the five top employer-desired skills are very close, with only a few percentage points separating them.

Students come to see how active learning strategies can help them develop those five skills, which cannot be developed passively. These skills are desirable for those going into professions that are directly connected with your discipline and also with your course. Listening to lectures and reading will clearly not suffice. The evidence for active learning group exercises, writing assignments, team projects, and problem-solving challenges could not be more relevant to students' goals.

Applications

1. For one of your courses—past, present, or future—consider how you plan to exploit the benefits of active learning and meet its challenges.
2. How might you help your students develop a sense of agency?
3. Which active learning strategies do you think might be most effective for the students in this course?
4. How might you encourage student buy-in for active learning in the course?
5. How can active learning strategies help you achieve your course learning goals?
6. What skills are necessary for someone working in your field? What activities might provide students with an opportunity to practice them?

Scientific Teaching

Scientific teaching is based on the idea that teaching should be approached with the same rigor as the best scientific investigation and research. Our NYU colleague Trace Jordan defines scientific teaching as "the application of scientific thinking to our teaching." In his workshops on the topic, he asks participants: "What would our teaching look like if we approached it as scientists?" Several traits and practices typical of scientific thinking and working emerge during the ensuing conversation. Scientists experiment, analyze, and ask questions; they review research and collaborate. And so what if, as Jordan asks, we approach teaching with these scientific habits in mind?

First, most of these habits are active, as scientists are doers; their practices align well with active learning strategies, like those we discuss in chapter 3. Second, science is research-based, and so scientific teaching should be as well. Scientific teachers should select methods that have been systematically tested and proven to reach a broad range of students.

For some of the same reasons that students may resist active learning classroom teaching strategies, science instructors may resist scientific teaching and its associated active learning techniques. Some may be unfamiliar with the research supporting the effectiveness of active learning strategies. Some may recall their own earlier successful learning through traditional lectures. Others may not want to develop new pedagogical approaches, thinking the effort will be time-consuming and only minimally effective. Still others may resist because such an emphasis on teaching will distract them from their research and perhaps even detract from their status as scientists.

Nonetheless, it has been conclusively shown that students who participate in lectures and laboratory work that require discovery and inquiry develop the essential scientific habits of mind that result in deep learning and productive research (Handelsman et al. 2004; Felder and Brent 2016). Scientific teaching grounded in active learning enhances scientific reasoning and conceptual understanding. It has also been shown to improve the retention of knowledge, resulting in longer-lasting learning (Brown, Roediger, and McDaniel 2014; see also chapter 4).

Many scientists who teach have developed inquiry-based labs in which students are required to develop hypotheses, design and conduct their own experiments, collect and analyze data, and write up their results—just as professional scientific researchers do in their labs. These authentic inquiry-based activities serve students far better in developing their scientific reasoning skills than do conventional "cookbook" lab exercises, in which students look for predictable outcomes that verify some scientific principle or reenact in simple fashion some previously discovered scientific concept.

Like lab work based on scientific teaching principles, scientific teaching in the classroom takes advantage of students' natural curiosity. It emphasizes inquiry and discovery. It involves students in problem-solving activities, even very brief ones, to engage them in their learning. And it requires students to explain their reasoning in solving a problem to one or more classmates as they calibrate their understanding and refine their thinking. Scientific teachers who employ active learning techniques communicate more directly, more frequently, and more effectively with their students—to check the extent of their understanding—than they would while lecturing to a silent audience.

Using scientific teaching principles with active learning for science pedagogy promotes serious thinking about science for students, some of whom will take only a class or two in the sciences before majoring in another discipline. What is the most important thing for these non-science-directed students to learn in their required core curriculum science course? Surely it is not facts and information, which will become quickly outmoded. It is most assuredly something about the way science works, the process of scientific inquiry and discovery, along with an understanding and appreciation for how scientific knowledge develops and evolves.

A major proponent of scientific teaching and the use of active learning in teaching science is Eric Mazur, a physics professor at Harvard University. A dynamic and popular teacher, Mazur discovered that his students were not developing a deep understanding of the scientific concepts he thought he was teaching them. Conducting an experiment on himself, he analyzed the depth of his students' understanding after they completed his courses, many of them having earned high grades. What he found surprised, even shocked, him. Disappointed by the shallowness of his students' understanding, he resolved to adopt the kinds of active learning strategies discussed in chapter 3.

Mazur has since become something of a poster professor for active learning in scientific teaching, having made a number of videos (available on YouTube) in which he explains his conversion and demonstrates his teaching techniques. It's eye-opening and game-changing to see students struggling with problems and exercises he designed for them. He pairs them up to explain their understanding of the problem to each other, however limited it may be. The difficulty, even failure, they experience in the process prepares them to absorb and better understand the correct explanation, and the reasoning behind it, that he eventually provides for them (see chapter 4).

Another way of using failure to aid and deepen understanding is advocated by Stuart Firestein, who suggests that failure is an intrinsic, inevitable, necessary, and extremely valuable part of science that students need to know about. Firestein argues that science teaching should include a history of failures and what was learned from them. In his book *Failure* (2014) he defines science as "a mechanism for making productive mistakes" (p. 93). Firestein argues that failure happens a lot in real science labs, and that students, both graduate and undergraduate, need to experience the reality of failed experiments as an element of their developing scientific understanding. He reminds us that questions are more important than facts; that active investigation of problems is more effective than passive absorption of information; and that answers, however accurate, are temporary, with data, models, and hypotheses always provisional and subject to revision. Firestein contends that students need to learn that scientific discovery is not a smooth arc of triumphant progression, but that it progresses instead by fits and starts, one step forward, another back, as scientists seek increasingly better explanations, while jettisoning those of lesser value and utility.

Firestein also emphasizes that it is curiosity above all that drives successful research and effective learning. After all, as the great physicist and Cal Tech teacher Richard Feynman often noted, science is about what we don't know; it's about "finding things out." If we already know it, if it's knowledge that is being transmitted, it's not science, but something else—established history perhaps, but not real science, which is about the unknown and the uncertain.

Chapter Four

Making Learning Last

One of the biggest challenges confronting teachers and their students is not learning per se, but making learning last beyond the immediate present, beyond the midterm and final exams, beyond the semester—making learning endure for the long haul. We want our students to leave our courses having learned for good what we have to teach. We hope that when the course is over, they leave our classroom changed in some way—looking at the world with a new perspective perhaps, or carrying with them new knowledge and new skills to apply throughout their lives and careers. Sadly, even for students who ace our exams, this is not always—or even often—the result.

One reason is the kind of studying that even successful students commonly resort to under the pressures of time and habit: cramming. Students tend to bunch up their studying in bursts rather than chunking it and spreading it out over time. Cramming has been shown to work for the short term—students pass their tests and remember what they need to know for their exams—but what they learn rapidly dissipates.

Much has been written about the deleterious effects of cramming, including lack of sleep, a reliance on drugs, and students' false sense of confidence in what they think they are learning. Yet students continue to confine their study to intense bursts, whether memorizing information for a test or writing a paper in one long stretch just before it's due. Research (Brown, Roediger, and McDaniel 2014; Dweck 2007; Willingham 2009) has consistently shown this approach to studying and writing to be ineffective for long-term learning and for writing successful essays, papers, and reports (see chapter 9).

Students benefit from understanding why cramming is counterproductive for learning. Cramming often results from procrastination—from students not spacing out their study over time and instead leaving everything to the last minute. Spaced study is far more effective for both short-term and long-term learning and allows students to focus on chunks of material they need to master, whether content- or skill-based. Spaced-out study allies well with active recall and repetition, which strengthen the brain's neural networks and embed what is learned more deeply in long-term memory (Willingham 2009; Brown, Roediger, and McDaniel 2014).

Learning is an acquired skill; it's not something we are expert at naturally, especially the kinds of learning that school requires. Our students have to learn how to learn. And as their learning becomes more complex, they need our help in managing the acquisition of knowledge and skills. This chapter considers how to help students become meta-cognitive—more conscious of their learning and better able to learn how to learn. And so we take up some key questions about long-lasting learning. We explain why some study strategies work and others don't. We identify the conditions necessary for successful learning, along with principles and practices that guide and sustain effective, long-lasting learning. Finally, we consider how to make learning itself an object of inquiry, exploring it from the perspective of strategic practice. We begin with less effective and more effective study strategies.

Ineffective and Effective Study Habits

Among students' most common ineffective study habits is highlighting—using colored translucent markers to mark passages of a text as they read. This technique is ineffective because it is passive; students make only minimal mental effort while highlighting. They often mark large blocks of text and not just occasional sentences, illustrations, definitions, key terms, and the like. In reviewing their reading, moreover, students tend to reread only their marked passages, sometimes highlighting even more of them. The process is superficial: it doesn't anchor in memory information in relation to concepts, and it doesn't situate ideas within conceptual frameworks. Highlighting limits students' ability to absorb what they are attempting to learn. To learn effectively, students need to do something that requires more thinking than highlighting typically does.

Instead, they should take notes and make notes. Students should annotate the text, marking it up with underlining and arrows that reveal connections and relationships among details and concepts. They should number key points as they occur in the text, jotting them in the margin in their own words. They should ask questions of the text in the same way. And after they have read a few pages, they should attempt to recall key concepts and their relationships without looking back at their notes. In short, they should actively engage the text, thinking through, with, and about it.

One approach to note-taking in this manner was developed at Cornell University in the 1950s and remains in use today. The Cornell note-taking method may resemble other strategies you have used yourself, and it's similar to one we advocate in chapter 9. Here are the steps to this approach, as adapted from Walter Pauk's *How to Study in College*:

1. **Record:** During the lecture, in a notebook set up with a "cue" column and a "note-taking" column (see the sample page in table 4.1), use the note-taking column to record the lecture using telegraphic sentences.
2. **Question:** As soon after class as possible, formulate questions in the left-hand column based on the notes in the right-hand column. Writing questions helps to clarify meanings, reveal relationships, establish continuity, and strengthen memory. Also, the writing of questions sets up a perfect stage for exam-studying later.
3. **Recite:** Cover the note-taking column with a sheet of paper. Then, looking at the questions or cue words in the question and cue column only, say aloud, in your own words, the answers to the questions, facts, or ideas indicated by the cue words.
4. **Reflect:** Reflect on the material by asking yourself questions. For example: "What's the significance of these facts? What principle are they based on? How can I apply them? How do they fit in with what I already know? What's beyond them?"
5. **Review:** Spend at least ten minutes every week reviewing all your previous notes. If you do, you'll retain a great deal for current use, as well as for the exam.
6. **Summarize:** After class, use the space at the bottom of each page to summarize the notes on that page.

Recent research offers a range of study strategies more effective than highlighting (Brown, Roediger, and McDaniel 2014; Willingham 2009). One way is to put new knowledge into a context, even into multiple contexts. New knowledge—whether concepts, examples, data, or information—needs to be attached somehow to students' existing knowledge. Students need to see and understand the relationship between what they already know and what they are learning for the first time. Contexts include frameworks of various kinds—historical, social, cultural, intellectual, and more. Frameworks allow students to put bits

Question and Cue Column	Note-Taking Column
Summary	

of knowledge together in order to see connections and divergences among theories and conceptual approaches. Putting Freudian psychoanalytic theory together with the theories of Carl Jung is one example; other frameworks that strengthen learning might be comparing Romanesque and Gothic architecture, contrasting Platonic and Aristotelian philosophical categories and concerns, or considering various kinds of causes and effects for diseases such as alcoholism—biochemical, behavioral, cultural, social, and so on. Learning lasts when contexts are established and connections identified.

Two related effective study habits are extracting key ideas from reading and then organizing those ideas into a mental model. In each of these active approaches to study, students must make decisions. They need not only to prioritize what's important but also to understand relationships between and among facts and concepts. In learning about Buddhism, for example, students need to understand more than just the "four noble truths": they also need to understand how those central Buddhist beliefs relate to one another, and also how they relate to the "eightfold path," a set of practices that address the life challenges presented by the four noble truths. And further, students can be expected to learn how Buddhist teachings were developed in response to Hindu religious beliefs and practices.

These more productive approaches involve active learning (see chapter 3), one powerful tool of which is writing (see chapter 9). Writing can solidify conceptual understanding by requiring students to *apply* a concept, even if only by identifying and explaining an example with a single sentence. Students can then further explore their understanding through a one-paragraph explanation of why or how the single-sentence example illustrates the concept. The key strategies here are to exemplify and apply, using specific examples and particular applications. (See interlude 4 on taking these strategies of explanation further.)

Other effective learning strategies include converting key points to questions and rephrasing main ideas. One benefit of converting key points from declarative sentences to interrogative forms is that the questions provoke answers. A point declared and then converted to a question allows for an expansion of that point. It invites explanations and applications. Consider, for example, the following sentence: "Enlightenment thinkers emphasized the mind's power to reason, in contrast to the mind's yearning for religious faith; they emphasized the common nature of human experience, ignoring differences in social, cultural, and religious values." We can rephrase this statement as an inquiry: "What did Enlightenment thinkers emphasize about the human mind and about human experience? How did these emphases differ from the concerns of earlier thinkers?" We might then follow those questions with: "What were the consequences of this shift of emphasis?" And so on, one question leading to another.

Asking students to rephrase main ideas in their own words helps them clarify what they understand and identify what they may remain fuzzy about. Getting students to convey their understanding in their own words gives them practice in explaining. It requires them both to generalize and to particularize, to extract concepts and then apply them to specific instances. Saying things in more than one way ("What's another way of saying this"? "How else might we explain this concept?") helps them see that there is more than a single, definitive way to explain an idea, analyze a concept, evaluate a scenario, or apply a general principle.

And as with extracting key concepts and contextualizing them, students are engaged in active learning when they create questions and rephrase statements. In doing so, they connect their new learning with their previous understanding, sometimes extending that understanding, sometimes deepening it, and sometimes subverting it.

Conditions for Successful Learning

What conditions are necessary for long-lasting learning? Willingham (2009) and Brown, Roediger, and McDaniel (2014) suggest these conditions, at the very least:

- Possession of an adequate *information/knowledge base*
- A spacious *working memory*

Without an adequate base of knowledge, a fundamental grounding in essential information, it is difficult for students to learn what is being taught. For example, if you know a great deal about a sport, such as professional baseball or soccer, you can follow discussions about games and matches and understand the fine points of plays and strategy. Shift the discussion to cricket or rugby, however, and you are likely to have a harder time understanding something spoken or written about those sports. Grounding in the fundamentals of the game and a degree of familiarity with it make deeper, more nuanced understanding possible.

The same is true of academic learning. If you know little about economics or tort law, reading an article about either subject is difficult, challenging, even frustrating. You struggle to decide what's important, extract key points, or follow the argument. A base of knowledge is essential for understanding, and understanding is necessary for developing deep, long-lasting learning. When students attempt to absorb too many things at once, they can't decide what's important, are unable to identify and relate key concepts, and quickly become intellectually overloaded and emotionally frustrated.

Consider how knowing and understanding key principles of mathematics—at whatever level, from the principles of multiplication to more complex theorems of geometry or equations of calculus—allows students to build on that knowledge, solving problems confidently and efficiently. Students who don't know basic number facts or who don't have a firm grasp of foundational concepts are at a disadvantage. While the better informed and knowledgeable students are adding small bits of information to their understanding of mathematics, those without an adequate knowledge base in stored memory are left trying to absorb too much information all at once. As a consequence, their short-term memory is overwhelmed, and their learning becomes compromised.

To avoid cognitive overload and have room in short-term memory for new information and new knowledge, students should have basic information and concepts already anchored in long-term memory. So how do we help students develop the base of learning in long-term memory that enables them to acquire new knowledge more readily?

As we suggested earlier, chunking learning in focused, short study sessions and practicing recalling that learning actively and building on it gradually are ways to build long-term memory and make room in short-term memory for new knowledge to be acquired.

Teachers often assume that their students have a knowledge base that they simply do not possess. This misconception frequently arises in intermediate and advanced courses that build on and extend basic knowledge and concepts. But it also occurs in basic courses, when instructors assume that students learned things in high school about which they have only the most superficial understanding. College students do not all arrive on campus with a common base of academic and social experience. More than ever before, they come today from diverse backgrounds—cultural, social, and economic—with varying levels and types of academic preparation.

Students can struggle painfully if they lack the knowledge base assumed by their instructor or have little grasp of concepts supposedly learned in high school courses. One way to ensure that those students can learn successfully in our courses is to provide them with the foundation they need to learn what we have to teach through extra help, such as tutoring, mentoring, and other forms of academic support. Possessing background knowledge is extremely important because, as Maryanne Wolf (2018) has noted, the more knowledge resources students possess, the better able they are to make inferences and deductions, engage in analogical thinking, and apply what they are learning (p. 56).

Taking regular study breaks also helps store learning in long-term memory. Studying for three hours or even two hours straight is not nearly as effective as studying for one hour or, at most, an hour and a half at a time. A ten-minute break after ninety minutes, or a five-minute break after forty-five minutes or even thirty minutes, gives students' brains a chance to rest and recover from their intellectual exertions. The result is stronger and longer-lasting learning. As teachers, we can explain how study habits like these can improve their academic performance.

A third strategy for making new learning stick is to develop memory aids—the use of mnemonics and other strategies that anchor new learning so it can be retrieved when needed. Most of us learned techniques for memorizing things—such as the mnemonics for the names of the Great Lakes (HOMES for Huron, Ontario, Michigan, Erie, Superior) and the colors of the spectrum (ROY G BIV for red, orange, yellow, green, blue, indigo, violet). Using mnemonics like these can help students put information into long-term memory, where it can be retrieved from time to time for practice or use. Retrieval is essential for solidifying new knowledge and rendering it ready for use. This is why recalling information without the aid of notes, even when the information is recalled only partially or without complete accuracy, is more effective than reading through a set of notes. And as research has shown, the greater the effort in cognitive retrieval, the greater the retention of learning. Once information is secured in long-term memory, it can be recalled, forming the basis for extending and deepening knowledge. Short-term memory space is thus available for acquiring new knowledge.

Key Principles of Active Learning

So far in this chapter we have considered effective and ineffective study habits and discussed the importance of being aware of our students' knowledge base, which is essential for calibrating our teaching. We have also suggested strategies for enhancing learning through making space available for knowledge acquisition in working memory. We turn next to some key principles that, though familiar, are essential for successful long-term, long-lasting learning: practice, struggle, and relevance.

Practice. Practice is critical for learning. This is certainly true for skills such as reading and writing, computing and analyzing, summarizing and synthesizing. At every level of schooling, skills are acquired through practice. As students achieve competence, they develop their skills through meeting increasingly complex challenges, scaffolded so that each is a bit more difficult than the last. Thus, we need to recognize the purpose and value of practice—and the different kinds of practice for different kinds of learning.

To be effective, however, practice needs to be conscious and deliberate. To develop skill in any form of learning—from playing piano to analyzing a balance sheet, solving complex mathematical equations, or learning the principles of nursing practice—students need to focus on the hardest elements and build their skill through concentrated, focused practice. Otherwise, they will find themselves simply rehearsing what they already know and can do, while glossing over what they don't yet know or haven't yet learned to do and developing an illusion of competence. The term most often used for a learning effort focused on the most difficult challenges is "deliberate practice"; this term reflects the importance of attention and intention while concentrating on the knowledge being acquired or the skill being learned.

Struggle. Researchers have discovered that there is a "Goldilocks zone"—a level of desirable difficulty that is "just right" for maximum learning. This level of challenge enables students to stretch beyond their level of competence. It taxes students just so much and no more, enabling them to meet the challenge with a reasonable degree of struggle. The struggle is necessary and productive for learning, even when a student fails to reach the desired level of skill or degree of knowledge retention. For example, having students try to solve math problems on their own with minimal guidance readies them, even when they fail, to better understand those problems when an instructor explains them later. They learn well because of their struggle—their effort is a prelude to more solid understanding. Their struggle to learn primes them for the teacher's instruction and readies them to understand it more thoroughly than if that instruction was provided without their initial effort at learning. A complicating challenge is that one student's "desirable difficulty" is an easy accomplishment for another, and a terribly out-of-reach task for a third. This makes our job as educators more difficult, of course. The challenge is to calibrate our expectations for how much, how well, and at what pace different students we teach can and do learn.

Relevance. Students remember what they care about and what they think about. Learning is stronger when it matters to students. It behooves us, then, to make the learning personal. Ask: "What does this mean to you?" Or, "Why does this matter for you? Why do you care about it? How does it impact your own life or the lives of those you care about?" We need to consider the implications of students' learning for their lives. We need to understand why what we teach might and can matter to them, and then factor that information into our course, syllabus, and lesson planning (see chapter 2).

The principles of practice, struggle, and relevance are grounded in the idea that intelligence is *malleable*. Intelligence can be developed through sustained effort. Students can improve their ability to learn with practice and expert guidance. The gold standard of research on this principle is presented by Carol Dweck in *Mindset* (2007), in which she contrasts the "fixed mindset" with the "growth mindset." Students with a *fixed* mindset believe that their failure to solve a challenging problem comes from their limited ability to do so. They are not smart enough, they think. Students with a *growth* mindset tell themselves that they need to work harder. These students come at the problem again with the attitude that, though the problem is difficult, they can do better. They just have to keep trying. It is this growth mindset toward problem-solving and toward learning in general that makes for success.

According to Dweck, learners with a fixed mindset consider their intellectual qualities to be fixed traits that cannot change. These learners prefer documenting their intelligence and showing off their talents rather than working to develop and improve them. They believe that talent alone leads to success, with only minimal effort required.

Students exhibiting a growth mindset approach learning tasks differently. They possess an underlying belief in themselves as learners and are confident that their learning and intelligence can grow with time and experience. When people believe that they can get smarter, they work hard, having realized that their effort leads to successful achievement.

Peter Johnston (2012) draws out the implications of Dweck's distinction between fixed and growth mindsets in his "dynamic knowledge frame." He explains how these contrasting attitudes appear in students' classroom behavior, in their approach to assignments and tests, and in their responses to difficulties and failure. "Fixed-frame" learners, for example, explain their own and others' performances in terms of natural ability anchored in permanent traits. They engage in activities that come naturally to them, including academic activities they can succeed at without much difficulty, thus avoiding the chance to make mistakes.

"Dynamic-frame" learners, on the other hand, explain their own and others' performance behaviors in terms of contexts and processes—according to what has been done. They choose activities that challenge them, from which they can learn, and through which they can develop. Difficulties don't distress them but rather increase their strategic efforts at self-monitoring, self-instruction, and self-development. They see failure as part of learning—unavoidable and even necessary—and they value education as a path to understanding others and the world as they prepare for productive work.

Helping students see the benefits of Dweck's growth mindset and Johnston's dynamic knowledge frame can have a significant impact on their learning. Getting students to view themselves as dynamic learners who benefit from working hard at their learning pays dividends not only in how much they learn but in how well and how long they retain it. When they overcome the negative attitude encapsulated in fixed-mindset thinking, they can become dynamic-frame thinkers with a growth mindset that helps them believe in themselves as capable learners—and with that belief, they can begin to realize their learning potential. Helping students cultivate a growth mindset and a dynamic learning frame is thus critical for our work as teachers.

It is important to note, however, that a growth mindset and a dynamic learning perspective cannot be simply proclaimed. Instead, they must be developed consciously and conscientiously over time and with effort. Students will inevitably lapse and find themselves in more of a fixed mindset and learning frame; Dweck advises acknowledging that reality and helping students recognize what triggers fixed-mindset behavior as a first step toward overcoming it and replacing it with the positive and beneficial learning habits of a growth mindset.

Context, Intermixed Practice, and Failure

Our goal as teachers is to enable students to deepen their understanding of concepts and be able to apply them in a variety of contexts. We want them to make connections between what they already know and what they are learning, and between what they learn in our courses and what they learn elsewhere. Our hope is for our students to develop a coherent, integrated understanding of not only our subject or discipline but of its place in their lives and in the larger world.

Deep knowledge is *contextualized*, *connected*, and *coherent*. Shallow knowledge is fragmented, disconnected, and incoherent. Shallow knowledge is better than no knowledge, but deep knowledge is better than shallow knowledge. It is deep knowledge, of course, that we need to aim for with our students. How can we help our students achieve deep knowledge that they can draw on long after they leave our classrooms?

One way is to interleave the various kinds of learning skills that students practice in our courses. In *Nonsense* (2016), Jamie Holmes recommends mixing up a learner's practice. Don't have novice golfers just hit balls off a tee at the driving range, one after another, he suggests. Mix up the different strokes, mix the irons and wood clubs, and mix the different-length irons. Similarly, he advises against baseball players taking batting practice by swinging at pitches thrown at the same speed and of the same type—one curve after another, or one fastball after another, for example. Mix up the pitches and their speeds, he recommends. Simulate the unpredictability of actual playing conditions, whatever the sport.

The same principle applies to solving academic problems, whether in math or physics, in economics or psychology. Knowing *when* to use a particular problem-solving strategy is as important as knowing *how* to solve problems and *which* strategies to apply. Testing students with different kinds of problems mixed together challenges them at a higher level of understanding than simply having them practice each type of problem separately. This kind of interleaving of tasks is essential for developing deeper and longer-lasting learning. As David Epstein (2019) notes, testing and spacing out learning make knowledge stick; they make it durable. Desirable difficulties, including mixing problem types—interleaving—make knowledge last; they also make it flexible (p. 96).

Holmes also argues that we need to think about the kinds of failure our students should practice—how often and under what circumstances they should practice failure, and when and how we should intervene. We need to think about the quality of failure—how close it comes to success, how interesting it is, and how it can be reframed as an opportunity to build resilience, pursue a new direction of thinking, or practice taking risks. "Fail better" was Samuel Beckett's self-admonition.

Now that we have identified some key principles for effective, long-lasting learning, it's time to discuss applications. What do we do with this information in the classroom? How do we help our students become deeper, more confident learners?

Seven Teaching and Learning Strategies

The following learning strategies summarize our key suggestions for making learning last.

1. Have students learn by re-creating their notes, not simply reading through them. That is, ask students to retrieve what they remember, say, from a reading. Ask students to check

their re-creation against the original text they have been studying. Also ask students to extend their thinking about what they are learning by expanding or otherwise embellishing their notes.

2. Break up the review of material for students. Have them practice retrieving information at reasonably spaced intervals. Let them accumulate and build up the knowledge retrieved, to gradually increase what they know. Begin a lecture not by summarizing the previous session, but by asking them what they remember. With each iteration of retrieval, they bring back a bit more of what they are learning.

3. Create desirable difficulties for students. Give them problems that stretch their ability and capacity. If a task is too easy, students can develop the illusion that they understand things better than they do. If a task is too difficult, it can cause students to give up in frustration.

4. Require practice with different types of problems rather than problems all of the same type or level of difficulty at the same time. Interleave these different types of problems. Doing only one kind of problem in math, for example, provides inadequate preparation for an exam that mixes many different types and levels of problems. Part of what students need to learn is to identify what kind of problem they are trying to solve—to distinguish among problem types. This skill is critical for deeper and more successful long-term learning.

5. Explain the importance of taking regular breaks.

6. Require students to begin long-term projects early. Stretch out their work and check on its progress regularly and frequently. Break down longer projects into smaller steps or stages, and check on those according to strict deadlines.

7. Help students understand the narrative and causal connections between and among facts and information, ideas and concepts. Provide them with a narrative arc for your course and its constituent elements (see chapter 6).

Applications

1. How might you help your students move away from ineffective study habits and toward effective ones?

2. How might you interleave different types of problems and questions for your students to test their understanding?
3. How might you create space for your students to struggle optimally with some of the more challenging material in the course?
4. How can you introduce the elements of practice and relevance into your assignments and class activities?
5. What kinds of contexts and connections might you provide in your course to make their coherence more apparent to students?
6. What questions could you use to help students develop a sense of agency?

An Explanation of Explanation

One of the most essential of all teaching practices is explanation. Much of what we do as teachers requires explaining. But just what are we doing when we explain? What is explanation anyway?

The basic meaning of "explain" is to make something plain or intelligible; to clear something of difficulty or obscurity; to describe it in a way that brings about understanding, accounting for its cause, origin, or reason for being.

Explaining involves different angles of approach. We *describe* something so a reader or listener can "see" it mentally. We *illustrate* a concept to aid understanding, anchoring the concept in something more concrete and specific. We *connect* one idea with another, presenting it in relationship to something else already understood—linking the new with the familiar.

Sometimes explaining requires *analyzing*—breaking a process down into steps or stages or parts and showing their relationship to one another. We explain, also, through *unfolding* layers of implication—through unpacking the meanings of a poem, for example, line by line, image by image, word by word, syllable by syllable, sound by sound.

Good Explanations

What makes an explanation good? What criteria define successful explanation? What are the qualities of a good explanation? Here are our candidates:

- Clarity
- Completeness
- Exactness
- Precision
- Integrity
- Elegance

Maryellen Weimer (2015b) offers the following observations and tips for crafting better explanations:

- Pitch the language at the level of the learner. Good explanations are understandable. Disciplinary language may be expeditious, but it's not always comprehensible to students.
- Pace the language to match the speed of the learner. Speak slowly enough to be followed by your students, yet fast enough to remain interesting.
- Provide malleable explanations capable of being reshaped, re-formed, reconstituted, or reconfigured; look for alternative ways to explain key concepts.
- Repeat as often as needed—perhaps in a theme-with-variations format.
- Illustrate with examples that are meaningful to your students—relevant, time-sensitive, and culture-sensitive.
- Offer multiple sources for explanations—not just from the teacher, but from students as well.

In *Improving Your Classroom Teaching* (1999), Weimer notes that learning how to provide clear and successful explanations that enhance student understanding takes time; it's a teaching skill to be developed gradually and with practice. She identifies three components to improving our explanatory practice: ascertaining when students do and don't understand; making content relevant; and developing and using concrete, specific examples effectively (p. 75).

We come to understand something, whether an idea, an object, a text, a person, or a performance, by approaching it from various directions—with our eyes, ears, and noses; with our minds via intellect and imagination; with silence and sound; by means of pain or embarrassment; and through history, science, religion, art, and experience. We discover a route and follow where it leads us.

Good explanations are often multidirectional: they explain in multiple ways and from multiple perspectives. How, for example, do we explain what rain is? We might explain it scientifically by describing clouds, climatic conditions, and the changing of water and vapor. To understand rain, we can observe it, see how it looks from different angles, notice how it falls. We can feel rain on our skin as a light and drizzly mist, barely identifiable as rain at all, or as a harsh and wind-driven downpour—or any number of sensations in between.

We can explain rain through its effects on plants and people. We can listen to the sounds it makes on glass, on blacktop, on stone and metal. We can consider the moods that rain induces before, during, and after the skies open. We can look at rain indirectly, obliquely, considering what we associate it with—tears, love, violence, sorrow. Taken together, these ways of understanding and explaining rain do not exhaust all the possible ways to comprehend it, but they do indicate that there is more than one approach to understanding and appreciating what rain is and does.

The Search for Good Explanations

In *The Beginning of Infinity* (2012), David Deutsch, a Cambridge University physicist, argues that the search for good explanations drives scientific understanding and discovery. The main effort of science, according to Deutsch, is to correct errors, which it does by searching for increasingly better explanations.

Good explanations result from a set of related empirical processes that possess what Deutsch calls "reach"—the capacity to solve problems other than those they were created to solve (p. 30). Reach is important because it suggests that our knowledge is always limited but also open-ended, our discovery of new knowledge being a stream of continuous explanation rather than a closed system with definite, absolute, and definitive answers.

David Hand (2015) suggests that explanations change as the data change; increasingly better explanations accumulate and capture better data. However, the patterns we use to describe the behavior of the natural world are not always accurate; they don't always encompass all there is, but rather all that we can see. And so we are stuck, most often, with something less than certainty, and, as a result, with a better explanation just waiting to be discovered.

Chapter Five

Discussion-Based Teaching

In college and university seminars and other small classes, teaching often takes the form of discussion. Discussion-based teaching provides a useful complement—or even alternative—to lecturing. Because discussion and lecture are the two most common forms of college classroom instruction, it's essential that we consider the merits, value, and benefits of each when planning and delivering instruction for our students. It's useful to remind ourselves of the central rhetorical considerations of audience, purpose, and occasion. What do we think is the best mode of instructional delivery for the particular students we are teaching in a given course on a particular day and for a particular course segment? Sometimes the answer will be discussion.

Leading productive discussion classes requires both preparation and practice. Effective discussions occur when they are prepared in advance, led with a purpose, summarized, and assessed. Good discussions are grounded in questions that generate further thinking for students and instructors alike. Moreover, to be effective, discussion-based teaching needs to meet course goals. That is, effective discussion-based teaching needs to be learner-centered and goal-directed.

Thus, this chapter is about discussion-based learning as much as discussion-based teaching. We explain why we use discussion in our own teaching and how to use it to promote student learning. We explore the types of challenges teachers confront in using discussion-based teaching, and how to address those challenges. We also consider ways to begin discussions in class and then sustain and conclude them, and we provide general guidelines for class participation in both small and large classes.

Instructors often have trouble developing and sustaining quality discussion in their classes. We remember occasions early in our teaching careers when we came to class armed with a set of questions that we expected would launch a vibrant discussion of the literary text assigned for the day. Instead, we were met with blank stares. As we raced through our questions, which we mostly had to answer ourselves, what we had thought would fill up a fifty- or seventy-five-minute class was exhausted in a fraction of the time.

Part of the problem was that many of our first discussion questions were closed rather than open-ended. They were not designed for discussion as much as for brief, clear-cut answers. That was one problem. A second was that our questions were too difficult. They called for deep understanding based on careful and thoughtful textual analysis, which students were only beginning to learn how to do. Yet another was that students were unprepared: they had not done the reading.

Let's take these up, briefly, in reverse order. To ensure that students can participate in a discussion about a text they have not read, we make copies of a few key passages we expect to focus on at some point during the class session. Sometimes it's the opening page or two, sometimes it's a passage describing a critical textual moment, and sometimes it's both. The idea, simply, is that all students can read the passage at the same time, with the prepared students seeing it for a second time. It's one way to get discussion up and running.

Another tactic is scaffolding questions so that the weaker and less well prepared students can participate early by answering opening questions that are easier than those that follow. One type of early question is to ask for observations. Ask students what they notice about the text. You will probably need to guide them a bit more specifically—helping them to notice, for example, that a poem has a regular or irregular stanza or rhyme pattern, that it is composed of a series of questions, that it describes an outdoor scene in one stanza and an interior space in another, and so on. From those observations, you can lead students to make connections and inferences and then on to interpretive conclusions about the text.

Another kind of opening question is to ask students for their personal responses to a text. Ask them what stood out for them, what struck them as memorable, interesting, or otherwise noteworthy—perhaps even something that upset, frustrated, or angered them.

Often, however, the problem is not with the reading or the questions, but with the discussion itself. The hesitancy of some students to participate may have cultural roots. Some of our students come from educational backgrounds in which they were expected only to listen and take notes, not to ask questions. Teachers, from their perspective, are the experts, and the ones who should be talking—explaining, demonstrating, elaborating—and not listening to students, who are there to pay respectful attention to their teachers.

What should we do when we encounter such hesitancy in our classrooms? First, we can recognize that our students come from a wide variety of educational backgrounds, and that class participation protocols vary across cultures, both within countries and between them. Many of our students are first-generation college students who are coming to our institutions with insecurities about their academic responsibilities; they often lack knowledge about higher education institutional norms and expectations. We should be sensitive to these realities and create a safe space for learning in our classrooms—a welcoming environment in which students who are new to higher education culture, and new perhaps to American college and university culture as well, can participate productively (see interlude 1).

At the same time, we can make the case that students attending an American college or university will find discussion-based classes to be, if not the educational norm, at least a common occurrence. Further, we might suggest that students who hope to seek employment in global companies, including American companies in the United States and abroad, need to participate productively in discussion and engage in collaborative work generally to develop important work-related skills that will be of value to them beyond college.

Nonetheless, some students, regardless of our efforts, may still not see the value of discussion. Why should they listen to other students, they think, instead of to the teacher? That's not what they're paying for. These students may see discussion as inefficient and ineffectual, as not giving them what they need to know to perform successfully on course examinations and other forms of assessment. They prefer learning directly from the expert instructor.

These are legitimate concerns.

As discussion is a form of active learning, one of the first things to do in introducing it is to explain its benefits for students. We present methods for doing so in chapter 3; we can add here that we need to let students know that we do not engage in discussion for its own sake. We conduct discussion-based classes not because discussion is interesting or enjoyable, or because it makes class go faster (though these are added bonuses of good class discussions), but because effective discussion-based teaching enhances learning. Thus, we need to explain the specific benefits of discussion as an aid to learning and to conduct class discussion in such a way that students experience its power to extend and deepen their understanding—to solidify, deepen, and advance their learning.

The Benefits of Discussion

Why have classroom discussion at all? What are the benefits of discussion for teaching and learning? The most important benefit of discussion is that it can strengthen students' learning so that it sticks better and lasts longer. This happens, however, only if the discussion is purposeful and goal-directed, and only if students are fully engaged in it. Discussion works when students have been hooked into the conversation. We thus need strategies to capture students' interest, provoke their thinking, and deepen their engagement with what is being taught through class discussion. This engagement is critical; everything else follows from it.

Students benefit in other ways from discussion-based teaching. They gain practice in explaining themselves to one another; they practice analyzing and responding, building on one another's thinking, and adjusting their thinking. As Michael Levenson (2018) has noted, students "test their voices" during discussion; they try out and clarify their thinking while opening their classmates' thinking to new angles of thought (p. 157). Discussion helps students learn to cooperate and collaborate, to work together in small teams; it gives them practice in oral communication, even the shy and diffident students. These skills will help them in future classes and the workplace.

Discussion keeps us connected to our students. We get to know one another better through the back-and-forth of conversation, and our bonds with our students and theirs with one another are strengthened. Discussion allows our humanity to emerge. And the classroom learning environment is enhanced by the greater ease of communication between teacher and students, and among students, enabled by the less formal qualities of discussion.

During discussion, questions often come up that were not part of the original teaching plan but that can lead to fruitful lines of inquiry, some of which may serve as topics for student research. Because class discussions can take such unpredictable turns, we need to be ready to take advantage of them. However, we acknowledge that discussion, as Jay Howard notes in "How to Hold a Better Class Discussion" (2019), involves risks. We risk losing control over the direction the class is taking. Although some instructors avoid discussion-based teaching because it requires improvisation, that is exactly what we need to learn how to do if we are to keep control of the class. For no matter how well planned a discussion-based class session may be, there is no guarantee that it will follow the prescribed lesson plan. Discussion's tendency to diverge and stray, to go off topic, can be a benefit for our teaching, as it makes room for moments of surprise and discovery, for us as well as for our students. But we must also meet the challenge of redirecting discussion that has deviated, however productively, back to the planned work of the class session.

A final benefit of discussion to consider is that it gives us a chance to see how our students think. In asking follow-up questions, we can probe their reasoning process to better understand why they think what they do. Discussion enables us to correct them when they are wrong—or, as often happens, when they are partly right and partly wrong. In short, discussion provides one of the richest means of formative assessment we instructors have, and one of the easiest to implement (see chapter 11).

Setting the stage for students to participate in class discussion begins with acknowledging the value of discussion and its importance in your course—both for student learning and for a student's grade. You may decide to count class participation as 10 percent or even 20 percent of a student's grade, defining "participation" as turning in short assignments on time as well as speaking up during class discussion. You might also count asking questions (and not simply responding to questions) as effective class participation.

Basic Principles of Discussion

Students need to know where they are in the midst of the discussion so that they can follow what is being said. For that to happen, we need to contextualize class discussion. We should explain the purpose of the discussion in relation to course goals and to larger contexts beyond the course proper, as well as make clear to students where the discussion begins, where it has gone, what it is doing at particular junctures, and where it ends up. When students get lost during a discussion, they turn off and tune out. Check in with them to ensure that they are remaining attentive. And when the discussion is about to conclude, provide them with clear key takeaways—what you want them to know and think about further.

To increase your chances of developing successful class discussions, keep the following suggestions in mind:

- Be clear about the purpose and focus of the discussion.
- Balance staying on track with allowing for digressions.
- Use open-ended questions with multiple possible answers.
- Validate student responses; correct when necessary.

- Adhere to the rules for discussion you establish with your students.
- Create an environment that welcomes student questions and responses, where all voices can be heard and all are listened to respectfully.
- Link the discussion to clear learning goals.

Conducting a Discussion: Several Principles Illustrated

Maryellen Weimer (1999) has succinctly summarized the value of effective discussion questions. She suggests that discussion questions are most productive when we give students time to think and to respond to incorrect answers constructively, as well as encourage them to engage in cross-talk—that is, to respond to one another (p. 55).

We elaborate here on Weimer's recommendations to create a set of guiding principles for conducting discussion:

- Give students time to think and write.
- Scaffold questions from easier to more difficult.
- Provide students with something interesting to discuss.
- Validate and use student contributions to the discussion.
- Encourage cross-talk among students.

One effective method for jump-starting discussion is to begin with a few minutes of writing. For example, on the first day of a critical thinking course, we can ask students to write briefly about the characteristic behaviors of critical thinkers with questions like: "What qualities do you associate with "critical thinking?" or "What distinguishes the thinking of successful thinkers?" Instead of following this writing period with a think/pair/share exercise, have the class as a whole share their responses and collect them on a whiteboard—perhaps recorded by student scribes.

Because students have had a few minutes to think via their writing, they have something to contribute to the discussion. Since everyone has something to say, all students can be called on should volunteers be slow to come forward. Under these conditions, it doesn't take long for discussion to get moving. The process includes one additional element: avoid criticizing or editing responses to the opening discussion question—for two reasons. First, you want to reduce students' anxiety, and second, you aim to generate and validate as many approaches, notions, and ideas as possible. While you are collecting responses, students have time to think. As they see and hear what others are contributing, they have additional thoughts, perhaps for the first time. And if they sense that all responses are welcome, they won't be afraid to contribute.

Following the initial collection of responses, continue the discussion by looking for patterns and connections—groupings and contrasts that lead to additional thinking. From there, further questions can be directed to key learning goals. For example, you can show students that there is far more to critical thinking than they initially thought, pointing out that critical thinking isn't always narrowly "critical" in the common sense of the term and that some of the elements of critical thinking they have identified are related to creative thinking; in fact, that critical and creative thinking complement and reinforce one another. By starting with what students themselves suggest, and with their initially limited understanding of critical thinking, you can engage them in further elaborating on what critical thinking entails, why it matters, and how they can develop their own critical thinking powers.

Strategies for Initiating Discussion

You can help students prepare for class discussion by giving them a pre-discussion assignment—for example, providing one or more key questions ahead of time on which the discussion will focus. We have seen syllabi that include discussion questions for the weekly required readings. Such questions can help students manage reading assignments effectively by directing their attention to what matters most. You might have students write brief online responses in a blog or forum posting, which you can then use to jump-start discussion in class. You can also have students keep a journal of their reading, which you collect periodically to read, comment on, and/or grade, and which can also serve as an entry point for them into class discussion. You can ask students to come to class with a question about a passage in the reading that confused them, disturbed them, or excited them. These and other kinds of small, low-stakes assignments and exercises share an important feature: they give students an opportunity to think a bit before you invite them to contribute to any discussion that takes place in class.

In "The Dreaded Discussion: Ten Ways to Start" (1981/2012), Peter Frederick offers a number of other suggestions for getting discussion going, including these three:

1. Ask students to identify one concrete image, scene, or moment from an assignment they read or viewed. They don't have to

analyze or interpret their choice, but they do need to describe it so that their classmates know what they are referring to. You can follow up by asking the reason for their choice.

2. Have students write down two questions they have about the day's assignment.

3. Ask students to pair off and decide together on the primary value of a reading due for that day's class, and how it connects to the goals of the course.

We have successfully used these additional strategies:

4. Have students identify one passage from a reading assignment that resonated for them because they found it interesting, provocative, important, confusing—give them a range of options.

5. Ask students to find a second passage that can be related in some way to the first passage they selected. Have them write a sentence or two explaining the connection. Ask for volunteers to share their thinking after first reading their selected passage or passages.

6. Present students with a brief scenario to think about, with one or two guiding questions. Give them two or three minutes to think and jot a few notes; then pair them or group them in threes to discuss their thinking. Have each pair or group contribute to the class discussion overall.

7. Show students the first few steps of a scientific experiment. Ask them to predict what will happen next under conditions you set out for them.

For each of these exercises, be sure to clarify what you expect students to do. Once an exercise has been completed, let students know what it is you expect them to have learned from it. Be clear about what you want students to take away from the discussion overall, as well as what they should learn from its individual elements.

Strategies for Sustaining Discussion

One familiar difficulty you are likely to face in sustaining class discussions is having only a few students contributing—the same few for most of a class session, and then, if you allow it, those same students again and again, class after class. Some students enjoy discussion so much that they are consistently eager, even insistent participants. When one or two students are dominating a discussion, respond by thanking the vocal few for their contributions and letting them know that their ideas are appreciated, but that it's time to hear from some other students, whom you can then solicit.

Another challenge comes when a discussion falters or comes to a halt. When this happens, pause the discussion (since it has stopped anyway) and turn the situation to your advantage. Have students write for a few minutes—no more than two or three, even as little as one minute—to ask a question, identify a key idea or insight, or predict or suggest what they expect or want to hear about next. Then ask them to share their thinking about what they were writing. You can have them do this first in pairs or groups of three, or you can go straight to full-class discussion.

You can kill a discussion by doing the majority of the talking yourself. If you dominate the discussion—by speaking first, by tipping your hand about what you think, by monopolizing the conversation—the discussion will die, if it ever acquires any momentum at all. Listen more and listen better. Speak last or not at all. Jot down what you hear students saying—on the board, or on paper. You can comment on their observations later in the discussion, after other students participate. You can ask questions directed toward your learning goals. You can point out connections among the comments your students make during the discussion and identify key questions that their comments raise.

Facilitate, guide, direct—but don't take over. At a later point in the class period, you can distill key ideas, explain essential concepts, connect the dots, reveal your hand. You might also ask a couple of students to serve as discussion note-takers. Often in discussion, students will miss some key points you want them to understand. You can use your own notes taken during the discussion to clarify, calibrate, and develop the discussion further in the direction of your learning goals.

For sustained discussion, students need to practice the skill of careful and attentive listening. Teach listening skills; require serious listening. During class discussion, ask students to reformulate in their own words what other students say. Insist that students respond to each other before you respond to them.

Two other pieces of advice about sustaining effective class discussions are provided by Maryellen Weimer (2015a). First, keep the discussion segments short—fifteen minutes is a reasonable length for students to stay engaged and focused. At that point, you can highlight key points, explain what was accomplished, and describe where the discussion needs to go next. Then take students in that direction with the next focused discussion element for another ten or fifteen minutes. And so on. Her second piece of advice is to conclude with something clear and noteworthy. Weimer suggests returning to the question that launched the discussion and having students write a one-sentence summary in response. You can have one group of students do this, another group list questions the discussion has answered, and a third group identify any questions that remain unanswered. If time permits, you can use the responses of each group to wrap up and close out the discussion. You can also collect students' responses for review, perhaps incorporating them into your teaching plan for the next class meeting. And when you run out of time during a discussion class, you can always email the students later with a few key takeaway points you want to highlight for them.

Responding to Students during Discussion

Instead of responding yourself immediately to a student's question or comment, ask for one or perhaps two students to respond first. Require students to observe these kinds of discussion protocols consistently. Be sure, as well, to affirm and confirm what students are saying. Question students and prod them to clarify their ideas. Connect the comments they make; build upon them and thank students for offering them. When you need to contradict a student's contribution, find a way to accept part of what that student has offered. Validate the comment and the effort to contribute. You can say something like, "You make an interesting but provocative point. The first thing you said was clear and to the point. It's the second part of your comment I would like to challenge or have us think about together."

When you need to complicate, develop, or otherwise extend or expand what a student offers in discussion, be sure to indicate the importance of the student's comments before developing them further in your teaching. Always seek to connect, to integrate, to validate, and to build on what students contribute in class discussion. And be sure to let them know when they are doing good and productive work in their class discussions.

When a student gives a decidedly incorrect response to a question, instead of simply telling the student that the response is wrong, ask why he or she is thinking along those lines. Ask for evidence ("Where in the text do you find support for this claim?") and get at the reasoning ("Why do you say that—or think that?" "Explain how you arrived at this conclusion"). Often you will find that the student has misunderstood a detail, misconstrued a term, or otherwise gone off track at a particular point that you can now identify. You can then explain how the student made the error and how it can be corrected. You should validate the correct part of the student's thinking—up to the point where the mistake was made. Let the student know what he or she got right. Also let the student know that you understand the process of reasoning by which the mistaken conclusion was reached.

You can demonstrate your interest in the discussion and students' participation in it, their responses during discussion, and their questions by maintaining eye contact with students, by nodding at them, by listening attentively, and by moving around the room as well as through other physical gestures and movements that indicate interest. You can also bring up comments that students have made outside of class, perhaps something a student said informally before class or after a previous one, or brought up during office hours or in an email, that you think can add productively to class discussion of a relevant topic.

For small classes, try to bring every student into the discussion, at least part of the time, even in a brief and simple way. Mention that you will try to hear from every student at least once during a class discussion (if class size permits, of course). During the discussion proper, you might say things like: "We have heard now from four students, let's hear from some new voices." Or: "One side of the room has been dominating the conversation so far; now it's time to hear from the other side." To ensure more equitable and complete participation, put students in small groups, perhaps assigning particular roles to each group member so that everyone will have something to contribute, if only during their small-group discussion.

Keep track of which students you call on. Shift your attention to different parts of the room. Ask easy questions of more reluctant participants. Direct the more difficult, complex, and challenging questions to the eager and better-prepared students. Consider what kinds of questions you will direct to whom and at what point in the discussion. Also, let students who didn't participate in a particular class discussion know that you missed hearing from them, and that you will be calling on them early in the next class meeting. Rather than make assumptions about their reasons, you can reach out to them to find out why they were not participating. They might simply need your human touch.

Ways to Discourage Discussion

In an article posted to the website of the American Astronomical Society, Douglas Duncan (Duncan and Southon 1976) presents half a dozen ineffective ways to encourage and sustain discussion. The most common of those he mentions are teachers not waiting long enough for students to answer, and teachers asking closed, low-level questions. We mentioned earlier how open questions are far more effective in engaging students in thoughtful class discussion. If you ask a productive question, it takes students time to think of a thoughtful answer. Research suggests that you should wait at least four or five seconds before commenting on the question. We have waited longer—sometimes ten seconds or more. With that extra time, students can better process the question and begin to decide on an approach to answering it.

Other practices we have seen that discourage discussion include the vague request for questions: "Any questions?" Or, "Do any of you have a question? No? Okay, then let's move on." This approach almost always elicits silence. To encourage students to respond we need to ask more specific questions, such as "Who can provide an example of the concept of confirmation bias?" Perhaps to be followed with: "Let's get three or four different illustrations."

Another type of problematic question that shuts down discussion is the leading question. Duncan provides some examples: "Why doesn't the moon have an atmosphere? It has very weak gravity, doesn't it?" And, "What happens when we add the sums of the rows? Do we get skewed results?" No thought is required to answer such questions, and students are probably not going to bother. When they do this, teachers are answering the questions themselves.

Two other ways to discourage discussion, inadvertent though they might be, are to reward through praise the first student who answers a question, and to establish an unwelcome, even critical atmosphere. We may offer rapid praise as a way to encourage other students to offer answers because we think they will want to enjoy a similar burst of praise from us. Yet doing so cuts off other students from answering if they have a different take or another way of approaching the question. If it's discussion we desire, we would be better off saying something like: "Yes, that's one interesting way to think about this question. Let's think a bit more about this answer. Where else might it take our thinking?" You can also ask for other students to respond with different answers before offering any commentary yourself at all, saying, "Thank you. What do others think?"

Creating an atmosphere in which students feel uncomfortable responding because they fear being grilled, embarrassed, or even humiliated inhibits discussion. We may create such an atmosphere with comments that imply that our students are stupid or lazy, that they aren't trying hard enough, or that they just aren't getting what we are teaching—and that it's their fault. Comments like these exemplify this behavior: "Do I have to explain this problem again?" "Does everybody understand what I just said now for the third time?" "How many ways do I have to explain this?" These comments are surefire discussion killers (and ones we have all too often, unfortunately, heard in the field).

A Note on Online Discussions

Online discussions can be guided by many of the same strategies we use for discussion in face-to-face class conversations. Some students who are shy and reticent in physical class settings are more comfortable discussing their ideas and asking questions in online courses. All students, however, need to be prepared to participate in online forums and to contribute to blogs and wikis, or any other medium you require. The key is to require everyone to participate and explain what level of participation you expect. For example, if students write a weekly blog or forum post, you might also require them to respond to the posts of two classmates. You can provide structure by setting length requirements: at least 200 words for the post, for example, and at least two or three sentences for each response to the posts of others.

You can also demonstrate for your students how you would like them to participate. Model for them an acceptable response or comment in a forum post. You might, for example, post a comment and then ask students what they noticed about what you said. Their comments and questions can lead to further online discussion.

Lolita Paff, in "Coaching Strategies to Enhance Online Discussions" (2015), suggests thinking of yourself as a "coach" for your online students, perhaps enlisting your better students as "assistant coaches." As a coach, provide timely feedback on students' online work, whether it be low-stakes forum postings or higher-stakes assignments for your eyes only. With frequent low-stakes work, this feedback need not be extensive. You could also spot-check a different set of students each time, rather than all of them for every assignment.

Check in with students about their learning. Find out from them whether they are able to keep pace with the assignments, perhaps on a weekly or biweekly basis. If you see that some students are failing to submit forum posts or other assignments, contact them directly. If they don't respond, contact their advisers. Don't let them slide, which is sometimes easy to do online.

Applications

1. Think of a lecture you delivered or a lesson you taught without a class discussion. How might you revise that lecture or lesson to incorporate discussion-based teaching? What questions would you ask to achieve your learning goals for the session? How might you use discussion to arouse curiosity about your lecture topic?
2. What challenges have you personally confronted in teaching through discussion? What adjustments do you plan to make to improve the effectiveness of your discussion-based teaching?
3. What motivational strategies and active learning techniques do you think could help you improve your discussion-based teaching?
4. What might you do for students who are hesitant about participating or perhaps have not been participating at all?
5. How might you establish expectations for decorum in both on-site and online discussions?

Embarrassment and Learning

One of the greatest impediments to learning is fear, and one of students' greatest fears is a fear of embarrassment. Students are often afraid to expose themselves in class discussion and possibly be perceived as stupid or revealed as not having done their homework adequately. Students fear exposure of their ignorance, of their failure to understand key concepts or applications, and may worry that they don't belong in a particular course or program—or perhaps should not even be in college at all.

Embarrassment and its attendant emotional baggage cut close to students' sense not just of what they know and understand but of who they are. When a fear of embarrassment reflects a student's sense of unworthiness, or of being an incapable learner, it may be to protect their sense of identity and self-regard, their personal and social capital.

Students' fear of embarrassment is bred of anxiety rooted in a lack of confidence in their ability to perform academically. Students fear that they will "mis-perform" or underperform, and thus embarrass, even humiliate, themselves. As a result, they may avoid participating in class discussion in an attempt to deflect attention from themselves.

Contributing to the fear of embarrassment is the "spotlight effect," in which students feel that everyone is looking at them, that all eyes are focused on them. Far more often than not, of course, this fear is groundless; typically, others are attending to themselves far more than to the individual in the imagined spotlight. Even so, the imagined spotlight feels blindingly bright and unforgiving to one experiencing its effects. And though students overrate the attention others pay them and may feel that the spotlight is shining on them unfairly, it feels acutely real and painful nonetheless.

Another factor contributing to the fear of embarrassment is a sense of threat—especially the threat of being outed, being shown as unworthy, as not belonging to the group. This sense of threat might be felt by a student who is different in some way from the other members of a class, whether in language or culture, in race or ethnicity, in sexual orientation, in prior educational experience, or in extracurricular and co-curricular experiences that the other students share and the student who feels threatened does not.

Students who fear such exposure and harbor a sense of threat may experience class discussion as a danger zone. Others whose fear of embarrassment is less intense may take a cooler, more analytical approach. These students analyze the costs of revealing themselves, through participating in class discussion or asking a question of their instructor, against any benefits their comment or question might yield for them. They make a cold cost-benefit calculation.

One reason that embarrassment can impede college success is that embarrassment is closely linked with a fixed and rigid approach to learning. Students with a fixed mindset about learning believe that they are either smart or not, completely right or wrong, able or unable to meet an educational challenge or demand. For students with a growth or dynamic learning mindset, such binary either-or, all-or-nothing categories are superseded by more flexible ways of thinking about themselves as learners. These students understand that they are smart enough to understand some things and not yet knowledgeable enough to understand others, and that they can be partly right about an idea or almost right about a solution they present. They see their learning as making steady and gradual progress toward a goal. Their dynamic understanding of learning promotes growth by allowing for failure and learning from failure. And so these students take for granted and accept that they will make mistakes because it's part of the game of learning. Being both expected and acceptable, failure has no bearing on their sense of themselves, and hence it brings with it no emotional baggage rooted in embarrassment.

As Thomas Newkirk points out in *Embarrassment and the Emotional Underlife of Learning* (2017), one of the biggest problems with embarrassment as an inhibitor of learning is that a student may experience humiliation and shame, feelings deeply rooted in our emotional lives. It may not be logical or rational for a student to see him- or herself as being in the spotlight. It might not be accurate that this student is being laughed at for a lack of knowledge, a mistaken assumption, an inaccurate perception, or an egregious error. Other students may be—and are likely to be—equally confused by what confuses the embarrassed student. But a more logical analysis of a perceived social and public failure and its accompanying embarrassment only comes later—ex post facto. During the moment of failure, during the actual mis-performing or underperforming, the student's failure and embarrassment are real and inescapable—and most often felt as humiliating or shameful.

The first step in helping students overcome their fear of embarrassment is to acknowledge its reality. We teachers need to understand that our students possess these fears, especially students in their late teens, who are still figuring out who they are, and who care deeply how their peers perceive them. The second step is to devise strategies not only to address the social and psychological realities of students' lives but also to create conditions in our classrooms that enable students to experience failure and partial success without embarrassment.

How can we create environments in which all of our students feel able to take risks, make mistakes, and learn from those mistakes without feeling acute emotional distress? What can we do to ensure that students become willing and active participants in their learning such that their anxieties and fears, if not completely eliminated, are sufficiently mitigated so that they assist rather than inhibit their learning?

Here are a few suggestions to help students navigate their participation in fast-paced class discussions and to ensure that all students are heard:

- Give shy or reluctant students a chance to participate early, when the going is easier and there is much less risk of becoming enmeshed in complicated aspects of the conversation.
- Give everyone a few minutes to think and write before beginning a class discussion, thus ensuring that all students will have something to contribute—if only a question.
- Ask students to turn to a classmate and take a minute or two to share what they have written, to compare notes and see where they are in sync and where they diverge, and to articulate the tack that each took in their response. (See chapter 3 for additional suggestions of this type.)
- Build on what students can do in order to help them develop the capacity to close in on what they cannot yet do.
- Describe their performances in terms of process—that is, in terms of progress toward a larger goal. Explain how the larger goals are shared goals for all students and that students vary in their pace in reaching those goals.
- Provide opportunities for students to help each other make progress. You can employ peer review, not to evaluate performance, but to provide feedback for what to do next. You might present questions to help students think about what they are trying to do—for example, in a draft for an essay, report, or presentation—but have not yet accomplished.
- Encourage students to notice what they like about each other's work so that they can say things to each other such as: "Do more of this," "Help me understand what you are saying here," or "If you provide more details like these, I will see even better what you are showing us."

An underlying principle of these suggestions is that not only is it okay to seek help and accept assistance from others, but it's a good idea and a useful practice. Also built into these suggestions is the importance of second and subsequent chances, of revision, of returning to develop, expand, clarify, enlarge, enrich, or otherwise improve on whatever work a student is presenting. And finally, in commenting on student work, whatever its genre or form or degree of complexity, you can direct your remarks toward the student's product or performance rather than the student. It's a student's performance at a particular time that is being discussed, commented on, questioned, guided, and perhaps assessed or evaluated—not the student's character, and not the student's abilities.

Tom Newkirk—on whom we have already leaned heavily in this interlude—notes that our failures are not usually due to personal deficiencies, such as lack of effort, but derive more often from a lack of preparation. He suggests that, when your students experience a setback, you can pinpoint something specific to improve, rather than make generalized suggestions and vague global remarks about what is deficient. Localize a particular problem instead, and provide explicit guidance in what the student can do about it. It's a bit like coaching: the feedback typically provided to athletes by their coaches is specific, focused, and timely.

Embarrassment, Newkirk (2017) writes, "is inextricably linked to some of our most powerful and debilitating feelings: shame, fear, regret, caution, and avoidance" (p. 176). As behavioral economists such as Dan Ariely (2010) and Daniel Kahneman (2011) have repeatedly shown, everyone—including our students—has a tendency toward loss aversion; we minimize our risk in situations where the calculus suggests that the dangers outweigh the benefits. And so students may pretend to be attentive but remain silent to avoid exposing their awkwardness. For us teachers, Newkirk suggests, "the complex task of teaching is to structure the risk/reward equation so that we minimize what might be lost by being awkward and approximate" (p. 177). We should maximize what might be gained by creating opportunities for successful participation—for helping students engage willingly, and ultimately successfully, in their learning.

Newkirk's ideas are supported by recent research that highlights the importance of emotion in motivating and deepening learning. As David Brooks suggests in a *New York Times* op-ed piece (2019), when we share our passion for what we teach and our reasons for it, we invite students into a new community of learning. In sharing with them our love for our subject, we give them something they too can learn to love. Brooks cites the work of Patricia Kuhl and her colleagues (2016), who have shown that the social brain is a significant factor in all kinds of learning, from babies learning two languages simultaneously to adults learning music. Brooks also cites the work of Suzanne Dikker and her colleagues (2017), whose research demonstrates how teachers' and students' brains are synchronized when things are going well, but out of sync when negative emotions—fear, dread, confusion, worry, anxiety—prevail in the classroom. Their research and Newkirk's work on embarrassment suggest that we need to consider how to harness the social and emotional aspects of students' lives to improve their learning. We need to find ways to invite them to join us in inquiry, to help them loosen up, to encourage and support their halting efforts to advance their education, and to participate with us, their teachers, in the great communal enterprise of learning.

Chapter Six

Lecturing and PowerPoint

Here's a story that may sound familiar. Perhaps you have even experienced some version of it yourself. We know we have.

A fresh-faced faculty member—having spent the closing weeks of summer compiling notes, building media-rich slide decks, making sure everything that needs to be covered will get its due over the course of the next fourteen weeks—stands behind a podium. Dozens of students stare back at him, expectant. As he begins, that expectancy becomes attentiveness. A quarter of an hour passes, and then another. More and more heads begin dipping, nodding, looking out the window, or more likely at a phone. The silence and stillness filling the room—apart from the professor's voice—feels oppressive. The sound of students shifting in their seats is unnaturally loud. The professor begins to notice brief bursts of keyboard clicking and cannot shake the suspicion that it's for shopping and messaging, not note-taking. Forty-five minutes in—right at the heart of the day's material, the meat of the lecture—he's lost them.

Unfortunately, next week brings no improvement. The pattern repeats session after session, but with the initial stages of expectancy and attention becoming shorter.

I know so much! he thinks. *I have so much to give! Why is no one interested?*

One obvious answer is that people tend to be more interested in themselves than anyone else (just like, one could argue, the professor in this story). This is only natural: without self-interest, the human species would not survive. And as individual human beings, we can't help but experience the world through the lens of the self—that's all we have. It's hard to blame students for losing interest in a topic to which their personal connection is unclear or nonexistent—or that simply can't compete with whoever's instant-messaging them during class.

But we don't need to become grim fatalists, bemoaning our students' dwindling attention spans. Quite the contrary: being aware of student self-interest, and the sources and limitations of student interest, provides the basis for many of the productive teaching strategies covered in this chapter, as well as in chapter 1 on how to motivate student learning. In that earlier chapter, we discussed the importance of relevance and purpose to student learning; here we will consider ways to arouse curiosity, sustain attention, and ensure understanding. It may not simply, or even mostly, be boredom or disinterest that's causing our audiences to drift; confusion and fatigue are also common culprits.

Paradoxically, our best intentions are sometimes to blame. *I have so much to give*, we think. It's our responsibility to share as much of the knowledge we have worked so hard to attain as we can. It's our social and civic responsibility and, depending on our field, it may even be a matter of public safety that we equip students with the knowledge and tools that they will need in their chosen profession (nursing, for instance). Our institutions and departments may also hold us to certain curricular standards relating to that perennial concern of so many educators: *coverage*. But while there are obviously many legitimate reasons for considering the issue of coverage in designing our courses and lectures, and for setting coverage requirements at the curricular level, it is equally important to consider what students do and experience in class to learn what is being covered.

You may recall the philosophical parable: if a tree falls in the woods with no one around to hear it, does it make a sound? Here's a new version: if all the material has been covered in lectures but the students haven't learned it, has it been taught?

Sometimes covering too much in a lecture is counterproductive: it may overwhelm students who, by the time they formulate a question about something that has confused and stalled their comprehension, may have missed the next three minutes of your presentation. Covering too much also often prevents instructors from creating space for engagement during the session—an essential antidote to overwhelming lectures—because breathless coverage eats up all the time.

So how do we create a space for engagement? And to begin with, how do we present material so that it's interesting and clear? In short, how do we solve that age-old problem of not losing our students? The heart of this problem is also the problem of how we help them learn during our presentation of content, material, or subject matter—assuming, of course, that some form of presentation is the most appropriate pedagogical mode for the occasion.

Our answer to these questions, and the overarching principle of this chapter, may seem obvious, but its obviousness is precisely what makes it all too easy to take for granted—and easy for us to forget to apply: *Think of your audience. Think of your students.* Design and deliver your lectures with their subjective experience of the classroom in mind.

These considerations will lead you to make informed choices about when and how to lecture, and how to lecture in ways that can engage students and enhance their learning rather than put them to sleep. In this chapter, we explore some approaches to maximizing the benefits of lecturing for students, while minimizing the more common causes of disengagement.

The Lecture: Benefits and Drawbacks

The lecture (from the Latin *lectura*, which means "reading, a text to read") has a long and distinguished history. From the origins of the university in medieval Europe, lectures were the primary mode of instruction. Even earlier, during the Athenian golden age, Aristotle and Plato lectured, and Aristotle's lectures were preserved by his students; today we still read his lectures on *Poetics*, *Politics*, and *Nicomachean Ethics*. The lecture persists in university education worldwide as the primary mode of instruction—across disciplines, programs, and schools, spanning centuries, countries, and continents.

Why has the lecture become the dominant mode of college and university instruction? What are the advantages of the lecture and what are its drawbacks? First, the lecture presents information and ideas by a knowledgeable authority. The faculty lecturer holds the stage, ideally capturing the attention of the student audience. The lecturer instructs the students, who listen patiently and attentively, receiving knowledge and perhaps wisdom as well.

Second, this no-nonsense approach to teaching is efficient. The lecture's format privileges information delivery. From the point of view of the lecture, discussion and questions are an unnecessary luxury—a kind of soft approach to teaching and learning. Lecturing is all business.

Third, the lecture, which can be recorded, serves as a repository of course material that can be accessed electronically and from a distance, allowing students who cannot attend the lecture to access its content—its information, explanations of concepts, and applications of ideas.

And fourth, the lecture can do things that other "materials" in the course cannot. Through lecture, professors can discuss the most cutting-edge research, summarize or connect topics and concepts that appear across the assigned readings, and contextualize and introduce readings so that students are more likely to complete and comprehend them. Lectures can identify or highlight what is going to appear on the exam; they can even serve as the primary content of a course. Lectures also give professors a chance to express their enthusiasm for their subject and transmit to students some of that passion and interest—which they are less likely to acquire from reading a dry textbook (McKeachie and Svinicki 2014, p. 59).

What might be some drawbacks of the lecture as a tool of instruction? What are its limitations? And what alternatives can be offered either to replace the lecture as an instructional mode or to supplement and complement it?

First, the lecture, in its pure form, offers no opportunity for the teacher to know whether students understand what they are hearing or for students to check their understanding with questions. Unless the lecturer pauses to solicit questions and then responds to them, students cannot ask the lecturer to clarify the content presented, to provide examples of concepts, or to suggest applications for the information they are absorbing.

Second, the lecture mostly requires students to be passive listeners. Implicitly, it encourages docility and, explicitly, passivity. The lecture form prevents students from engaging in dialogue, not only with one other but often with the instructor. The lecture fosters a form of subservience, even adulation, of students toward their master teacher.

Third, the lecture is a one-way street and a top-down structure. It's authoritarian.

Fourth, the lecture format emphasizes the sage on the stage, preempting the chance for the instructor to be the guide on the side. The lecture prevents the instructor from serving as coach or mentor for students.

And last, the lecture may disadvantage the already disadvantaged, including first-generation students and underrepresented groups, as well as women students in the many STEM fields in which they remain the minority. Research increasingly indicates that all students benefit from classes that incorporate active learning and other inclusive approaches, rather than relying solely on the traditional lecture, but that the benefits are even more pronounced for these more vulnerable populations (Freeman et al. 2014; Haak et al. 2011; Lorenzo, Crouch, and Mazur 2006).

The lecture, like any proven tool, is not inherently good or bad—it's more a question of how and when it's used. A hammer is great for so many things, but for fixing a computer? Not so much. When is lecturing the right tool for the job? What does the lecture enable instructors to do that other modes of instruction do not? And how do we best implement it? We need to answer these questions for ourselves, in light of the material we're teaching. And once we decide that we are going to lecture, we need to consider how we can maximize the lecture's virtues and create lectures that truly advance student learning.

Effective Lecturing

Given the inherent benefits and limitations of the lecture as an instructional tool, what are some ways we can make our lectures more effective as incitements to student learning? What makes for a successful lecture from the perspective of learning that lasts?

The first thing to consider is the purpose of the lecture: What is it for? What is it designed to do? We must also consider where each lecture fits into the overall scheme of our course or a unit of instruction within the course. An additional consideration is the extent to which we can combine the lecture with other instructional approaches, such as discussion and other active learning strategies as explored in chapters 3 and 5.

A lecture can be entertaining, but this is not its primary purpose. A lecture primarily teaches. The lecturer informs and educates students, explains and illustrates ideas and concepts, makes connections among them in some kind of framework, invites students to think and apply concepts, and in other ways extrapolates from the information being presented. Most often, the lecture's primary purpose is instruction through disseminating information. More ambitious lecturing goals include provoking students to think while making connections between ideas and examples, facts and frameworks, or concepts and applications.

This is not to suggest that making lectures entertaining is unwarranted, but rather that entertainment should be subsidiary, ancillary, and added only in the service of instruction. In making a lecture entertaining, an instructor might well excite students' imaginations, engage their feelings along with their intellects, and motivate and perhaps even inspire them to learn. But the instructional objective assumes priority. And so the first question we need to ask is: What are the goals of this lecture? What do we want students to know, understand, or be able to do after listening to the lecture?

Next, we need to consider what prior knowledge students might need to understand the central concepts of the lecture. What background knowledge should we provide, either in the lecture itself or in a prior handout or online posting? And what might we do to compensate for students' limitations and prepare them to understand and value the heart of the lecture? These questions of student background are especially important in the multicultural, global classroom, where they extend not only to prerequisite content knowledge but also to cultural assumptions some of us may not even be aware of: for example, when using a baseball analogy to explain a concept of evolution, or drawing an offhand comparison between the novel being taught in class and a television show popular in the United States in the 1980s. The need for this awareness is not limited to the international campus: varying levels of preparation and a diversity of cultural and academic backgrounds will be found in any classroom with a diverse student makeup—which is to say, every classroom.

Interactive Lectures

After we identify the goals we want to achieve—or that we want students to achieve—through our lectures, we need to decide on the best means for reaching them. As already discussed, the lecture as a mode of teaching and learning has its benefits and drawbacks. But not all lectures are created equal. In traditional lectures, the instructor talks and students listen. Sometimes, near the end of the lecture, time is allotted for questions. Interactive lectures, on the other hand, allow for periodic pauses for questions and structured active learning exercises. Here are a few additional important differences:

- In traditional lectures, student cross-talk is discouraged. Any Q&A that occurs is between student and instructor only. Interactive lectures allow for student-to-student talk during active learning exercises.
- In traditional lectures, students work independently, taking notes. Interactive lectures, on the other hand, set students working with partners or in small groups at strategic points during the lecture.
- In traditional lectures, there is no explicit monitoring of student understanding. Interactive lectures provide opportunities for direct assessment of student understanding.
- In traditional lectures, there is no opportunity to correct student misunderstanding. Interactive lectures allow for misunderstandings to be corrected at a number of junctures.

To some extent, every lecture is a performance. As the instructor, you are onstage, the center of attention, an actor in motion, both physical and mental. As such, you need to transfer your energy, thinking, and feeling into corresponding energies for your students. If they are to learn well and remember the heart and soul of your lectures, students need to become active participants in them. And if part of your lecture performance is to demonstrate how to engage with ideas, concepts, applications, problem-solving, and the like, you need to provide students with opportunities to join you in that work. It's not enough for us to model a process of think-ing, to demonstrate and explain, to show and tell our students what we are doing—though all of those things are important. We also need to incor-porate our students' thinking and engage them in thinking—to make them active learners during our lectures.

The Lecture as Story

Once we decide on goals and a general approach, how do we shape our lec-tures? A lecture's structure is intimately related to how readily it can be followed and absorbed; structure enables us to frame and highlight the key messages we want students to take away from the class session.

One classic and effective way to structure a lecture is to take the narra-tive approach. A lecture can be thought of as a story, with a beginning, middle, and end—a story that develops and that contains conflict and res-olution. For example, a science lecture on the periodic table of elements can include the story of its origin, including the competition among sci-entists and other investigators to create the table. That lecture can include stories of individual elements, of how those elements were discovered, and of the people after whom the elements were named. It can include accounts of how the elements are used, how they can be combined, and how ele-ments fit into a pattern with similar elements in the periodic table.

To take another example, a first lecture on English Romantic literature could tell the story of how William Wordsworth and Samuel Taylor Coleridge came to write and publish their groundbreaking book of poems, *Lyrical Ballads*, in 1798. It could include the story of the book's reception and explain why the authors revised and republished it two years later, in 1800. These and similar stories serve to anchor scientific and literary con-cepts in history. They humanize science and literature and help students remember what they are learning—in these cases, about the nature and function of the periodic table, and about what Wordsworth and Coleridge attempted and accomplished with the publication of *Lyrical Ballads*, with its famous influential preface.

We need to keep two things in mind when working with the concept of lecture as story. One is the lecture's organization—how to start the lecture, how to structure the middle of it, and how to end it. The second is to keep an eye on the key takeaways we want students to understand from the lecture. These considerations require that we isolate and clarify our learning goals for the lecture, first for ourselves and then for our students, and that we then design the lecture in a way to best achieve those goals. Structuring a lecture is a matter of both alignment and backward design (see chapter 2).

A story establishes a setting and involves human characters. A story has a trajectory: it develops, typically includes conflict of some sort, and comes to some kind of resolution—or not. A story may also be episodic, part of a larger story. For instance, English Romanticism can be linked to developments in continental and American Romanticism, and literary Romanticism can be connected to developments in Romantic music and art in England, on the continent, and beyond. Romanticism can also be linked to what came before—as a reaction to eighteenth-century neoclassicism—and to what emerged afterwards in the Victorian era, in post-Romantic literature, art, and music.

We need to consider, then, which parts of the story to tell in any lecture, and how the lectures fit together to tell a larger story or set of larger related stories. Making connections for students among and through stories helps them understand concepts and developments in relation to one another, and those connected relationships help them remember what they learn (see chapter 4). Well-constructed lectures built on and around stories can help students understand what we have to teach and remember what they are learning.

In the lecture as story, we can connect the information, concepts, principles, and frameworks we teach through the connections that hold narrative together: causality, conflict, and complication. Causality explains relationships; it's itself a type of relationship. Is something a cause or a consequence? Perhaps it's a cause of one thing and a consequence of another, an outgrowth of something that leads up to it and a stimulus for something else that follows.

Conflict stimulates interest and generates curiosity about its potential resolution. Identifying conflicts among ideas, approaches, theories, and the like helps bring them to life for students.

Complications deepen understanding, and stories are rife with them. Finding ways to illustrate complication in your lectures, a little at a time, brings students to a deeper understanding of what you are teaching them.

Through stories, we can identify patterns, connections, and relationships among situations and phenomena, concepts and disciplines, questions and solutions. How might our courses and our teaching practices include stories—to engage our students, enhance their learning, and humanize the abstract concepts we teach? What might be the overarching story of any particular course we teach? How might that story be embedded in the larger stories of our discipline as a whole?

These are key questions to ask when considering the lecture as a story. But there are others we can ask as well. What conflicts of idea and concept, of purpose and value, are embedded in the materials we present to students? What complications in that material might we find and highlight via the medium of story?

In teaching about evolution, for example, teachers can tell the story of Darwin's competition with Alfred Wallace to publish his theory before Wallace did. They could tell the story of people's response to the publication of Darwin's ideas. Similarly, in teaching about the discovery of the double helix or of the progress of the space program, stories about the contributions of women can be told, including the difficulties they faced in gaining the recognition they deserved for their contributions. In the STEM fields especially, stories about the human beings whose contributions have gone unrecognized provide rich opportunities to redress systemic demographic imbalances among students.

Stories about women scientists and scientists of color can provide students from underrepresented groups with role models, enable them to envision how people like themselves belong in these fields, and help them understand the injustices that historically have prevented their fuller acceptance. One example is the story of how Watson and Crick consistently downplayed and downgraded the contributions of Rosalind Franklin to their discovery of the double helix. Another is the story of the women, a number of them women of color, who made important mathematical contributions to the accuracy of space flight, as described in the book and movie *Hidden Figures*.

The Lecture as Solution to a Problem

Besides story, we can approach the design of a lecture in terms of an answer to a question or a solution to a problem. Question-answer, problem-solution lecture structures work well for explaining origins—such as the emergence of the big bang theory, the discovery of the Rosetta Stone, the development of vernacular literatures in Europe, the invention of the automobile or airplane, the discovery of radiation, or the emergence of psychiatry, fractal geometry, or behavioral economics.

We can get students' attention with authentic problems and arouse their curiosity with intriguing questions. If we bring story to a problem-solution or question-answer lecture, we can multiply the ways in which we bring the lecture material to life, thus engaging our students and making them more active participants in their learning.

To make students truly active participants, however, we need to introduce pauses into our lectures—moments for reflection and opportunities for students to think about how they would respond to a question, a problem, a scenario, or some other provocation. We can use the techniques described in chapter 3 on active learning to accomplish these goals.

A lecture that lasts an hour (give or take ten or fifteen minutes) should have built-in stopping points. The lecture should be "chunked" in some way. If the chunks are not natural parts of a story, we can create segments that individually have a discrete focus but connect with each other in a logical and coherent way. It is at those pauses in our lectures—those stopping points every fifteen to twenty minutes—that we have the opportunity to engage students in writing, thinking, and active learning.

At this point you may be thinking that interspersing your lectures this way with active learning exercises will take time away from providing information and that you will cover less material as a result. This is an important issue, perhaps the most difficult for instructors who rely primarily or even exclusively on lecture in the classroom. Here is how we respond to this concern.

"Coverage" is a metaphor rooted in an instructional model based on information transmission, a model we think is ineffective for student learning. Considerable research has demonstrated that students learn more and retain what they learn longer and better when they are actively engaged in their learning. Passively listening to lectures does not engage students in ways that enhance learning. That's why we strongly advocate breaking into a lecture at strategic points—every fifteen or twenty minutes, ideally—to ask a question, pose a problem, or introduce an active learning technique such as a minute paper or a pair-share conversation.

Coverage is a counterproductive metaphor for teaching and learning. If you cover less and go deeper into what you teach, students can learn more and retain it longer. That's the goal of teaching anyway, isn't it? If you feel that you must provide students with large quantities of highly detailed information on slides chock-full of text and images (about which more a bit later in this chapter), post the slides on your course site as study aids. Design your lectures to address the critical elements—the central topics, key issues, and essential questions—so that you can add instructional value during your time in the classroom. Don't simply repeat in the lecture what's on the study slides. Use your lecture time to promote critical thinking, to explain and explore the key issues and ideas that matter for the lecture topics you address.

Less is more in this case. When lecturing is the modus operandi for your course, design and develop your lectures less from the standpoint of coverage and more from that of student engagement and learning. One way to do this is by using narrative and problem-solution structures to make your lectures coherent, interesting, and memorable.

Principles of Lecturing

We may easily forget that the experience of the lecturer differs dramatically from the experience of the students listening to a lecture. While lecturing, you are active, engaged, in explanation mode; you are speaking and gesturing and thinking. Your students are quiet, in reception mode; perhaps they are thinking, perhaps not. They are listening, or perhaps daydreaming, or surfing the web. And even if they are thinking, how might you sustain and advance the benefit of the thinking stimulated by your lecture? That's the real challenge—not only to stimulate our students' thinking, but also to advance it, sustain it, deepen it, and make it last.

The first step is to create room for thinking—for students to think about not just the information contained in the lecture but the problems the lecture identifies, the questions it raises. This, of course, is an important reason to focus your lectures on questions, problems, challenges, or cases.

Second, present your lecture in language suitable for and understandable by the student audience. Good lectures, like good written expository texts, blend the specific with the general; they make abstract concepts concrete through the use of multiple examples. Clarity emerges from the details related to the ideas that the lecture illustrates or otherwise supports. Too many details, however, can muddy the waters and overwhelm the listener, especially when not organized around concepts, stories, and other schema.

Which raises the third point: effective lectures are logically organized and flow from one part to another. Their structure is often made apparent through the use of transitions: "We have just discussed X; now we turn our attention to Y, which is related to X in these ways . . ." A more specific example: "Now that you understand the structure of the atom and its component particles, we turn next to how atoms bond together to form molecules." Or: "Now that we have sketched out Marx's general economic theory of labor and capital, we need to consider the contribution of Lenin to the development of the ideology of communism. And after that, the ways in which Marxist-Leninist theory has been translated into practice in Asia and South America."

Throughout the lecture, it is important to remind students of its key messages, what they should take away, what they need to understand and remember—as well as where they have been and where they are going. Such moments of emphasis can punctuate the beginning and end of a lecture and the moments of transition between sections, topics, and units.

A final point about effective lecturing: consider how you will begin— how you will gain your students' attention and interest. We put this point last because you can't know how to draw your students' attention to what will come in the lecture until you have identified its purpose and goals, and until you have figured out how to organize it logically and coherently.

A Note on Conceptual Frameworks

Because students are often unfamiliar with the concepts and terms they will encounter in a course and the details of the subjects they are beginning to study, it is difficult for them to understand how everything fits together. They need help from their instructors in creating *coherence*— linking details with concepts and understanding how concepts relate to one another. They need our help in separating essential, critical ideas from less important, peripheral ones.

Depicting a conceptual framework or model visually with a diagram can be helpful. Using flow charts, pie charts, line and bar graphs, and other visuals to represent processes and show information can clarify, concretize, and contextualize the unfamiliar. Keeping these frameworks and models simple makes them easier for students to comprehend. Avoid overloading them with excessive detail. Clarity is best achieved with streamlined, stripped-down explanations. Simplicity early on yields a basis for more elaborate explanation and understanding later.

Engagement and Feedback

As we have suggested, the key to engaging an audience and keeping it engaged is to present a question, problem, or other attention-grabber, such as an image or a story. Get students thinking about the question, problem, image, story, or scenario. Give them time to think, perhaps a chance to jot a few notes or even lean over and talk to a classmate about the challenge you have given them to think about (see chapter 3).

Connect your opening gambit with what will follow. Either ask students about this connection—for example, what do they predict will come next in the lecture?—or tell them directly how the next part of the lecture links up with your opening and with their thinking about it. Be sure also to relate the lecture content to what students have already learned in the course, to what they know generally, and, to the extent possible, to their overall experience.

During the various parts of the lecture, observe how students are responding and, if you can, assess their degree of attention and interest. Depending on how well they are responding (or not), you may need to adjust your pacing, shift your focus, pause to ask a question, stop to give a brief quiz, or intervene in any number of ways to regain students' attention.

You can ask for both informal and formal feedback in a number of ways. At the end of the lecture, for example, you might have students write for a minute or two about the "muddiest point"—about what remains unclear to them. Or you might have them list what they think are the two or three main concepts of the lecture, or what for them are the key takeaways (what they learned or what they value from listening to the lecture). Depending on time constraints, you might ask students to volunteer their responses orally, collect them and review them between classes, or not collect them and simply have students think further on their own.

Barkley and Major's *Learning Assessment Techniques* (2016) provides a cornucopia of activities to assess student learning in the classroom. An increasing number of technological tools are providing effective ways to check in with students, perhaps the most common being clickers and polling apps. (See chapter 7 for more on these tools.)

You can also survey students anonymously partway through the course to see what is helping them learn or what might be hindering their participation. Such a temperature check at the halfway point of the course, or earlier, is less about what students might like or dislike and more about what they are learning and what teaching practices might improve their learning. If your institution supports a center for teaching and learning, or if you can recruit a willing colleague, you may be able to request that someone conduct a small group analysis—a kind of focus group process—in which students discuss in small groups what is and isn't helping them learn in the course.

You can use what you learn from any of these forms of feedback to calibrate your teaching, often while the semester is still proceeding. And if the feedback comes too late, there's always next time.

Preparation

Prepare carefully for your lectures. Preparation involves not only decid-ing on a lecture's content—its overall topic and subtopics—but also com-ing up with examples, scenarios, cases, quotations, supporting evidence for its key ideas, and the like. Consider as well how you will prompt stu-dent thinking and engagement. Preparation involves thinking about not only *what* you will teach but also *how* you will teach it.

You also need to consider more prosaic matters, such as the physical space occupied by lecturer and students. Visit the space before class starts if possible. What will students be able to see, or tend to look at during the lecture, given the layout of the room? How will you make sure that even students in the back can hear you? How will you emphasize main points so that everyone in the room understands?

Preparation also involves rehearsal—practicing your delivery of the lec-ture, including timing yourself. To what extent will you follow a "script"? How much of your lecture should you write out word for word? How much of your lecture do you want to deliver more spontaneously? When you do work from a scripted text, where, how much, and for how long will you step away from the text and speak directly and less formally to your students?

Keep in mind that you do not have to read or memorize a written script. For many, a script is simply a means for clarifying and organizing their thoughts and a tool for identifying the main points to be covered, which can then be jotted down on a simple notecard.

When you have identified your goals and key points, consider prioritiz-ing them: that way, if you find yourself running out of time, you'll know what can be cut or dropped.

Delivery

You need to think about not just the content and structure of your lecture but how your delivery can enliven the lecture's content and clarify its organization. To emphasize main points or key issues, particularly con-tested issues and questions, you should modulate your voice and modify your body language. You can repeat the most important points, and you can use emphatic gestures to accentuate them further.

Be sure to pause at key junctures. Give students a chance to shift gears with you, especially as you transition from one part of the lecture to another. Marking transitions directly, clearly, emphatically—making transitions both audible and visible—keeps students located in the lecture, prevents them from getting lost, and helps them understand the relationship of the lecture's parts.

PowerPoint for Learning

For some time now, PowerPoint and similar presentation software has been the default way to project visual media during college and university lectures (as well as during academic conference presentations). How this has come about is less important than that it is now an inescapable fact of academic and professional life. Since PowerPoint remains ubiquitous and pervasive in college and university classrooms, it is worth considering how to use it for teaching and learning (or when to use it at all).

How might PowerPoint slides be used to enhance and not obstruct student learning? As with effective lecturing generally, effective use of PowerPoint depends on clarity, focus, and purpose; requires structure and coherence; and succeeds best by not overwhelming the audience with an abundance of visual detail. All too often we see slides overloaded with bullet points and text and that are difficult to read, especially for students simultaneously trying to listen to the lecturer.

Every PowerPoint slide deck is designed to accompany a spoken text. The goal is to make each slide serve a specific aspect of the lecture, not the other way around. Your slides should complement your verbal message rather than compete with it. Slides loaded with text or irrelevant images detract from the lecture by distracting students. Keep PowerPoint slides simple, clutter-free, and easy to take in at a glance.

As Cliff Atkinson reminds us in *Beyond Bullet Points* (2011), working memory—through which all information that lands in long-term memory must pass—is not a pipeline. It's more like the "eye of the needle" (p. 27). We can hold only so much in mind as we transform new information into lasting learning. Consequently, we need to be selective and focused about the material we present—throughout a lecture, as well as on any given slide.

Each slide's purpose and function should be immediately apparent; otherwise, students will be confused, left wondering what they are looking at and why and how it relates to what is being said at the time by the speaker.

Avoid duplicating in your slides what you say in your lecture. If your slides simply print on-screen what you are saying in front of a class, why should students bother coming to hear your lecture? Why not simply have them read and study the slides at their leisure in a convenient location? More important, duplication can interfere with learning, overtaxing the networks that process both spoken and written information (Schwabish 2017). The student may also expend effort comparing the spoken and written versions of the lecture (Clark and Mayer 2011). We want this precious mental energy directed toward calculus or political science, not proofreading.

Consider the following when creating slides for your courses: (1) messenger, message, and medium; (2) signal-to-noise ratio; (3) fonts and colors; and (4) charts and graphs.

Messenger, Message, and Medium

Our NYU colleague Will Carlin (2016) highlights three aspects of using slides for teaching and presenting: messenger, message, and medium. Carlin reminds us that we should not overlook the messenger—ourselves as teachers. How do we come across with our slides? What image of ourselves do the slides convey? What tone do we create with our slides? To what extent do our slides reveal us—explicitly or implicitly—as credible sources of information and instruction? What might be the unintended implications of our slides about us as a messenger for what we have to teach, show, and explain?

The message of our slides, both individually and collectively, needs careful consideration. What is conveyed through each slide? Is the message clear, direct, and identifiable? Does it compete or interfere with other messages on the same slide? (It should not.) To what extent do our slides together tell a story, convey and explain an idea, dramatize a situation, or make an argument with a claim and supporting evidence? How is our message organized? What are its parts? Is there a clear beginning, middle, and end? Have we given the viewer or listener a sense of what's coming? Have we announced moments of transition to clarify the structure of our slide set? Have we properly emphasized key concepts and takeaways? In *Better Presentations*, Jonathan Schwabish (2017) recommends using what he calls "scaffolding slides"—agenda and header slides among them—to communicate the structure of the presentation and help audiences follow along.

In considering the message of our slides, we should also ask ourselves what part the slides play in our class session—how do they relate to other teaching tools and strategies we plan to use for the lesson?

And finally, the medium—the presentation software templates and tools themselves. What does the PowerPoint medium allow us to do that we couldn't do without it? What is the added value of using Power-Point in any particular lecture? What does it contribute? How does it enhance our presentation? And more importantly, how does it strengthen and support student learning? How, that is, can we use PowerPoint to improve our teaching so that it yields effective and long-lasting learning?

Signal-to-Noise Ratio

A common problem we have encountered when visiting classes is Power-Point slides on overload—slides packed with so much information that it's hard to know what to take in first, and equally hard to decide what is critical information and what can be usefully ignored. One way of thinking about slides is to consider their "signal-to-noise ratio" (Reynolds 2008). We should ask ourselves what elements of the slide communicate the intended information or concepts. Anything that does not directly contribute to that communication is "noise"—a distraction from what we intend to accomplish with the slide. For example, a slide that uses color without a clear and distinct purpose introduces "noise," as does a slide that uses 3-D effects, or one that includes data outside the bounds of the slide's purpose. Slides with a low signal-to-noise ratio are difficult to process as students struggle to determine what's important—what they should attend to and what they should ignore.

Simplifying slides increases their signal-to-noise ratio; simplicity reduces distracting information and detail so that students can focus on what's important. One way to simplify slides is to follow the 6 × 6 rule: no more than six lines per slide, with no more than six words per line. What can't be contained on a slide following this guideline should be cut, perhaps to be used on a subsequent slide. For some PowerPoint slide gurus, however, even this 6 × 6 rule allows for too much clutter. They propose, instead, a 3 × 3 rule: no more than three lines per slide, with no more than three words per line. Seth Godin (2007) has urged a six-word total limit per slide. Nancy Duarte (2008) has taken a different tack, but to the same end: she posits a "three-second rule" that would allow viewers to process each slide with little more than a glance.

And of course, there are some who suggest *never* adding words to slides. They advocate instead for text-free slides that contain only images—and not too many of those either. Adapting Michael Pollan's advice about eating (eat food, mostly plants, not too much), we might say: use Power-Point, mostly images, not too many.

The point is not to insist on any particular rule over another—different presenters may abide by different guidelines depending on the particular presentation—but to emphasize the principle behind all of them: focusing your slides and using them to amplify rather than distract from your lecture.

To this end, when providing feedback on slides (a frequent component of our work with faculty), we most often recommend reducing the amount of text. Usually this means cutting out unnecessary words, using phrases and sentence fragments rather than complete sentences, and removing chunks of text from slides to deliver orally instead. Here are a few other tips to help you streamline your slides:

- Use sticky notes and a magic marker to design a first draft of your slide deck (Duarte 2008). The sticky notes can be moved around as you refine the structure of the presentation. Their small size, combined with the big print produced with a marker, force you to economize with any text you incorporate.
- Use the notes function for your detailed lecture notes, not the slide itself. If your students clamor for detailed slides from which to study, produce and distribute handouts of the notes (which PowerPoint allows you to print).
- If you're including lists of bullet points (while adhering, at the very least, to the 6 × 6 rule), avoid wrapping any single line into a second, and consider revealing the bullets one at a time, highlighting the one you're currently talking about. Schwabish (2017) recommends a "layering" method: duplicate the finished slide as many times as there are bullet points on it; then remove all bullet points but the first for the slide's first appearance, all bullets but the first two for the second, and so on. Alternatively, if you're handy with PowerPoint, you can use its animation tools.

Be spartan in your use of slides. Be stingy with the words you put on them. Limit what each slide contains. Make the slides do work that can't otherwise be accomplished without them.

And make your message clear.

Introduction to *Walden*

Thoreau conducted his "experiment" in living
"deliberately" at Walden Pond from July 4, 1845 to
September 6, 1847. There he would write most of the
first version of *Walden*; after seven drafts he would
finally publish the book in 1854.

Though seemingly a retreat from
society, Thoreau's stay on Walden
Pond had a public context:

◆ His was an individualized version
of many other utopian social
experiments (Fruitlands, Brook
Farm) set up in the early 1840s to
counter the negative social
effects their members associated
with capitalism.

◆ Slavery/The annexation of Texas
in 1845. Thoreau was stirred by
Wendell Phillips, who spoke
against the annexation bill in
March, 1845 in Concord.

Figure 6.1. A PowerPoint slide introducing Thoreau's *Walden*.
Photo of pond courtesy of Anton Borst. Photo of cabin courtesy of Austin Bailey.

Focusing the Message: A Case Study in Slide Design

Figure 6.1 shows a slide from a survey course on early American literature
that introduces the nineteenth-century writer Henry David Thoreau. As
you can see, it's chock-full of useful information and appealing images.
Not bad, right?

Though slides like this are pervasive within the academy and out, its
design runs counter to many of the principles we have discussed. It has
way too much text, creates far too much noise, and attempts to send too
many messages at once. Vacillating between reading the slide and listening to you, students will be able to attend only partially to each. And so it
needs to be streamlined.

In working with faculty on their slide decks, one of the most frequent
recommendations we make is to split a slide into multiple slides. Figures 6.2 through 6.5 show one example of how we might remedy the
noisiness of the slide in figure 6.1. We could begin with an image of

Figure 6.2. Slide of photograph of Henry David
Thoreau.
Photo by B. D. Maxham, 1856.

Thoreau that fills the entire screen, maximizing its impact (figure 6.2).
While this slide is up, we'd talk generally about Thoreau, who he was,
when and where he lived, and what he is known for writing.

Then we'd advance to the next slide (figure 6.3). Before saying anything about this slide, we could ask students to describe what they see.
Maybe they'll say they see a shed, or a barn, or a schoolroom. They may be
surprised to learn that the image shows a replica of the cabin that Thoreau built and lived in on Walden Pond for two years, but we will wait to
tell the class this until two or three students have made a guess. With this
slide up, we could then describe in greater detail Thoreau's retreat to
Walden Pond and the book, *Walden*, that came out of that experience.

The next slide will allow us to delve even deeper into that topic. Here
again, we might pause for discussion, as the image (figure 6.4) affords the
opportunity to *see* details that reflect some key themes of *Walden* and that
can serve as powerful aids to memory and understanding. To provoke
thinking about these themes, we could ask students: "What do you see in
this picture?" After gathering some details, we'd then ask another question
(though students might have already begun to answer it): "Given this living
space, how do you think Thoreau lived here? How did he spend his time?"
Students are likely to notice the sparse furniture, the cooking implements,
and, of course, the writing desk. This brief discussion would move organi-
cally into the instructor's more detailed explanation of Thoreau's life on
Walden Pond and the process of writing and publishing *Walden*.

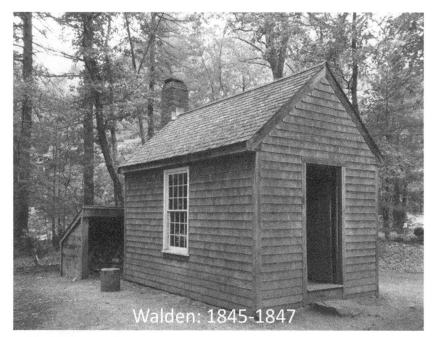

Walden: 1845-1847

Figure 6.3. Slide of replica of Thoreau's cabin—exterior.
Photo courtesy of Austin Bailey.

Figure 6.4. Slide of replica of Thoreau's cabin—interior.
Photo courtesy of John Eiche.

Figures 6.5a, b, and c. Three slides contextualizing Thoreau's Walden experiment.

That's a lot of material so far, and we still have more than half of the original slide to deal with. We will present that remaining portion in brief. In figures 6.5a, 6.5b, and 6.5c, notice that all the lengthy complete sentences are gone. Instead, we have a slide that announces a shift in topic: we will now be contextualizing Thoreau's project in antebellum America by looking at two contexts in particular: the prevalence of utopian communities in the first half of the nineteenth century, and the annexation of Texas in 1845. The first of the three slides locates students in the lecture. The second and third provide relevant visual cues or associations to accompany the subsequent segments of the lecture—utopian communities in the first segment and the annexation of Texas in the second. While each of these slides is up, we describe the historical issue (one at a time, one slide at a time) and explain what it had to do with Thoreau's antislavery position.

Fonts, Colors, and Other Forms of Noise

What is true generally for the words and images on slides—stripping them down and simplifying them—is true for the use of fonts and colors as well. Simpler sans serif fonts, like Arial and Calibri, are easier to read than serif fonts, like Times New Roman, because they lack the "feet" of serif fonts.

Colors can make for eye-popping and beautiful slides, but they can also be distracting. Any use of color needs to be purposeful. Ask yourself what the color means, what it says. If it doesn't mean or say something specific, don't add it. Use instead the default color, most likely black on a white background, which is the most comfortable and easiest to read because it's the most familiar and the most common.

Exercise extreme caution with the fancy "bells and whistles" with which slide software often tempts its users. In the example depicted in

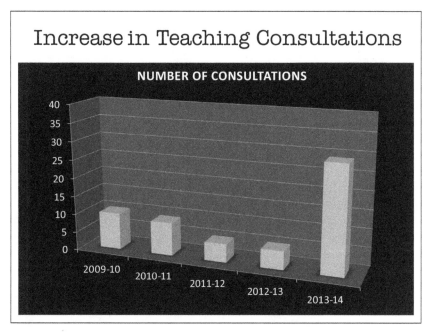

Figure 6.6. "Increase in Teaching Consultations" as a 3D bar graph.

figure 6.6, note the inconsistent (and serif) fonts, the 3D effects, and the use of a low-contrast color scheme: Are these features helping viewers? Or taxing their attention? And are they serving or undermining the intended message? The 3D effect, for example, has the inadvertent consequence of implying a decrease in the number of consultations, when clearly an increase is meant to be communicated.

In our revised version of this slide (figure 6.7) we added a little color (though not visible in the reprinting here): the rightmost bar was made purple to emphasize our point and to celebrate our institution's colors. We also maxed out the y-axis at 30, rather than leave an empty gap of 20 units, which only served in the original slide to make the success of "Fall 2014" look smaller. And lastly, we consolidated the heading and subheading into one punchier title.

Our point is not that this slide is now perfect. It may not comport with your own style—maybe it's not minimal enough (away with the purple!)—and even in the revised version, two more potential issues remain: we don't know what the y-axis represents, and the last bar represents a semester instead of a year. Our point is simply that slides, and the lectures they supplement, are always subject to revision and refinement.

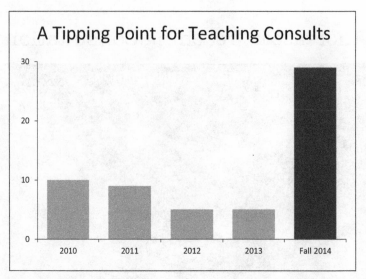

Figure 6.7. "A Tipping Point for Teaching Consults," a stripped-down version of the 3D bar graph.

Charts and Graphs

Although we could say much more about using PowerPoint slides, we offer only a few last suggestions here. When you use charts and graphs, put the legend indicating what the colors or pie slice sizes represent *on* the chart rather than alongside it (see figure 6.8). Use clearly marked labels that can be readily distinguished by a visually distinctive detail— broken versus solid lines, for example, or contrasting colors for different elements. Be consistent in what the columns on a bar chart represent. Clearly label the *x*-axis and *y*-axis of your charts. Use standard and regular increments to represent the units represented on the axis (time, volume, distance, and so on).

In general, adhere to the two key principles we have relied on throughout this section on PowerPoint: (1) effective slides send a single clear message, and (2) effective slides help you deliver your lecture while not competing with you for your students' attention.

Recap Review

Figure 6.9 presents a slide recapping some of the more basic tips for PowerPoint we've considered in this chapter. This is a pretty minimal slide, as far as slides go. But you may be surprised what you can remove when you

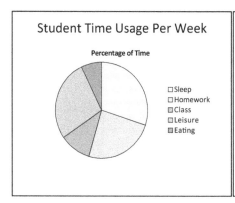
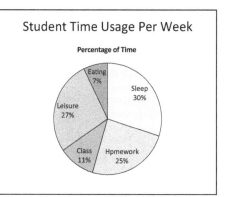

Figure 6.8. (a) Pie chart of "Student Time Usage per Week" and (b) a revised version of the same chart.

apply the same critical eye to your slides that you do to your writing, your lab work, or the actual script of your lecture (see, for example, how we revised it in figure 6.10).

How else might you approach this slide? What other edits might you make to clarify the slide's message and help students learn? Do whatever will help students follow your lecture, and remember to keep their focus where it belongs: on you.

Slide Design Tips

- Colors must contrast
- Use colors minimally
- Follow 6×6 rule
- Use simple sans serif font
- Use 32pt or larger
- Avoid clutter

Figure 6.9. Slide of bullet-point list of "Slide Design Tips."

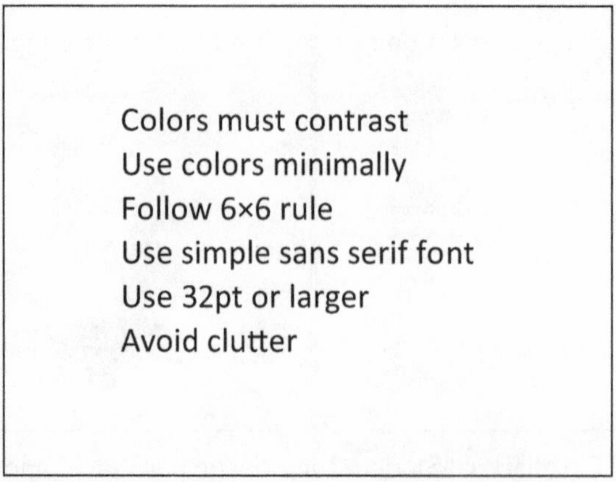

Colors must contrast
Use colors minimally
Follow 6×6 rule
Use simple sans serif font
Use 32pt or larger
Avoid clutter

Figure 6.10. Revised slide of slide design tips.

Applications

1. What did you do to create your best lectures? What might have prevented you from delivering successful lectures on other occasions?
2. How might you introduce a story, question-answer, or problem-solution element into your lectures?
3. Think of a recent lecture you gave or of one you need to prepare. How could you chunk the lecture, organizing it for ease of comprehension? What kinds of transitions could you use to highlight the lecture structure?
4. Evaluate one of your slide sets from the standpoint of the "less is more" approach advocated in this chapter.
5. As an audience member, what do you appreciate in a presentation? What taxes your attention? Apply the same judgments to one of your own lectures, including your slides.

Group Work

Research consistently suggests that group work promotes learning. That's one reason to have students work together in groups. Another is to provide students with practice in explaining their thinking to others and in learning to listen to others' perspectives and reasoning. But students need to understand the purpose of their collaborative learning. We need to be transparent about why we are asking them to work in groups and about what the group's focus will be. Students need to understand how working in groups strengthens their learning, and what that has to do with course goals.

In summarizing research done by Steve Trickey, Keith Topping, and others, Peter Johnston (2004) identifies a number of ways in which the reasoning ability of students who learn how to think together improves, including their ability to examine assumptions. They show an improved aptitude for expressive language and for creative thinking. They are more willing to speak in public and to listen to and consider others' ideas. And not surprisingly, they are more comfortable in and more supportive of group interactions, while also demonstrating a higher quality of interpersonal relationships.

Johnston also notes that just because students work *in* a group does not mean that they work necessarily *as* a group. For that to happen, they need to work together productively toward the common goal reflected in the group's assigned task—for example, coming to consensus about a proposal; solving a complex problem in math, science, or engineering; explaining, illustrating, or applying a concept; analyzing a text; or summarizing an argument. Groups achieve success *as groups* when their members learn in a supportive environment in which they can explore ideas together, challenge each other's thinking respectfully, learn to listen to each other, and build upon one another's contributions. In addition, the development of the individual minds of group members derives not only from the analytical, logical, and informational work the group does, but equally from the emotional and relational support the group provides for its members (Johnston 2012).

Groups can be formed in a number of ways. You can have students count off by three, fours, or fives, for example, and then have all the ones, all the twos, and so on, gather together in one section of the room. Each group might then be assigned a single task that, when completed and reported on, will contribute to an overall group project. Instead of randomizing group makeup, you might deliberately diversify the groups, mixing students according to race, gender, skill levels, and other characteristics. You can also allow students to form their own groups. Each of these methods has merits and limitations. Decide whether it's more important for students to work with people they don't know, whether you want to encourage a mix of perspectives in the groups, whether peer teaching is a goal, or to what extent students might take ownership of their learning and the process of that learning. In general, we have found that variety in the size and the formation of groups keeps students interested and engaged better over the course of a semester than using the same method and the same group size, which can become stale.

John Bean (2011) recommends five students as the optimal size for in-class group activities and no more than six. Smaller groups of three or four have been shown to be effective for longer-term projects. Pairs can be successfully used for peer review, including multiple iterations in a kind of speed-dating pattern. Richard Felder and Rebecca Brent (2016) advise limiting groups to three or four members for in-class activities to avoid free-riding and to increase individual participation, while recognizing that larger groups may accommodate a wider range of perspectives. You can, of course, vary the size of the groups to align most effectively with the purpose and goals of the group activity.

Group work presents a number of pedagogical challenges. One challenge is resistance: some students find group work inefficient and unproductive and want to be taught by the expert teacher, not by novice classmates; they may also be averse to figuring things out for themselves. This challenge can be met with transparency—explaining the purpose of the group work, its usefulness for developing important life and work skills, and its value for making learning last.

A second challenge is keeping groups on task, and a third is ensuring that all members contribute productively. You can meet the second challenge by providing a clear purpose and direction for the group assignments, and identifying a product to be presented at the end of a specified time limit. Providing each member with a particular role and responsibility ensures productive participation by all members. Along with assigning specific roles and responsibilities to group members, you need to monitor group work—intervening, supporting, and encouraging students while they are engaged in the process. You need to know when to step in and when to step back, when a group needs guidance, and when it needs to be left alone to struggle productively with a task.

Assessing and grading group work present yet other challenges. You need to decide if the group work task is low- or high-stakes, whether the assessment feedback or grade will be provided to the individual members or to the group as a whole (or both), and the extent to which the grade assigned contributes to a student's overall grade. Will you be grading the product only, or does the process factor into the grade as well? Many teachers include group work as part of a participation grade, allocated overall as between 10 and 20 percent of a student's final course grade.

Numerous options exist for assessing and evaluating group work beyond grading the individual or the group as a whole. For example, you can assign students two grades, for their individual work as well for the ultimate product of the group, whether it's a research paper, presentation, or lab report. Or you can count only the group grade, but make it the average of their individual grades.

Students can also grade themselves and each other; they can describe their contributions in a short written self-assessment, leaving the actual grade to you. Whatever grading option you use, it's a good idea to let students know ahead of time how they will be graded and to give them your grading rubric—the criteria you will be using (see chapter 11).

Lastly, here are a few questions to consider when planning group work:

1. What is the learning goal of the exercise?
2. How is the activity connected to the class session and to the course overall?
3. How can you ensure that students understand the purpose and goal of the activity, as well as its alignment with the course goals?
4. What product will you require the groups to produce? What will they do at the end of the group work time allotted?
5. What time limit will you put on the overall group activity? Will you divide it into parts and provide time limits for each of those? How will the timing be enforced? By you, by a group member, or in some other way?
6. What will be your role while the groups are on task?
7. How will you frame the group assignment? How much guidance will you provide? Will you present assignments orally or in writing (on the board, with an instruction sheet)?
8. How will you assess the group's activity and provide feedback to the group?
9. How will you connect the group's work to what may have come before it during the class session, to what may follow it during that session, and to what precedes and succeeds it in the course overall?

Chapter Seven

Teaching and Technology

For better or worse, technology is everywhere, including in our classrooms, whether we intend it to be there or not. In some ways this is nothing new: writing and books were once cutting-edge media technologies, and it's hard to imagine the history of the classroom without them. Likewise, teaching today without using digital technologies is not only increasingly difficult (no email!) but also likely to result in missed learning opportunities for you and your students.

Unlike writing and printed texts, however, which have remained roughly the same across the centuries, today's technologies are evolving constantly and not just rapidly but, as some have noted, exponentially. Students and teachers are presented daily with new digital tools for learning, and also with new distractions. Teaching and learning with technology can thus mean a number of different things. We can use technology to enhance what we teach and make it more engaging; we can use it to give students new opportunities to create and apply what they're learning; and we can cultivate students' digital literacy, in terms of developing both the digital skills they will need in the twenty-first-century workplace and their ability to approach critically—and use purposefully—the technologies emerging all around them.

Given the pace of technological change, a chapter on teaching and technology runs the risk of becoming dated by the time of publication if its purpose is to discuss specific tools and technologies. These are always changing and competing with one another. Therefore, we keep our focus here as much as possible on principles and general tips and on proven tools and categories of technology rather than the latest development. For the latest in instructional technology, you will probably want to consult the internet—or better yet, your institution's instructional technology specialists, as we explain later.

As with so much we have discussed in this book, using technology in the classroom effectively begins with a question that on the surface has nothing to do with technology: What are your learning goals for your students? Once you answer this question, you can then ask: What technology will help your students most effectively reach those goals and allow you to measure their progress?

Approaching Technology in the Classroom

Another difficulty for a chapter on technology, in addition to the pace of change, is the breadth of the term "technology." In the classroom, we can use technology to extend and expand discussions through social media or online forums (and if we're teaching online, these may be among our only forms of communication, along with email). We can make our presentations more engaging through the use of clickers, polling apps, and multimedia interludes, such as short videos, all of which effectively break up long lectures. Students can collaborate on annotating a text, making a documentary, or building a website to present their research to the world (or at least their classmates) with freely available tools and platforms. And we can give students unprecedented opportunities to visualize and apply traditional "content" in ways unimaginable a decade ago, as our colleague Trace Jordan has done by incorporating augmented reality and 3D printing into a chemistry class about modeling molecules.

Thus, on one end of the spectrum, "teaching and technology" can refer to basic technological infrastructure, such as email, library databases, and the learning management system (LMS) used by your institution, including Blackboard, Moodle, and Sakai (NYU's LMS). Depending on your college or university, you may have access to other tools as well: web publishing (to build websites), a streaming platform (to upload videos), or a videoconferencing application (such as Zoom or Blackboard's Collaborate), which may or may not be bundled within your LMS. On the other end of the spectrum, "teaching and technology" can refer to efforts like those of Professor Jordan, who uses cutting-edge technologies that are still in development or that are even being developed *for* and *by* the course itself. Trace, for example, collaborates with colleagues in computer science on developing some of the AR software used in his class.

The sky's the limit. But it doesn't require specialized personnel or a 3D printer to innovate in the classroom. Both faculty and students can experiment with a wealth of open-source and free tools (or free versions of paid tools). Even a simple online publishing platform, like WordPress or Medium, affords limitless possibilities for assignments and activities that cannot be exhaustively described here but that you and your students can invent and discover.

What we can provide you with are questions, principles, and examples to guide and stimulate the process and make using technology less daunting. Even the most tech-savvy among us can be overwhelmed at times—how do we choose from so many available options? When you take on the challenge of adding a new technology to your course, whether or not you already have a specific tool or platform in mind, we recommend that you consult with your institution's center for teaching and learning or its instructional technologist group (or person). There are many different terms for these types of units and personnel: besides centers for "teaching and learning," some are called centers for "teaching innovation," "educational technology," or "teaching excellence." These specialists can advise you on the types of technology available to you, given your course goals, and guide you through the tools licensed at and provided by your institution.

Of course, not every institution offers this kind of resource. If yours does not, a useful first step is to familiarize yourself with the features of the LMS—some great features (online discussion forums, annotation tools, blogging platforms) may be readily available to you and your students.

Before selecting a technology, consider these guiding questions:

- What are the learning goals for your course? Not only in terms of what students will know, but what they will be able to do—or what they will be able to *become* by virtue of the course.
- If you have taught the course before, what are some problem areas you experienced? What elements of the course remained challenging for students? What skills did they need to develop in your course but often did not?
- What activities, forms of media, and digital products (websites, wikis, podcasts) are most related to the goals and problems you want to target in the course? What required technological skills would your course give students the opportunity to practice and apply?
- What technologies are most readily available at your institution (within the LMS, for instance)?
- To what extent are general technological skills, or facility with specific programs or platforms, an essential part of your course? For example, in a sociology course on quantitative research methods, familiarity with R programming language might be essential.

- What kind of general technological skills, or facility with specific programs or platforms, will your students need to succeed in the courses or careers that typically proceed from work in your course or discipline? In an introduction to journalism course, for example, podcasting might warrant a place it didn't ten or even five years ago. Depending on your answers to this question and the previous one, more class time might legitimately be devoted to getting students up to speed on the technology itself.
- What logistical "hiccups" are typical for your course? What issues have you had in, for instance, distributing materials, communicating with students, or taking attendance that might be resolved or streamlined with an automated process, digital tool, or program?
- What do you want to do in your course—or have students do—that until now has not been possible? What do you want to improve but have not been able to? Like the old proverb says, there may be an app for that.

Better Learning through Technology

At its best, technology in the classroom allows us to do things with our students we couldn't do otherwise (for example, shooting research-based PSAs with our phones). It also enables us to improve what we already do, such as engaging a massive lecture hall with a polling app; and it helps us to keep doing what we have been doing, but in ways or contexts that were previously impossible—creating a virtual classroom, for instance, attended by students at universities in New York and Abu Dhabi. At its worst, technology is just bells and whistles, its benefits clear to neither instructor nor students.

To ensure your own purposeful use of technology—to clearly connect it to the learning happening in your class—consider these questions as you review potential digital tools and projects:

- Why are you planning to use a particular technological tool? What is its purpose? How does it support your course learning goals?
- What is the added value of the technological tools you or your students are using? How do they enhance, extend, or deepen learning?

- How much training and support will students need in the use of the technology? (In group work, some of that training and support can be offloaded onto the more tech-savvy group members.)
- What does the technology do for your teaching and your students' learning that can't be done without it?

These are important questions. Considering them thoughtfully is essential for keeping the elements of teaching and learning aligned, keeping our courses coherent, and improving student learning. Moreover, as we discussed in chapter 1 on motivation and elsewhere, communicating your rationale for the use of the technology will increase student buy-in and ensure it benefits student learning.

This is not to suggest that you can't leave room for improvisation, experimentation, or play in the classroom. In fact, while trying out a technology for the first time, you'll have to leave room for the unexpected. But these less predictable elements of technology use, far from being drawbacks, are among the distinct benefits that technology can bring to your course; dealing with the unexpected and unplanned can give students (and instructors) rich opportunities for adapting and creatively applying what they are learning. Keep an open mind about what constitutes a "benefit to student learning." While the rationale for using a particular technology may sometimes be obvious (as with incorporating a social media–related project in a class on online marketing), in other cases it may be less direct or clear, but no less beneficial to student learning. The technology's added value may be as simple as adding an element of fun or collaboration to the process of achieving the learning goals of the course.

New Opportunities for Learning

What are some of the technologies you can use to enhance your courses? Or rather, to repeat one of our earlier questions, what are some of the things that technology allows you and your students to do in the classroom that can't be done without it? To address this question, we will discuss ways to extend the classroom, enhance lectures, increase collaboration, create for an audience, and learn through visualization.

Extending the Classroom

We will not discuss online or even blended classes extensively here, as that topic is beyond the scope of this chapter. (That said, many of the same pedagogical principles apply across media and to both tech-enhanced and analog approaches to teaching.) But what is essential to asynchronous courses, in which students participate at different times, can also benefit synchronous ones, in which all students "tune in" together at the same time: namely, the online discussion board, or any other platform (a blogging platform, for example) on which students can post and share their writing and comment on each other's ideas.

These tools allow you to expand the bounds of the classroom community and conversation. Before the semester begins, you might greet your students by email and ask them to introduce themselves to the class on a forum dedicated to the purpose. If you have a class blog set up on the LMS, WordPress, or Google's Blogger, you could ask them to include a photo in their post of something that interests them or reflects their personality in some way. Or you could wait and have this be the first assignment on the syllabus after the semester begins. When all of the student introductions are up, email the class to let them know.

Once the semester is under way, the online forum or class blog can serve to continue classroom discussions by giving students a way to reflect on or synthesize or generate questions about what happened during a class. They are also a powerful means of preparing for a session. If you ask students to write about a reading or discussion topic before it's covered in class, they'll be better prepared to participate. You will be better prepared as well, having had a chance to survey their initial thinking, which you can refer to during your lecture or the discussion.

As with in-class discussion, online discussion is most engaging and productive when students are in dialogue with each other, not only with the instructor. Set expectations and requirements for when and how often students should post and comment on the posts of their peers, and set expectations and requirements for *how* they should post and comment. If you want robust, thoughtful paragraphs with references to course material, your students may need models and practice before successfully producing them.

Students' work in online discussion needs to be purposeful. Having their work read and responded to by their classmates is one source of purposefulness. The instructor should also respond in some way—by briefly commenting, responding more substantially, referring to students' posts in class (perhaps even projecting them on-screen), or some combination of the three. In larger classes, it can be helpful to split up online discussion into small groups so that participation is not diffused across a large cohort. Similarly, even in a small class it may be hard to respond to all students as extensively as you would wish if they are posting frequently. But responding to several different students each time and discussing the online discussion in class will show them that you care and are interested in their work.

As will a grade. Making students accountable for a certain number of comments, or for a certain length of response, is often needed to ensure participation. Your grading and feedback need not be overly extensive or formal (which in fact can be counterproductive if the goal is to loosen them up to think and write freely); some kind of low-stakes, credit/no-credit method tends to be ideal in this case.

There are many ways to extend classroom discussions and build community besides blogs and online forums. You can videoconference with your students, for example, making your office hours more accessible and potentially less imposing. Google Hangout or Skype works for this just as easily as whatever tool your LMS may provide. You can invite guest speakers to your class this way as well (though it should go without saying that you should get to class early to set up a connection and have a plan B if it fails). You could even invite guest *students*. What if a former colleague is teaching a course in another state, or another country, that complements yours? Say you're teaching an environmental science course near an urban Superfund site and your friend is teaching the same course near a severely deforested region in South America. Or you're teaching a course on Walt Whitman and a grad school chum is teaching an American literature course in Japan. What kinds of notes could students in the two courses compare? And what kinds of differences in perspective could they discover through videoconferencing or simply reading each other's class blog?

Enhancing Lectures

Multimedia technology—videos, images, audio recordings—can add interest, emotion, context, and real-world situations to a lecture to illuminate and concretize the concepts you're teaching. Using technology in this way can also break up a presentation and reengage your students' flagging attention. As we have observed in the classrooms of professors across the disciplines—and from the front of the room ourselves—maintaining engagement after twenty to thirty minutes of any one topic or format becomes increasingly difficult without some kind of change in mode or method.

Make the most of these multimedia formats, and make sure that the connection to what you're teaching is clear; if it's not, explain the connection or give students time to wrestle with it. If students are going to watch a video, would they benefit from understanding its context beforehand? If the video is archival footage of the civil rights movement, you may want the class to be surprised and to experience the emotional impact of what they are about to see. This intention is fine, as long as you have considered what it is you want the class to get out of the video and the best way for that to happen. You could also give students questions before they view the video to focus their attention: What kinds of facial expressions do you notice? Who seems to hold authority in the march depicted in the video?

If you're showing a PowerPoint slide with a detailed image of the respiratory system, give students a chance to take it in; then ask them what they notice. If you have just been describing the case of a patient who experienced a peculiar pain while breathing, ask the class to speculate on the source of that pain, based on the patient's description and what they see on-screen in the diagram.

Other especially useful and increasingly prevalent tech tools in large classes and lecture-style classes are clickers and polling apps. They allow the instructor to poll the class, checking for preexisting knowledge (or misconceptions, as the case may be), students' understanding following a lecture section, general reactions and responses, or solutions to a problem just worked on in class. The results are typically projected on-screen in real time—in the form of a bar graph if students, for example, are answering a multiple-choice question, or a word cloud if students are answering an open-ended question about their responses to a line of poetry or to a case study in ethics. (Word clouds present all responses, but in different sizes: common responses appear larger and less common responses are smaller.)

The benefits of these tech tools are manifold. They enable you to collect feedback from the class to assess their understanding. They enable you to reengage students' attention by taking a break from the lecture and giving them time to process what they have been hearing. Polls can also be used to stimulate small-group and class discussions: after students, for example, see how many of their peers answered the same way they did (or didn't), they can talk in pairs about whether they will stand by their response or change it.

Because clickers are separate handheld devices and each student would need one, you will probably have to request them from your institution or department. But there are freely available polling apps that students can use on their phones, such as Poll Everywhere, Kahoot!, and Mentimeter. You can also use such apps to project the poll results from within your PowerPoint presentation.

Increasing Collaboration

Technology isn't required for classroom collaboration, but tech tools can make it much easier and open up previously unavailable arenas for collaborating. With G Suite for Education, Google's apps for education, students can share and work together in real time on documents, spreadsheets, presentations, forms and surveys, even websites (using Google Docs, Sheets, Slides, Forms, and Sites, respectively). They can message each other while working to discuss changes. They don't have to pass hard copies back and forth, and they don't have to schedule on-location meetings outside of class.

Peer review, too, benefits greatly from these tools: students can suggest revisions and make comments on classmates' drafts. These marked-up documents can be shared with the instructor for assessment.

As writers and current or former instructors of writing ourselves, we recognize just how collaborative writing so often is—and must be—and we appreciate these kinds of tools for making that aspect of writing visible to our students. (We rely on Google Suite the most, for its familiarity, availability, and widespread use, but it's not the only available option.)

Students can collaborate on myriad projects, not only on traditional papers and presentations. For instance, it takes a team to design and build a website to present student research (on Google Sites or WordPress), but such a project also gives students a unique opportunity to think about how they might combine, connect, and arrange bits of research collected from members of a small group or even the whole class. This is what is done in "People of New York," an interdisciplinary seminar that is part of the required curriculum at Macaulay Honors College at the City University of New York: students develop websites to share their research on a particular New York City neighborhood.

A project as ambitious as a website may require significant amounts of class time for discussion, planning, and implementation, including instruction on use of the technology. The website will probably be the centerpiece of the course, a focal point of practice through which students learn about their research topic and its relationship to the topics of their peers. All this work must be justified in light of the course learning goals, which could include developing the ability to make connections across topics or disciplines, to organize and present information in a compelling and clear fashion, and to work collaboratively on large-scale research and design projects.

If these are not your particular goals, you wouldn't want to devote so much time and effort to a project like this, or to require it of your students. But there are smaller-scale alternatives. Setting up a class Twitter or Instagram account, or simply a hashtag on either platform, enables students to share comments, links, articles, and images relating to the course. We have known professors whose use of a class Twitter account to address questions or comments during a class session gave students too shy to speak an avenue into class discussion.

Whatever you choose to use, remember that it should be meaningful, with students required to post in some fashion. Utilize or discuss the feed in class, or have students write a short reflection on a post or comment of their choice. One of the potential benefits, particularly in linking to content relevant to the course, is that students will connect what they're learning to the media they probably already consume and may be prompted to discover other sources of information to find useful material. Another prime benefit of such tech-enhanced collaboration for students is learning from their classmates' posts.

One last example of technology-enabled collaboration, and one you might not expect, is collaborative reading. Students can collaboratively annotate digital texts, as well as images and videos, by using tools or platforms such as hypothes.is, MIT's Annotation Studio, Perusall, Xodo, Kami, or Stanford's Lacuna Stories. Although digital reading is sometimes viewed with suspicion (and not without reason), collaborative annotation can make visible and cooperative a fundamental stage of critical and close reading with which students otherwise must struggle in isolation, if they do it at all. Using these tools, students can see and respond to each other's annotations, building on one another's ideas, seeing how parts of a text that didn't speak to them spurred reactions and interpretations in their peers, and vice versa. Collaborative reading can provide students with a granular, dynamic model of the reading process. And as the instructor, you will be able to see, assess, and guide their efforts.

Creating for an Audience

One of the drawbacks to the time-honored research paper—and many other traditional assignments—is that only the instructor reads them. Who else matters, you might ask, if it's the instructor who gives the grade? Laboring over a carefully researched ten-page paper for a single reader may still feel like a disproportionate amount of effort for such limited impact, as well as not at all reflective of how most writing is done outside of school, on the job, in the media, or online. Professors of composition have long understood the importance of rhetorical context for effective writing: without a clear sense of who they are writing for, our students may flounder, unable to make the kinds of rhetorical decisions that writing constantly demands. In addition, as we discussed in chapter 1, students are more engaged if their work is purposeful and meaningful. When students know that their fellow students, or even the broader public, will read their writing—that they are actually writing *to* and *for* someone—the wider potential reception creates for them a sense of urgency and a clearer rhetorical context.

We have already talked about several modes or platforms for online writing—participating in forums, blogs, and social media or building entire websites—all of which may be set to varying levels of privacy. But even if only class members are given access to student writing, and not the general public, students' work can become purposeful in ways that projects submitted only to the professor cannot. One of us (AB), for example, asked his American literature survey to build a shared annotated bibliography hosted on the class blog. Each student had to find a reputable online source, link to it, and describe in a blog post why it was reliable and useful for research. The students' writing was not only being read by their peers but used: students drew ideas and sources from the bibliography as they developed and completed their end-of-semester research papers.

Writing online gives your students all the learning benefits of writing, but with the added value of ownership, meaningfulness, and audience response conferred by online publishing.

When class projects are made fully public, students have the opportunity to not only create and share knowledge with each other, but also to add to and shape the web—to have a real social impact. Our colleague Amy Hamlin (2017) at St. Catherine University has her students, as a culminating activity in her "Women in Art" course, participate in a Wikipedia edit-a-thon. Their assignment: to conduct research on a neglected female artist and contribute a new entry to Wikipedia. Students are thus required to read Wikipedia critically for its skewed representation of gender in the arts, conduct research on their chosen artist, and craft an informed, critical appraisal to be shared publicly in an effort to counter the sexism pervasive in online environments like Wikipedia. The potential insights from this activity are profound: students see the constructed nature of knowledge and history and are empowered to take control of the narratives that have excluded others, including themselves.

Learning through Visualization

A picture can be worth a thousand words. So can a chart, bar graph, 3D model, diagram, map, timeline, immersive virtual reality experience, or GIF. In fact, some of these, when done well, can be worth considerably more.

What concepts, forms, processes, or environments do you wish your students could see? How might students better understand a set of data or information through a particular shape—a pie chart or line chart or illustrative infographic—that helps them focus on what's significant amid all the numbers? Natural and social science disciplines using quantitative research methods have long relied on such data visualizations; now, through the "digital humanities," these and other methods of interpreting and presenting data have made deep inroads into teaching and research in the humanities as well.

Another way to think about the pedagogical potential of visualization is in terms of context—both spatial and temporal. Digital timelines can be plotted with multimedia entries, allowing students to align political events with cultural ones. Digital maps can be used to bring literary movements to life, showing, for instance, where Walt Whitman might have crossed paths with other significant New Yorkers of his time, or where we can still enjoy some of the vistas that inspired his poetry. Such visualizations can help students, on the one hand, achieve a wider angle of historical vision and, on the other, connect a historically distant person or event to the present time and place.

As useful as such visualizations may be in a lecture or on a course website, the process of *making* them provides even richer opportunities for active learning. In the process of visualizing data, students have to interpret data, identify the message that data communicates, and decide how best to present the data to convey the same message to others. In building timelines or maps with multimedia components, they make connections across disciplines and media and must identify, clarify, and prioritize the most salient content to include. Such activities are prime forms of active learning, and a way to solidify lasting learning, because they require students to connect old and new information, relate concepts, and create visual and experiential associations with what they're learning. Students end up applying their learning, and creating from it, in multiple ways.

What's next? Mixed reality, according to EDUCAUSE's 2019 "Horizon Report" (Alexander et al. 2019), among other things. With augmented and virtual reality, we will be able to ask, where do we want our students to go? What do we want them to see and do when they get there? Is there a historical event that we want them to experience? Perhaps looking at the East River through their phone to see what it looked like in 1856, when Whitman first published "Crossing Brooklyn Ferry"?

Digital Literacy

We could have organized the preceding section on the benefits of technology in the classroom in many other ways, adding or giving greater emphasis to other types of active learning, such as *curation, multimedia composition, remixing and recombining, making thinking visible,* and *creative means of synthesizing information.* All of these activities are implicit in the preceding discussion, and we might have covered them at greater length—as well as many other topics—but for the limited scope of this chapter.

There is, however, one last overarching benefit of teaching with technology that is essential to consider. Whatever subject we might be teaching, part of our job is preparing students for life and work in the twenty-first century, and if we are to prepare them for success, it's hard to imagine digital literacy not being part of that preparation, whether it occurs in your courses or elsewhere.

Any of the activities and projects already discussed will provide your students with practice in the use of different platforms and tools, in addition to achieving the learning goals more directly related to the disciplinary content of your course. Some students may already be familiar with a particular technology—or be a quick study in the digital arena—and these students can help their classmates. (For group work, it's advisable to distribute this kind of expertise.) Encountering some amount of trial and error and having to figure things out as you and your students go along is natural, and even desirable. Even if it's a messy process, learning how to use a new platform or tool and adapting to it has advantages over developing expertise in a single tool over a sustained period of time, as it promotes the ability to adapt. The specific tools, after all, will always be changing.

And in some ways, using technology—and especially forms of digital composition and design—is analogous to using writing as a tool for learning across the curriculum. Technology use can often involve writing, but even when it doesn't, it prompts students' reflection and creativity in applying what they are learning in the course.

Another and no less significant side of digital literacy is developing the ability to think critically about the technologies quickly proliferating throughout every aspect of our daily lives. One obvious application relates to the proliferation of information online; much of it is useful, of course, but much of it is unreliable. Although the evaluation of sources has always been a key component of research, the potential obscurity of a digital text's source and the careless habits that such convenient access to information can encourage raise the stakes and difficulty of assessing validity and require a new layer of instruction in traditional research skills. A number of online resources, including those from university teaching centers, provide useful guidelines for doing just this; one of the more helpful, in our view, is offered by Purdue University's Online Writing Lab (OWL). (See interlude 7 for some suggestions about how students can evaluate sources.)

But it's not only the content delivered by technology that warrants critical appraisal; it's also the technologies themselves—the tools, platforms, forms of media, and algorithms and code from which they are built. Numerous recent books have looked at the biases and prejudices that carry over into the machines and programs that human beings design; see, for example, Sara Wachter-Boettcher's *Technically Wrong: Sexist Apps, Biased Algorithms, and Other Threats of Toxic Tech* (2017) and Cathy O'Neil's *Weapons of Math Destruction: How Big Data Increases Inequality and Threatens Democracy* (2016). Professor Hamlin's Wikipedia edit-a-thon project is a good example of this kind of critical engagement in action in the classroom. In focusing on Wikipedia, her students consider both message and media, developing an awareness of the current limits of Wikipedia's stated aim: to make *all* knowledge freely available for *all* people through open, collective design and development.

There are many avenues for such reflection—questions of privacy, automation, the attention economy. Closer to home, perhaps, and a frequent source of frustration for instructors, is the distraction of devices in the classroom. Research has shown that open laptops, even those of *other* students, can interfere with student learning in class. Mandating no devices in class, or during certain portions of a session, may thus be the right option for many instructors. Talking to your students about the reasons for the policy or even asking for their input on creating a policy has the added benefits of increasing their buy-in and raising their awareness of the potential effect of their screens on their learning. Another option is to incorporate their laptops and phones into the activities of the class so that they are put to educational use rather than some other use.

The goal, as with all things teaching-related, is to empower students—in this case, to be able to use technology effectively and understand it critically. Don't assume that students possess this technological literacy. Some will have had greater interest in and exposure to the kinds of digital tools you may want to use than others. Moreover, some will have had greater prior access to them than others, and for all sorts of social, cultural, and economic reasons (economic access and the "digital divide" being another potential avenue for critical reflection). And even the most practically adept technophiles among your students may not have questioned technology's always evolving societal and personal impact.

A Dirty Little Secret

What if you're not a "tech person"? Can you become one? How?
Google.
We're being serious. You use technology to learn technology. Robust communities of amateur and professional developers populate online forums and message boards to share their knowledge. Often, whatever question you have will have been answered somewhere already; it's just a matter of hitting on the right—or right enough—search terms.

When searching for the most up-to-date tools, use some of the terms and topics you've seen mentioned in this chapter, or variations thereof. For example:

- Collaboration tools for higher education
- Annotation tools
- Collaborative annotation tools
- VR/AR in the classroom
- Best free data visualization tools
- Best timeline makers
- Using Instagram in the college classroom

One of us (AB) began graduate school (in English, not computer science) without a Twitter account—or any social media account for that matter. Email and web-surfing were about the extent of his technology skills. But by the time he finished he held a position as an instructional technologist with a sideline building websites on WordPress for a couple of private clients.

A pivotal moment in this evolution came when he had to deal with a problem on a website that required coding. He didn't know how to code (you can get pretty far on WordPress without knowing how), so this was potentially a crisis. But then he remembered Google. He Googled the problem and found lines of code someone else had written to address the same issue. He didn't understand the code, of course, but the person who had written the code also explained what it did and where to cut-and-paste it. Problem solved—and he learned something new in the process.

Tips for Teaching with Technology

Some final, general tips on using technology in the classroom:

- Consider the tools and platforms provided by your institution. All else being equal, choosing a tool with which your students are already familiar and have ready access to over one that has the same functionality but is not supported by your college or university can save on time and effort to train and register students.
- For small-group projects, distribute the more technologically skilled students across groups.
- Don't take your students' knowledge of technology for granted. Some will know more than you, some will know less, and some will be about as knowledgeable as you.
- As with any activity, digital or otherwise, explain the rationale. What are the benefits for students and their learning?
- Keep it simple—for your students. It's easy to get caught up in all the possibilities that some of these platforms offer (text, images, embedded audio!), but it's better for your students if their work remains focused, manageable, and purposeful.
- Keep it simple—for yourself. As with introducing any new element to your teaching, make manageable, gradual tweaks.
- Make the technology you choose a central component of the class, not an add-on. For a blog, this could mean making it a regular part of their work, with clear expectations from the beginning of the semester to the end (requiring one 250-word post and two comments per week, for example). For a website project, this could mean working in stages over the semester through scaffolded assignments and activities and regular discussions concerning student progress.
- Have a plan B when using new technology. And when using any technology. And sometimes a plan C.

You can do a lot with technology in the classroom that you couldn't do otherwise. You can do a lot without technology that you couldn't do otherwise. And there's a lot of overlap between teaching with and without technology. The key, as always, is to keep your learning goals in mind and to identify, revisit, and refine your methods for meeting them. Technology can help in that process in ways that continue to evolve, and it's up to all of us to figure out how.

Applications

1. Think of one course in which you would like to introduce one technological tool that you have not yet tried. Which would you choose and why?
2. How might you train yourself or be trained in the use of that technology? Begin taking the necessary steps to become adequately adept with it.
3. What is your position on students using their phones, tablets, and computers in the classroom? Why do you take that position?
4. What assignments could you create to help students learn to evaluate information and to lead them toward understanding and knowledge?

Information and Knowledge

We are awash in information, which has never been more available or accessible. And yet the information that comes to us and our students is not always accurate and not always trustworthy. One of our challenges as teachers is to help students vet and validate information, wherever they find it, if it is to become useful knowledge. Information requires analysis and interpretation. Inaccurate, erroneous information leads to faulty interpretation and inaccurate understanding.

We need to help our students remain vigilant about the information they encounter and to be skeptical about it. They need to learn to sift information, to sort and examine it, question and challenge it. In their book *Blur* (2011), Bill Kovach and Tom Rosenstiel propose using the following questions about information:

1. Where did this information come from?
2. What is the evidence for it?
3. Why is this information important to know?
4. What is missing from this information?

Daniel Willingham (2012) suggests a related way to evaluate information:

1. **Strip it**: Boil the information down to its key claim. Identify its essential supporting evidence.
2. **Trace it**: Identify who is providing the information and what others may have said about it and about the provider.
3. **Analyze it**: Consider how trustworthy the information is.
4. **Accept or reject it**: Decide whether the information and associated claims are sufficiently well supported to warrant acceptance.

Information and the Internet

Some people argue that in the internet age learning facts and amassing knowledge are no longer important. "You can look it up," they say. To some extent, of course, they are right. But there is more involved in finding things out than "looking it up." First, much of what is available on the internet is simply wrong. Not only does the internet contain much unintended error, but it has become a storehouse for all kinds of deliberate falsehoods. Unless students are equipped with a method of sifting out errors and detecting "fake news" and other forms of dishonesty and false information, they are prey to perpetrators of deception. Second, even when students can find useful information the easy way—by surfing the open web rather than searching the library—this may encourage them to believe that knowledge acquisition is always easy. All they have to do is click a few times on their devices. This is a dangerous misconception.

So, too, is the notion that we don't need to have facts at our fingertips. Consider, for example, how knowing with confidence the multiplication tables through twelve makes it easy to estimate numbers, products, and percentages. If we never learn the times tables because they are readily available at the click of a mouse, we will never be able to estimate numbers with ease and confidence. We need to know things—as many things as we can absorb and retain. Knowing more about many things allows us to seize opportunities to combine them in surprising and unexpected ways. That way innovation lies.

Chapter Eight

Experiential Learning

The central idea of "experiential learning," as the term suggests, is the process of learning through experience. The "learning" part requires an additional element: *reflection*. Thus, a fuller concept of experiential learning includes reflection about the learning experiences in which students participate. The teacher's responsibility is to create worthwhile educational experiences so that students will have something of value on which to reflect.

Like active learning, experiential learning involves many different forms of student engagement. Our NYU colleague Todd Cherches (2019) has identified these as "inquiry, exploration, discussion, involvement, engagement, collaboration, connectivity, knowledge-sharing, cross-pollination, problem-solving, decision-making, risk-taking, analysis, synthesis, creativity, innovation, reflection, testing, application, and more" (p. 3). Cherches's experiential learning model emphasizes presenting and facilitating skills; it also highlights the importance of coaching, especially providing timely constructive feedback (p. 4). We have discussed many facets of this model in previous chapters; others we address in this and subsequent chapters, and in our epilogue on teaching as creative problem solving.

As a form of active learning, experiential learning differs from rote learning and didactic learning, both of which are passive rather than active (see chapter 3). Experiential learning is learning by doing. In this kind of hands-on learning, students assume responsibility for their learning, taking control of both the learning experience and their reflection on it. Without those intertwined elements, there is no real experiential learning.

Experiential learning differs from traditional academic instruction in other ways as well. Students learning experientially manage their own learning; they determine what to do, when to do it, and how. In addition to a venue change from the classroom to some type of field environment, there is often no textbook, though other resources may well be made available to students. And although experiential learning courses are embedded in a curriculum, that curriculum may be more malleable and less solidified than the curriculum for traditional classroom-based academic courses. With experiential learning, there tend to be fewer limits on and more latitude in what students are permitted to do—more leeway in *how* they learn as well as in *what* they learn.

Among the earliest and most influential advocates of experiential learning were John Dewey, Paulo Freire, Maria Montessori, Jean Piaget, Carl Rogers, and Rudolf Steiner. Although their reasons for employing it and ways of embodying and teaching it varied dramatically according to their pedagogical, political, and psychological viewpoints, these proponents of learning through experience, like others, espoused a constructivist philosophy of education in which knowledge is not transmitted but rather constructed by students in the process of learning. What students learn is less something they are "given" than something they discover themselves. Inherent in experiential learning is Dewey's idea that "the process and goal of education are one and the same thing" (quoted in Kolb 2015).

In the *Nicomachean Ethics*, Aristotle argues that we learn things we cannot yet do simply by doing them. Aristotle did not develop a full-fledged pedagogy around experiential learning; that would have to wait until the late twentieth century, when David Kolb published *Experiential Learning* (1984). Kolb's model emphasizes firsthand primary source learning—going to the zoo to learn about animals, for example, or watching animals in the wild, rather than reading about them or viewing a documentary about animal behavior. Another kind of experiential learning occurs in work environments: through internships or job-shadowing, students learn from authentic real-world experiences and in actual rather than simulated work environments (though simulations, case studies, and other applications of concepts learned have become accepted experiential learning practices).

Kolb's (2015) experiential learning model includes four different kinds of abilities: "concrete experience abilities (CE), reflective observation abilities (RO), abstract conceptualization abilities (AC), and active experimentation (AE) abilities" (p. 42). This cycle of experience, reflection, conceptualization, and experimentation is not only cyclical but iterative. That's both its challenge and its power. For Kolb's cyclical model to work, however, certain conditions must exist: students must be able to be actively involved in their learning experience; they must be allowed to reflect on their experience; they must have the analytical and conceptual skills to understand what's at stake in their learning experiences; and finally, they must have decision-making and problem-solving skills. Two ideas are central to Kolb's model: learning is "best conceived as a process, not in terms of outcomes" (p. 37), and learning is a "continuous process grounded in experience" (p. 38).

Successful experiential learning also requires certain learned dispositions. A willingness to engage actively in learning is essential, along with an equivalent willingness to reflect on the experience undergone. Experiential learning also thrives when a student welcomes feedback and wants to learn from it. These positive attitudinal dispositions are affected by a student's feelings, which play a role in experiential learning, as they do in other forms of learning (see chapter 1 and interlude 5).

Because experiential learning involves iteration and recursiveness, students need to learn from repeated opportunities to practice. For example, consider the experiential learning required in learning to drive, speak a foreign language, or play a musical instrument. We know from our experience in learning these skills that repetition and practice are necessary. The same is true of other kinds of experiential learning—as it is, moreover, of academic learning generally.

We also know that a degree of challenge is required if students are to improve—if they are to get to "the next level." Thus, students' learning experiences outside the classroom should push them beyond their current level of understanding and nudge them into new learning territory. Experiential learning offers students the opportunity to try new things that they may fail at initially or eventually achieve only partial success in pursuing. Through analysis and reflection, however, students can improve their performance and deepen their understanding. These aspects of the experiential learning approach are congruent with measures taken to help students retain their learning—with making learning stick (see chapter 4).

One key to experiential learning is to bring the outside world into the classroom. Teachers can create different kinds of learning experiences through role-playing, simulations, case analysis, gamification, and other forms of active learning. These pedagogical practices enable students to look both backward, through reflection, and forward toward real-world applications.

And of course, we can make the outside world our classroom by incorporating various kinds of co-curricular and extracurricular learning elements and environments into our courses. A common approach is taking students on a traditional field trip to visit, for example, museums, battlefields, or science and other research labs to extend and enrich their learning. We need to break down boundaries that separate and seg-regate learning in order to help students see the larger world as an exten-sion of the classroom and come to understand that learning can take place anywhere—and indeed, that it should take place everywhere they find themselves or put themselves.

In addition, although it's not absolutely essential for these and other types of experiential learning—learning to teach among them—feedback from a teacher or other accomplished professional helps immeasurably. Experiential learning can be accelerated as well as elevated by the inter-vention of an experienced facilitator. For their part, students must take to heart the facilitator's targeted feedback and continue to make the cali-brated corrections required for improving their performance. (For addi-tional discussion of feedback, see chapters 9 and 11).

The Benefits of Experiential Learning

One benefit of experiential learning is that it enables students to develop new habits, which often require behavioral changes. At its best, experien-tial learning results in significant transformation of both learning be-haviors and attitudes. Attitudinal change is often overlooked in our think-ing about teaching and learning. However, as we noted in chapter 1, helping students develop a positive attitude and a flexible mindset is one of the most important pedagogical challenges we face.

Another potential benefit is the opportunity to learn from the experi-ence of others. In courses steeped in experiential learning—and even in courses in which experiential learning is only modestly embedded—students have opportunities to share their field experiences, both their successes and their failures, along with their reflections about their expe-riential learning situations. In-class discussions of students' experiential learning in a course can be supplemented with cases, games, interviews, scenes from films, and other types of scenarios and simulations.

Other potential benefits accrue when experiential learning bridges the gap between theory and practice—between abstract understanding and concrete application via experience. There is also much evidence that ex-periential learning increases student engagement. It's no surprise that when students invest themselves actively in collaborative problem-solving, a central ingredient of experiential learning, they become more interested, more enthusiastic, and more committed to securing a positive outcome. Part of this engagement is attributable to their personal stake in what they are doing. Students care about their learning experiences when they are able to make decisions, when they are given latitude, when they have opportunities to make choices in their academic assignments and in how they conduct their fieldwork, and when their emotions are tapped and their feelings valued. Under these conditions, coursework becomes much more than an academic exercise.

Although experiential education is a common feature of professional and vocational programs, its field-based dynamic has gained less of a hold in the liberal arts. (The sciences, of course, have their labs.) Nonetheless, the benefits of experiential learning can also accrue for traditional classroom-based educational approaches, as the lines between practical and academic learning continue to blur. Part of the rapport between classroom and extramural learning derives from a renewed interest in civic literacy. Even more of this rapport, however, derives from the increased desire on the part of business and the professions for graduating students with a broad suite of skills, including communication and critical thinking, teamwork and collaboration, and problem-posing and problem-solving, along with the dispositions of persistence and perseverance through difficult challenges (see chapter 1).

A central goal of liberal education is mastery of both broad and specialized knowledge domains (general education coupled with the major). What is often missing from this educational paradigm, however, is an opportunity for students to apply and use the knowledge they acquire, especially during their undergraduate years. Allied with being able to apply knowledge is being able to transfer newly developed skills to different contexts—educational, personal, and professional. Such knowledge transfer requires the kind of deep learning best developed in educational settings that provide opportunities for students to learn by experience and reflection.

Students often prefer that problems be defined for them and that clear, understandable solutions that they can be shown or can figure out for themselves are available. Experiential learning situations, however, often introduce students to complex problems that admit of multiple solutions—or that have no available solution at all. Rather than posing pre-identified problems for students, experiential learning scenarios can be structured to require students to frame and reframe problems themselves. Such problems typically require students to confront dissonant information as well as to deal with ambiguity and rapidly changing circumstances. Wrestling with authentic real-world problems, both individually and collaboratively, helps students develop the problem-solving skills required for deeper learning.

Lifelong Learning

Even more than being able to adapt to the practical learning "on the job" that employers typically favor, students need to be able to continue their learning beyond the demands of any particular job or any particular career domain. Information and knowledge are changing ever more rapidly, rendering many jobs, careers, and businesses obsolete within a matter of years rather than decades. To survive and even thrive in the future workforce, students will need to become masters of their own learning. Their capacity for learning how to learn is likely to be the deciding factor in their work future.

Accomplishing this pedagogical objective is a major goal of experiential learning approaches. Research on service learning and internship programs has found that students who regularly combine structured reflection with in-the-field experiences more often develop strategic learning orientations to meet new challenges (Eyler 1993; Eyler and Giles 1999). When students' need for knowledge springs from an actual problem in the field rather than from a concern about knowledge required to pass a test, they become authentically invested in their learning. Personal need creates an intrinsic motivation because it serves an immediate practical purpose.

Traditional classroom learning differs markedly from community field learning in other ways as well. Unlike classroom learning, which is often decontextualized and focused on individual learners, workplace community learning is context-specific, centered on problems and practical approaches to their solution sought through collaboration. Lifelong learning develops best in situations that allow for the demands that field learning makes on students. It stands to reason, then, that to help students become lifelong learners, we should seek ways to create these kinds of challenges for them, integrating those experiences in appropriate ways in the courses we teach. To this end, we can introduce experiential learning elements into our more traditional academic courses—to tap into the power of experiential learning even in those situations where we may have to deal with school, program, departmental, or other constraints.

Considerations for Experiential Learning

Other considerations to take into account when implementing experiential learning are designing experiential activities, classroom activities, and external activities. A few words about each of these design opportunities.

In *designing experiential activities*, you need to decide which parts of your course are best suited to experiential learning. Consider precisely how those experiential learning activities link up with your course objectives. Also consider to what extent the experiential learning feeds into larger objectives beyond your particular course goals. And consider as well how you will evaluate and grade student performance. Designing experiential activities requires an approach that sees student learning as an encounter with problems to be identified and solved instead of information to be remembered and concepts to be understood (Wurdinger 2005). Also important is incorporating a clear structure for activities undertaken both in the classroom and outside it. The structural elements should include establishing clear goals for all activities; explaining how the experiential components fit into the course's big picture; and defining specific roles for student participants, the course instructor, and on-site personnel.

In *designing classroom activities*, take account of how you will direct and monitor student inquiry, perhaps using Dewey's "pattern of inquiry" model, in which inquiry occurs throughout the learning experience (Wurdinger and Priest 1999). A pattern of inquiry is undertaken when a student identifies a problem to be investigated and creates a plan to address it; this is followed by an opportunity to put the plan into action and have the extent of its success evaluated, with further adjustment and calibration as needed.

To be consistent with the principles of experiential learning, remember to keep activities student-centered and hands-on. Allow students opportunities to make mistakes and learn from them; provide timely feedback and time for quick revision; and coach and encourage students along the way and provide critical evaluation of their performance.

In *designing external activities*, recognize that whatever you set up for students is likely to be affected by contingencies beyond your control. Everyday workplace realities—from people issues to weather changes, schedule adjustments, disrupted routines, competing ideas and perspectives, and other issues—need to be acknowledged. This is why it's important to brief students with information about the site and the people involved before they embark on an external environment learning experience (Moon 2004). Take care when setting up external learning opportunities to gain the commitment of employers and other project supervisors to the program and the students. And ensure that the people working at the field site with students are in sync with your learning goals for them.

Essential Conditions for Experiential Learning

To enhance, extend, and deepen student understanding, try to create experiential learning opportunities that meet the following conditions (Eyler 2009):

1. The work, service, or field experience clearly connects with the course's academic goals and objectives.
2. Carefully developed assessments provide evidence of achieving the academic goals and objectives.
3. Supervisors and mentors from the field and the classroom work together to monitor student learning and provide feedback.
4. Students receive preparation for their field experience ahead of time, along with guidance in how to learn from and through the experience.
5. Students prepare and receive feedback on well-structured, ongoing opportunities for reflection that link what they learn in the classroom with what they learn in the field.

Along with other experiential learning advocates, Janet Eyler (2009) emphasizes the critical importance of structured feedback and repeated reflection throughout the course on both its academic and experiential components. Reflection, she suggests, should be embedded in the learning experience from beginning to end. It should be continuous and iterative rather than an end-of-course retrospective exercise. Reflection should take place in class and in the field, before, during, and after field experiences and class discussions. Having students keep a reflection journal enables them to keep track of their gradual accumulation of knowledge and their gradually increasing understanding. It reflects the speed bumps they hit, the confusions they suffer through, the obstacles they encounter (which they may or may not overcome), and the give-and-take nature of their learning experience as they progress and regress throughout the course.

Regular and continuous reflection helps students think about their learning as a process, as something that is achieved over time and that entails some degree of uncertainty and confusion along the way. Moreover, continuous reflection better approximates what actual authentic learning looks like. And thus, continuous reflection better prepares students for the kind of learning that, in their working lives, they will be exposed to and will need to adopt and demonstrate.

Types of Experiential Learning

Here are the major types of experiential learning you might consider for your students. We provide a quick note about each, except for service learning, which we discuss at length.

Apprenticeships

Apprenticeships give students a chance to try out working in a field of interest to get an inside look at a particular type of work. Ideally, an apprenticeship includes a mentor, an experienced professional, to guide the apprentice in learning and doing what's required in entrance positions in, for example, architecture, engineering, or data analysis (see also interlude 8).

Clinical Experiences

Clinical work provides students with opportunities for hands-on learning of particular skills associated with a field, such as nursing, medical and computer technology, and teaching. Clinical practice is part and parcel of hospital work as well as of social work and many teacher-preparation programs. The key to successful clinical learning experiences is timely, targeted, regular feedback.

Fieldwork

Fieldwork has long been a staple of study in anthropology, sociology, and the biological and environmental sciences. It offers students the opportunity to take their classroom and textbook learning outside those boundaries and apply it in communities and in the natural world. The "field" is the student's "laboratory" for experiential learning, whether a neighborhood, a village, a school, a forest, an archeological dig site, or any other physical space.

Internships

Internships function much like apprenticeships: they offer students a chance to test their suitability for a career field, as well as how deeply interested in it they are. As with apprenticeships, internships have the added bonus of providing students with valuable work experience. In addition, students benefit from being supervised and coached by professionals in the field. Internships can provide students with a window into a profession or industry, which may wind up encouraging (or discouraging) them from pursuing it further. Some internships include financial compensation.

Research

One of the most familiar and common forms of experiential learning for students is doing research under the supervision of a mentor (see interlude 8). Students benefit when they can systematically investigate and research contested questions. As many discover, learning from empirical observation, cutting-edge technologies, and collaboration can be exciting. True collaboration is a key element of student research experiences; in whatever project they find themselves working on, the research must be authentic and real, not a made-up exercise.

Service Learning

A common and well-known type of experiential learning is service learning, which combines academic study with real-world experience. The learning element of service learning often links concepts and knowledge explored in traditional academic fashion with experiential learning embedded in some type of community service.

The learning experience for students depends on the nature of the service and the academic course in which the service learning is embedded, and so it can vary dramatically. A key issue is how much each of the two components—service and learning—is emphasized. Another concern is how authentic the service is and the extent to which student participants contribute to the community they serve, however modest that service may be and for however long it may last. MaryAnn Baenninger (2018) argues that in successful service learning volunteer and recipient merge in ways that benefit all participants.

More than four decades ago, Robert Sigmon (1979) developed the following typology of service learning categories:

- *Service* learning, in which learning is secondary to the primacy of the service activity
- Service *learning*, in which learning is primary and service is secondary

- *Service learning*, in which the goals of the service and of the learning are given equal weight and emphasis
- Service learning, in which the goals of service and learning are separate.

How Service Learning Works

In service learning, academic course material—information, knowledge, frameworks, concepts, and the like—is taught and learned through practical applications accompanied by reflection on the connections between the learning and the service. This reflection component is critical; without it, the learning element is minimized. Moreover, the service and the learning are integrated and reciprocal, balanced and blended.

As part of the reflection process, students engage in discussions about their service learning experience and write about what they learned from doing it. The learning that students experience in these courses includes not only practical applications of course concepts but also other kinds of real-world practice, such as working with others as members of a community. Students who participate in service learning courses report that this interpersonal learning is one of the most positive and beneficial aspects of their service learning experience.

Whatever the balance between the two components of service learning, different kinds of activities can form part of the experience. Examples include volunteering, internships, fieldwork, and various types of community service. Volunteer activities tend to directly benefit those served more than the volunteers, who usually offer their service altruistically and without recompense. Internships provide direct benefits for student participants, whether or not payment is included, as they gain real-world knowledge. Similarly, various kinds of (almost always unpaid) fieldwork activities provide practical hands-on benefits, as participating students apply in real-world situations what they learn in the classroom or the lab. Fieldwork service learning experiences may also serve co-curricular rather than curricular functions.

Why Engage in Service Learning?

As a form of active learning (see chapter 3), service learning benefits students in many of the same ways that active learning strengthens, deepens, and extends learning outcomes. However, additional benefits accrue as well, such as coming to a deeper cognitive understanding of course concepts, developing social skills, and, especially, learning to work productively with others. Another frequent benefit is improvement in students' problem-solving skills, including their ability to evaluate contextual elements. A third benefit is an increased understanding of the social issues relevant to the community they serve as well as their own community. Finally, service learning enables students to extend and deepen their experience and understanding of cultural, social, ethnic, racial, and academic diversity.

Other potential benefits for students include stronger relationships with the faculty members who teach service learning courses, greater satisfaction with their college learning experience, and improved graduation rates. Student retention has been shown to be higher among students involved in service learning experiences. Instructors, too, tend to express higher levels of satisfaction with the quality of student learning in their service learning courses. In addition, instructors often develop strong networks with community entities, as well as with other faculty at their own and other institutions involved with similar service learning programs, projects, and courses.

To maximize the benefits of service learning for all parties—students, faculty, institution, and community—every element of the service learning program, project, or course needs to be carefully developed and thoughtfully integrated. It is critical to place students in communities carefully and to consider their function, purpose, and contribution in these communities. Additionally, students need to fully understand the purpose of their community service and its relationship to the course and its academic requirements.

As with other forms of experiential learning, the reflection component of the service learning course is essential. It should be rigorous and involve a significant amount of writing—reflective writing about what students have learned from their experience and how they might build on their service learning experience as they make choices about their major, their career, and their personal, academic, and professional goals.

Further support for the value of service learning experiences comes from the Carnegie Foundation for the Advancement of Teaching. In one of the foundation's *Carnegie Perspectives* newsletters, Tom Ehrlich (2005) suggests that integrating community service into undergraduate education helps students "connect thought and feeling" and offers them ways to consider what matters to them, and why. He suggests, further, that service learning promotes leadership skills and knowledge, which are best gained through authentic, real-world experiences. A third benefit that

Ehrlich identifies is an increased interest in and commitment to civic engagement and responsibility along with subsequent political engagement.

Service learning thus has significant potential to connect students to their learning and to their community. In so doing, it offers the prospect of making learning matter for students long after their college years are past.

Applications

1. Select a course you teach for which you would like to incorporate an experiential learning component. What type of experiential learning would be best suited to the course and the students you expect to take it?
2. What kinds of activities and assignments would you design for the experiential component of the course? How would these link up with classroom activities and assignments? How would both classroom and external activities and assignments meet your course goals and objectives?
3. What set of evaluation and grading criteria would you use for both in-class and external experiential work (see chapter 11)?
4. How would you describe the experiential learning component in your overall course description? How would you pitch the experiential learning component and persuade prospective students of its benefits for them?

Mentoring and Teaching

Mentors guide students in understanding the *unspoken rules and practices* of a given disciplinary, professional, or institutional culture. The mentor makes the implicit explicit, which is especially important for students new to higher education. Mentoring can be crucial to student success and retention. Because the mentor cultivates a personal relationship with the mentee, and because mentees may not understand the academic culture they are entering, articulating expectations, goals, and boundaries for them is a crucial part of the mentor's job.

Mentoring and Expectations

Expectations about the mentor's and student's roles need to be established from the outset of a mentoring relationship, and they can be clarified in writing. One way to establish clear expectations for mentors and their mentees is for mentors to create an "advising statement." Such a written statement can serve as a checklist of what each can expect of the other. It can also provide a rationale for those expectations. Because there is an inevitable power imbalance between mentors and mentees, it's important that the mentor be the one to initiate the creation of this statement. It's equally important, however, for mentors and their mentees to discuss the document, mostly to ensure that it is clearly understood.

For example, Professor Moin Syed, an associate professor of psychology at the University of Minnesota–Twin Cities, provides his mentees with an advising statement that covers a wide range of topics, including, among others, guiding philosophy and career paths, diversity, time management, ethics, conflict resolution, meetings, communication, lab work, funding, and authorship.

The following questions can help you design and structure a mentoring relationship:

- What are your learning goals? What are the mentee's learning goals? How will you meet them?
- How frequently will you meet with your mentee? What will you do when you meet?

- How will the mentee communicate with you? By email? By phone? Under what circumstances can he or she contact you?
- How will you reach out to a mentee? How will you know what the mentee needs from you?

Mentoring as Teaching

To some extent a mentor is a teacher. But mentoring involves something more as well. What do mentors do that coaches or teachers don't necessarily do? Mainly, they form a personal, supportive relationship with their mentees. Here are some teaching recommendations for working with your mentees.

- Assess prior knowledge at the beginning of the mentoring relationship through low-stakes writing exercises or activities designed to demonstrate existing knowledge. Asking, "So what do you know about research?" is not enough; students don't know what they don't know.
- Assume nothing about your students.
- Repeat and review key principles that you want them to learn.
- Don't immediately provide all the answers. Know when to let students struggle and give them space to wonder, think, and question before you give them the answer (unless they reach it themselves).
- Encourage your mentees. Let them know that failure and error are necessary parts of learning and discovery.
- Demystify the practice of research by explaining how you, a professional practitioner, do research. What kinds of successes and failures have you had? Share your personal experience with students—let them know that research is a human endeavor.
- Meet your students where they are: some may need guidance in reading critically and writing clearly, as well as in their research and presentation skills.

Chapter Nine

Writing and Learning

First, students learn to write; then they write to learn. Writing and learning, like writing and reading, are reciprocal acts; they inform and sustain each other. Putting pen to paper or fingers to keyboard prompts thinking as writers consider what to say and how to say it effectively.

Writing is a form of inquiry, a way to explore thinking. Writing leads to discovery, including finding out things we didn't know we knew. Writing enhances memory and stimulates the imagination. It allows us to hold on to what we have learned and to wander into realms of thought we have not yet visited. Those are just a few reasons why writing is critical for learning. Here are a few more.

Writing nudges our first fragmentary thoughts toward coherence. It reveals gaps in our thinking that need filling, gulfs that need bridging, disparate thoughts that need connecting. Sometimes we fill those gaps, bridge those gulfs, or make those connections with further writing and thinking. Sometimes we do it through research and talking with others, sharing our drafts, and getting feedback on them. Writing also solidifies our understanding: by helping us see what we don't yet understand, writing enables us to figure things out and eventually come to a more coherent, deeper, more extensive understanding. An unfinished act of learning itself, writing advances our learning as it aids and abets the process of learning. When we write, we take ownership of our ideas and assume a sense of agency, as writing is active and dynamic rather than passive and static.

We write to learn in various ways and in many contexts. Some of our writing is exploratory (to see what we know and to figure out what we don't understand), some is explanatory (to explain things both to ourselves and to others), and some is evaluative (to express our views, our opinions, or our perspective on what we have read, seen, heard, or discussed). Some writing is mandated by others, as when we write in response to a need, an invitation, or a requirement. No matter the stimulus and regardless of purpose, any occasion to write is an opportunity to learn. This is as true for us as it is for our students.

Our concern in this chapter is with how writing can be used to enhance, extend, and deepen students' learning. As a first step toward those goals, we need to help students experience the pleasures and not just the pains of writing.

Students normally think of writing as difficult and challenging—as a kind of work. And to some extent, of course, it is. Even so, writing also has its pleasures, including the pleasure of discovery through the act of writing. One of writing's greatest pleasures is using our minds actively and imaginatively—considering ideas, exploring them, and finding ways to express them effectively.

Our goal as teachers is to help our students experience writing as an opportunity to grow intellectually and imaginatively, to develop their thinking, and to enrich their learning. Simply telling our students, however, about the pleasures and rewards of writing is not enough. We need to design assignments that engage them in meaningful, productive intellectual work. These assignments can often be linked with reading, another critical faculty we need to help students develop.

Writing about Reading

One of the most important kinds of writing our students do is writing about reading: writing about historical events, perhaps using primary sources such as original documents; writing about literary works, including poems, stories, novels, plays, and essays; writing about texts in philosophy and religion, the social and natural sciences, music and art, photography and film, health and medicine, business and engineering. When students write about texts, they need to read them attentively and notice things typically overlooked on a more casual reading.

Annotating

Throughout our own education, we have often experienced the value of annotation. We may be embarrassed now by some of the annotations we made in our books as undergraduates, but those annotations allowed us to engage with what we were reading. This is a basic lesson we need to ensure that our students learn.

We have often seen instructors use annotation to get their students started in writing about their reading. Among the most consistently effective ways to have students begin writing about what they read is to annotate and question texts and to do free writing in response to them. These techniques are easy to employ and accessible to students. They provide a jumping-off point for analysis of all kinds of texts. And they prove useful as fodder for further development as students write more formal papers, essays, and reports.

In annotating a text, students respond actively by writing in the margins around and within a text—underlining words, circling phrases, bracketing sentences and paragraphs and stanzas, drawing arrows, adding question marks, exclamation points, or other abbreviations. Underlining and highlighting are not enough, being passive responses to texts. Students need to annotate actively by adding comments to the passages they underline or highlight. They need to make notes about those passages.

What we can help students understand is that annotating a text offers a convenient and relatively painless way to begin writing about it. Their annotations get them thinking, helping them zero in on what's important. Their annotations help them clarify their understanding of their reading while also flagging certain textual details as puzzling or disconcerting.

Writing their notes, however briefly, encourages students to focus both on the writer's idea and on their reaction to it. They need to experience how annotation stimulates their thinking. A further advantage is that, if they write nothing more, they have at least marked up the text for productive rereading and later perusal. And when they write about the text in a more formal way later, their annotations direct them to the key passages where they have noted significant details and raised questions for subsequent consideration. The purpose of annotation, in short, is to serve the writer's thinking, to aid discovery, and to assist remembering.

Here is a sample set of annotations for a paragraph from Gretel Ehrlich's "About Men," an essay about cowboys. We present the first paragraph of Ehrlich's essay followed by a few sample annotations.

When I'm in New York but feeling lonely for Wyoming I look for the Marlboro ads in the subway. What I'm aching to see is horseflesh, the glint of a spur, a line of distant mountains, brimming creeks, and a reminder of the ranchers and cowboys I've ridden with for the last eight years. But the men I see in those posters with their stern, humorless looks remind me of no one I know here. In our hellbent earnestness to romanticize the cowboy we've ironically disesteemed his true character. If he's "strong and silent" it's because there's probably no one to talk to. If he "rides away into the sunset" it's because he's been on horseback since four in the morning moving cattle and he's trying, fifteen hours later, to get home to his family. If he's "a rugged individualist" he's also part of a team: ranch work is teamwork and even the glorified open-range cowboys of the 1880s rode up and down the Chisholm Trail in the company of twenty or thirty other riders. Instead of the macho, trigger-happy man our culture has perversely wanted him to be, the cowboy is more apt to be convivial, quirky, and softhearted. To be "tough" on a ranch has nothing to do with conquests and displays of power. More often than not, circumstances—like the colt he's riding or an unexpected blizzard—are overpowering him. It's not toughness but "toughing it out" that counts. In other words, this macho, cultural artifact the cowboy has become is simply a man who possesses resilience, patience, and an instinct for survival. "Cowboys are just like a pile of rocks—everything happens to them. They get climbed on, kicked, rained and snowed on, scuffed up by wind. Their job is 'just to take it,'" one old-timer told me.

ANNOTATIONS

She cites images of the cowboy, clichés about cowboys. Her
    attitude toward these images and clichés?
Chisolm Trail—where's that? Important?
Cowboys work in teams—not solo. A necessity.
"Toughness" vs. "toughing it out"; an instinct for survival—how
    to do that?
Visual details—riding into the sunset. Marlboro man ads.
    Mountains.
Romanticizing—central issue? Beyond cowboys? Romanticizing
    things we don't know.
Macho cowboy—a cultural stereotype? Rugged. Silent . . .
A hard job—cowboying!

Questioning

Another useful writing strategy that helps students engage with texts is questioning. For example, you might have them reread the paragraph from Ehrlich's essay and jot down some questions about it. You can invite them to ask about the writer's details, her idea, her evidence, perhaps her use of language, like the term "rugged individualist." Have them consider or ask about what she suggests with that term.

Questioning the text is a way for students to focus on evidence and idea—on what a writer is saying and how she supports what she claims. We can encourage students to focus some of their questions on whether Ehrlich's idea about cowboys is applicable to American men more generally. And then we could push them to ask some additional questions about her second paragraph:

> A cowboy is someone who loves his work. Since the hours are long—ten to fifteen hours a day—and the pay is $30 he has to. What's required of him is an odd mixture of physical vigor and maternalism. His part of the beef-raising industry is to birth and nurture calves and take care of their mothers. For the most part his work is done on horseback and in a lifetime he sees and comes to know more animals than people. The iconic myth surrounding him is built on American notions of heroism: the index of a man's value as measured in physical courage. Such ideas have perverted manliness into a self-absorbed race for cheap thrills. In a rancher's world, courage has less to do with facing danger than with acting spontaneously—usually on behalf of an animal or another rider. If a cow is stuck in a boghole he throws a loop around her neck, takes his dally (a half hitch around the saddle horn), and pulls her out with horsepower. If a calf is born sick, he may take her home, warm her in front of the kitchen fire, and massage her legs until dawn. One friend, whose favorite horse was trying to swim a lake with hobbles on, dove under water and cut her legs loose with a knife, then swam her to shore, his arm around her neck, lifeguard-style, and saved her from drowning. Because these incidents are usually linked to someone or something outside himself, the westerner's courage is selfless, a form of compassion.

EXERCISE

Ask students to respond to the following questions, and then to add one or two of their own.

1. Do you think that Ehrlich means to suggest that cowboys need to be maternal—that they need to develop the kind of caring instincts that mothers have for their children?

2. Do you think that things have changed very much since Ehrlich published this essay in 1985? Why or why not?
3. What questions would you ask Gretel Ehrlich if you had the chance to talk to her about her essay?

Free Writing

A third writing-to-learn technique to teach is free writing, a technique that has been around for decades. Free writing allows students to explore and record their preliminary thinking for later development. As with annotating and questioning, free writing is a way to record observations, reactions, and feelings about a text without worrying about organization, style, grammar, punctuation, and mechanics. Characterized by a freedom from correctness, free writing simply involves writing down what comes to mind without inhibition. The point is to get some thinking going, some thoughts flowing, and to get some initial ideas written down quickly. Free writing gives students a chance to explore their first thoughts to see where they might lead. It's a kind of low-stakes writing—preliminary, associational, exploratory.

Annotating, questioning, and free writing precede the more deliberative work of analysis, interpretation, and evaluation and the more formal ways of writing associated with them. Annotating, questioning, and free writing are ways to prepare for writing essays, papers, and reports. These three informal writing techniques work well together; the brief, quickly jotted annotations can be complemented with a second look via questions and then developed further with the more leisurely paced, longer elaborations of free writing.

EXERCISE

If your students are working with this essay, you might have them annotate Ehrlich's next three paragraphs for practice and jot down some questions about them. One or another of those practices will better prepare them to do their own free writing, either before or after reading the free-writing sample that follows Ehrlich's next three paragraphs.

The physical punishment that goes with cowboying is greatly underplayed. Once fear is dispensed with, the threshold of pain rises to meet the demands of the job. When Jane Fonda asked Robert Redford (in the film *Electric Horseman*) if he was sick as he struggled to his feet one morning, he replied, "No, just bent." For once the movies had it right. The cowboys I was sitting with laughed in agreement. Cowboys are rarely complainers: they show their stoicism by laughing at themselves.

If a rancher or cowboy has been thought of as a "man's man"—laconic, hard-drinking, inscrutable—there's almost no place in which the balancing act between male and female, manliness and femininity, can be more natural. If he's gruff, handsome, and physically fit on the outside, he's androgynous at the core. Ranchers are midwives, hunters, nurturers, providers, and conservationists all at once. What we've interpreted as toughness—weathered skin, calloused hands, a squint in the eye and a growl in the voice—only masks the tenderness inside. "Now don't go tellin' me these lambs are cute," one rancher warned me the first day I walked into the football-field-sized lambing sheds. The next thing I knew he was holding a black lamb. "Ain't this little rat good-lookin'?"

So many of the men who came to the West were southerners—men looking for work and a new life after the Civil War—that chivalrousness and strict codes of honor were soon thought of as western traits. There were very few women in Wyoming during territorial days, so when they did arrive (some as mail-order brides from places like Philadelphia) there was a stand-offishness between the sexes and a formality that persists now. Ranchers still tip their hats and say, "Howdy ma'am," instead of shaking hands with me.

Free-Writing Sample: Gretel Ehrlich, "About Men"
Androgynous? Cowboys as half-men and half-women? Cowboys are maternal and paternal, manly and womanly? Motherly and macho? Tough and tender. Surprising and more complex than usually thought of. Is this specific to cowboys alone? More generalizable to other men? Is it profession-linked, this doubleness? Cowboys have a multitude of responsibilities. Ehrlich seems to understand them. They seem to accept her. She respects and likes them. Does she want to be "one of them"? Where is she from? Fonda and Redford in the movie—what's an "Electric" horseman? Have to check that out.

Writing to Explain

When writing to explain a text, students are concerned largely with making their understanding of it clear to others. Such writing is based not only on impressions of the text but also on interpretation—that is, on a considered understanding of the text. In writing to explain a text, students need to be less personal, less informal, and less subjective than when they make annotations, develop questions, and engage in free writing. That earlier low-stakes, writer-based prose gives way now to a higher-stakes reader-based writing.

The work of annotating, questioning, and free writing about a text, however, is useful and essential preparation for more formal explanatory and analytical writing. The observations that students make during the informal writing process, the connections noticed, the patterns discovered, and the questions raised—all are crucial for developing their thinking further. These practices move students toward the next important step—developing an idea about the text.

When interpreting and explaining the meaning of a text, the goal is clarity. And clarity in writing to explain is twofold: both clarity of understanding and clarity of explanation are required. One way for students to begin clarifying their understanding of a text is to write a double-column notebook entry about it; another is to summarize it or paraphrase a crucial passage. We describe and illustrate each of these techniques.

KEEPING A DOUBLE-COLUMN NOTEBOOK

Keeping a double-column notebook is yet another aid to understanding a text and advancing textual explanation. In this type of notebook, students record thoughts about the texts they read, raise questions about them, and make connections with other things they have read, seen, or otherwise experienced. They can also collect and copy sentences, phrases, words, and ideas they might wish to preserve, as well as record their growing understanding of the significance and value of what they read. The notebook can serve as an arena in which to develop their thinking about issues that emerge from their reading. This writing strategy forms a bridge between the quick, subjective, personal response writing of annotation and free writing (writing for oneself), on the one hand, and analysis and interpretation (writing for others), on the other.

To create a double-column notebook page, have students draw a vertical line down the center of the page. One side of the page is for *taking* notes, to record what they notice about the text. On this side the goal is to capture what the writer is saying. On the other side, they record their own thinking about the text. That side is for *making* notes, recording their responses and questions. Here students can make connections with other things they have read, seen, heard, and otherwise experienced. They can challenge the text here as well. In both taking and making notes, students create a dialogue with and about the texts they read. They begin to create what we might call an "intertextual" web.

Here is an example of a double-column notebook entry for a portion of Gretel Ehrlich's essay about cowboys. First, we present the final three paragraphs of Ehrlich's essay and then the sample double-column notebook entry.

Even young cowboys are often evasive with women. It's not that they're Jekyll and Hyde creatures—gentle with animals and rough on women—but rather, that they don't know how to bring their tenderness into the house and lack the vocabulary to express the complexity of what they feel. Dancing wildly all night becomes a metaphor for the explosive emotions pent up inside, and when these are, on occasion, released, they're so battery-charged and potent that one caress of the face or one "I love you" will peal for a long while.

The geographical vastness and the social isolation here make emotional evolution seem impossible. Those contradictions of the heart between respectability, logic, and convention on the one hand, and impulse, passion, and intuition on the other, played out wordlessly against the paradisiacal beauty of the West, give cowboys a wide-eyed but drawn look. Their lips pucker up, not with kisses but with immutability. They may want to break out, staying up all night with a lover just to talk, but they don't know how and can't imagine what the consequences will be. Those rare occasions when they do bare themselves result in confusion. "I feel as if I'd sprained my heart," one friend told me a month after such a meeting.

My friend Ted Hoagland wrote, "No one is as fragile as a woman but no one is as fragile as a man." For all the women here who use "fragileness" to avoid work or as a sexual ploy, there are men who try to hide theirs, all the while clinging to an adolescent dependency on women to cook their meals, wash their clothes, and keep the ranch house warm in winter. But there is true vulnerability in evidence here. Because these men work with animals, not machines or numbers, because they live outside in landscapes of torrential beauty, because they are confined to a place and a routine embellished with awesome variables, because calves die in the arms that pulled others into life, because they go to the mountains as if on a pilgrimage to find out what makes a herd of elk tick, their strength is also a softness, their toughness, a rare delicacy.

Taking Notes—	*Making Notes—*
Representing the Text	*Commenting/Questioning*
Ehrlich debunks the stereo-typical image of the cowboy without denying that cowboys are tough, strong, silent individualists.	Is Ehrlich's own image of the cowboy overly romanticized, idealized? In making cowboys maternal, does she make too much of their gentleness?
She uses direct quotes from cowboys as one kind of evidence. She refers to images from popular culture—the Marlboro ad and a film—as examples of cowboy manliness.	Ehrlich's historical explanation may be an oversimplification, though its broad outline makes sense.
She provides social and historical context about cowboys and women.	Is her historical analysis correct?

SUMMARIZING AND PARAPHRASING

One of the most important writing skills students need to learn is to summarize and to paraphrase the texts they read. They should understand that a summary is a succinct account of a text. It compresses and condenses the text it summarizes and thus is shorter than the original. A paraphrase is different. To paraphrase is "to explain alongside"; it is more extensive than a summary and is generally as long as the original text. A paraphrase also follows the structure of the text paraphrased, which a summary may not attempt to do.

A paraphrase is inclusive; a summary is selective. In addition, a summary encompasses the whole of a text—it is an overarching encapsulation of the text. A paraphrase, on the other hand, focuses on a key segment of the text. A summary telescopes much into little; a paraphrase puts a small slide of the text under a microscope. Both summary and paraphrase are essential components of analysis. Students must master both skills in developing their interpretation of a text.

Here is a sample summary of Ehrlich's essay "About Men."

In her essay "About Men," Gretel Ehrlich disabuses readers of some common misconceptions people have about cowboys. Ehrlich identifies a series of clichéd images and ideas, such as that cowboys are "strong and silent," "tough" and solo individualists who "ride into the sunset." These clichés she demolishes by providing evidence to support a more complex view of cowboys as tough and tender, rugged but compassionate, manly while being maternal. Ehrlich includes brief anecdotal evidence along with quotations from cowboys she has known and worked with to support her more complex, less romanticized image of the cowboy than pop culture's iconic "Marlboro man" found on poster ads. In the process, she helps us appreciate how hard the life of a cowboy is, how much cowboys rely on each other, how deeply they are committed to the animals in their care, and how well they embody an ethic of community and compassion.

And now here is a sample paraphrase of the essay's final paragraph:

In the concluding paragraph of her essay "About Men," Gretel Ehrlich describes how the writer Ted Hoagland describes the fragility of the male cowboy. It is a fragility that cowboys try to hide as they depend on women to perform traditional female household tasks. For Ehrlich, the cowboy's "vulnerability" is real, authentic. Her final long sentence reveals the doubleness of a cowboy's experience— strength combined with softness, toughness mingled with a delicate sensibility. This complex feeling, Ehrlich suggests, is a product and consequence of the cowboy's love of his work, his appreciation of animals, and his deep reverence for the natural world.

Writing to Evaluate

Writing to evaluate a text has a twofold purpose: to make a judgment about the quality and value of the text, and to assess the social, cultural, moral, and other kinds of values the text embodies and perhaps endorses. To evaluate a text, students have to understand it. They need to be clear about what they think it says and suggests. Evaluation is thus grounded in interpretation. Writing to evaluate requires students to understand before they judge the text and consider its values.

The first challenge in evaluating a text is deciding on appropriate criteria, which will form the basis of our critical judgments of the text. Often evaluative criteria are implicit. In considering specific examples of texts and judgments of their relative merit and value, that evaluative criteria can be made explicit.

We might ask students to consider the following questions about Ehrlich's cowboy essay and then do the exercise that follows them.

- Do you find Ehrlich's thinking about cowboys persuasive? To what extent do you accept her evidence? Or her personal testimony?
- Do you think that she achieves her aim in this essay—to help us better understand the complex nature of cowboys?
- What cultural values are central to Ehrlich's argument? To what extent do your own values—your own sense of what a "man" is—mesh with those espoused by Ehrlich?

EXERCISE

Write a response to Ehrlich in which you question, qualify, debate, or elaborate on her portrait of the American cowboy. How or why might you modify it to account for your own thinking about her idea? Or what might you do to make her argument more persuasive? Consider the social and cultural values at play in Ehrlich's essay, including the values associated with gender roles.

The Writing Process

There are as many writing processes as there are writers. Even so, some practices are common to all writers, though they may use different terms to describe them. We describe here the broad features of the major elements of the writing process.

Considering writing as process reminds us that writing continuously evolves; with rare exceptions (Ken Kesey and Tom Wolfe, for instance), writing is not done in one sitting, in a single burst. Instead, writing requires planning and thinking; drafting and revising (with feedback); editing for style, clarity, and grammatical accuracy; and finally, proofreading to eliminate surface errors.

We briefly consider each of these stages, while recognizing that they recursively repeat, intertwine, and circle back on one another.

Pre-Writing

"Pre-writing," as the term suggests, refers to those activities undertaken before writing an initial draft. Students should understand that reading and annotating are aspects of pre-writing. Making lists and notes, jotting questions and keeping a notebook, including a double-column notebook, are also pre-writing activities. Students' thinking about what they will be writing is yet another element of their pre-writing.

These and other preliminary pre-drafting activities are important and necessary, whatever writing task awaits. They enable students to take small steps toward the work of creating a draft by aiding their efforts to figure out what they want to say. Both pre-writing activities and the draft writing that follows help students do that kind of thinking. We need to help them understand that they don't need to have everything figured out before they begin the actual writing of a draft.

An assignment's length, scope, complexity, and deadline affect the number and kinds of scaffolded pre-writing activities necessary to help students navigate the work. Some of this pre-writing can be done individually, and some in small groups; some can be done in class, some out of class, and some online. Some products of pre-writing can be collected, monitored, and evaluated, however simply.

The goal of pre-writing is to get students started, to get them thinking, to move them productively toward beginning their draft. The essential thing is to start the pre-writing work early. Students need help from the start with writing projects, however modest their scope, as well as early and frequent feedback on the components of their writing assignments.

Drafting

Students need to understand that first drafts tend to be rough drafts, even with pre-writing preparation. The purpose of a draft is to begin putting ideas together with supporting evidence. The idea may at first be fuzzy and not clearly defined. In drafting, a writer begins to bring an idea into focus. The student may not get to a clear and focused idea in writing the initial draft. It often takes a second or third draft to find an idea and develop an understanding of its potential. Because the hardest thing about writing is often just getting started, encourage your students to consider their first draft an opportunity to simply jump-start whatever writing challenge they confront.

The first draft charts a course—identifying a sense of direction for the writer's thinking. Students should understand that it's often a good idea to write the first draft quickly and think of it as an attempt to identify primary evidence and discover their main idea, however much both will need to be elaborated and refined. It can then be set aside for a short time and revisited for a second, more considered attempt. In the second draft, the student might expand on the first draft or refocus the first draft's idea and direction.

During the drafting phase, students need to consider their purpose for writing. Are they writing to analyze a text? To provide historical background? To contextualize the text, positioning it in a disciplinary conversation or debate? To explain something about the writer's position, perspective, attitude, or main idea? To argue for a particular claim? To persuade readers to take action? Whatever a student writer's purpose and idea, the explanation provided and the argument developed will gain persuasiveness from the kinds and amount of evidence offered in their support.

Organization need not be a major concern initially. However, the writer might begin with a general notion of what to do in the beginning, in the middle, and toward the end of a piece. In subsequent drafts, organization assumes a more prominent place as the serious work of revision begins, bringing into focus both the large-scale and smaller-scale details of ideas and evidence and refining the language, style, and structure.

Feedback

Student writers, like all writers, need specific and timely feedback. One of the most disconcerting and disappointing aspects of producing required writing assignments is not getting that kind of feedback but vague, general, formulaic feedback instead, such as "awkward," "unclear," "vague," or "needs improvement." What is awkward or vague? What is unclear and what exactly needs improvement? Equally unhelpful is excessively negative feedback that concentrates on fault-finding and pays little attention to what the writer is attempting to do and say.

Feedback differs from "correction," which is pointing out errors and rectifying them. Feedback should be responsive. It should emerge from an attempt to understand what a writer is working at saying, whether it's an idea being tested out, an explanation being offered, or an argument being developed. The best feedback is couched as authentic questions for the writer. It can include questions about clarity or a lack of clarity, about coherence or its absence. Those questions should help the writer recognize that something more needs to be done with a particular sentence to clarify its meaning, or with a particular paragraph's focus and arrangement of sentences to develop an argument. The instructor's feedback questions can guide the student without necessarily explaining how to improve the writing. That can come later, most usefully in a conference when teacher and student can discuss what is working in the draft, what is not, and how the student can improve it.

Revising

William Strunk and E. B. White say directly in *The Elements of Style* (2000) that "revising is a part of writing" (p. 105)—a very significant part, we suggest. There is no escaping this fact. What gets rewritten is the first rough draft—the messy, initial discovery draft—in which the writer begins thinking on the page and finding out what he or she wants to say, if not yet how to say it clearly and convincingly. Rewriting is where the action is, where the real work of writing gets done. After having permission to produce a poorly written first draft, the student can now revise it in the ways discovered during pre-writing and drafting to make it acceptable and even something to be proud of.

But first the writer must return to the draft and create as many follow-up and follow-through drafts as time, energy, willpower, and dedication permit before the inevitably approaching deadline, when the writing has to be completed and then handed over. French poet Paul Valéry once said that a poem is never finished, only abandoned—which is true, we believe, for all forms of writing.

In "Internal Revision: A Process of Discovery" (Newkirk and Miller 2009), writer and renowned writing teacher Don Murray argues that rewriting is not a burden but an opportunity for writers. He quotes the playwright Neil Simon: "In baseball you only get three swings and you're out. In rewriting, you get almost as many swings as you want, and you know, sooner or later, you'll hit the ball." That's the hope anyway.

Ideally, time should be allocated between drafts. How much time depends on scheduling constraints, the scope and scale of the writing assignment, the instructor and course deadlines, and the like. We encourage students to get a rough draft going as early as possible so that during the intervals between drafts the unconscious mind can work on the problems encountered during the writing. A considerable amount of research confirms the value of diffuse thinking—the kind of subconscious thinking we do after we work on a problem, in this case working on a draft.

We introduce students to a threefold rewriting, or revision, process: conceptual revision, organizational revision, and stylistic revision. They learn first and perhaps most importantly that revision involves "re-seeing" what they have been thinking and writing. We want them to understand that revision is not simply correcting grammatical errors, fixing punctuation mistakes, and moving sentences around. Our goal is to help them see revision as much more than a cosmetic final polish of the writing. Revision goes further, probing deeply beneath writing's surface features.

Conceptual revision involves reconsidering a main idea, usually by clarifying and deepening it. The original idea may be vague or overly general; it may be common and overly simple. Further thinking can improve and deepen the idea. Conceptual revision allows for rethinking, complicating, and developing an idea as it emerges from the writing and comes into focus.

With *organizational or structural revision*, the writer reconsiders the arrangement of the draft's parts. Is the organization clear? Does it make sense? Is anything out of order, missing, or in need of development? Does the conclusion follow logically from what precedes it?

Writers make moves as they develop a piece, especially as they work through its body, or middle. They ask themselves what kind of move they need to make at a particular place that will take them to the next place. Does the writer need to provide an example or two? Define a term? Introduce an analogy? Provide a contrast? Reference another text? Ask a question? Introduce an objection or a qualification? Cite an authority? And so on.

The other major challenge for organizational revision comes with designing and developing the middle of a piece of writing. How many parts should the middle of the piece have? What should those parts include? In what order should they be presented? How, in short, should the middle be constructed? How should it develop? How might it cohere so that it flows seamlessly, one segment into the next?

Stylistic revision revisits words, phrases, and sentences to ask: Are the chosen words the right words to convey attitude and idea? Do concrete and specific words balance and illustrate abstract and general words and concepts? Are phrases and clauses balanced and parallel? To what extent are the sentences clear and concise? If some sentences seem wordy, how might they be trimmed? Is the tone consistent? Is the level of the language appropriate for the topic and the audience? Is the writing engaging? Does the writing convey the real person thinking and speaking behind the language? How does the voice of the writing sound? Is there a discernible voice at all?

These three dimensions of revision—conceptual, structural, stylistic—provide students with an approach and a plan for rewriting. The revision strands invite and reward sustained attention and effort. In working with students' writing, we need to help them understand that revision helps them produce writing that is not only correct but clearer and more cogent. Recommend that they ask themselves these questions:

- What are you learning from this writing?
- What surprised you in this draft?
- What do you like best and what do you least like in this draft?
- What do you intend to do in the next draft, and why?
- What questions do you have for yourself, your teacher, your readers?

Editing and Proofreading

After the work of revision has been completed, it is time for editing and proofreading. Premature editing—correcting misspellings, dropped words, grammatical mistakes, wordiness, clichés, inconsistent tone and tenses—wastes time and energy if revision results in edited passages and pages being cut.

Editing focuses attention on small details—of spelling and punctuation, grammatical consistency, and proper usage. A current handbook or style guide can be used with editing.

The final step is proofreading: ensuring that typographical errors, misspellings, doubling of words, omitted words and phrases, and other infelicities have been corrected before the piece of writing is submitted. We have found with our own writing and with the writing of our students that it helps to read a final draft aloud. Reading aloud slows us down so we can better notice details of spelling, punctuation, and word choice; it helps us hear syntactic snags and confusing collocations of language. Reading aloud highlights how sound conspires with sense. The ear catches what the eye overlooks. The ear helps the eye to see. "The ear," Robert Frost (1995) has said, "is the only true writer and the only true reader" (p. 677).

Impediments to Writing

We fear that we may have made the writing process seem more efficient and more controlled than it is. The reality, of course, is that writing is messy. At every stage, we experience false starts, create awkward sentences, indulge in digressions, omit transitions, misplace commas, misspell words, and commit syntactic and grammatical blunders. Our notes and drafts—our first takes and passes at expressing our ideas and figuring out what we want to say—are fraught with confusion, more opaque than translucent, more fumbling than assured. That's the case with our own writing, with the writing of our students, and with the writing of others that we have had occasion to edit.

Students need to hear about these realities of writing. They need to know that getting it wrong is often a first step to getting it right and that all writers, professionals included, make mistakes and often get lost. We need to demystify the process for students and let them know that the smoothly finished products they read—from the briefest op-ed pieces and news accounts to more ambitious magazine articles and book chapters to published books—did not start off looking anything like what they do when completed and published. With publication, all the messiness of the work of writing is hidden and obscured and seems to magically disappear. Students need to know that the product is not the process; nor can the process be inferred from the product. Unless earlier drafts are available for inspection, a piece of writing cannot be reverse engineered.

Letting students in on this secret can be a major step toward allaying the anxiety they feel about writing. That anxiety has other roots as well. Some students fear that writing will expose their ignorance or reveal their incompetence—their limited control of grammar and punctuation, for example. Students in introductory courses, who are learning fundamental disciplinary concepts along with a discipline's vocabulary and ways of communicating, are especially anxious about their ability to manage those elements in writing.

Another challenge students face with writing assignments in both introductory and more advanced courses is learning to manage their time. Many students procrastinate, not realizing that starting early on a writing project and working at it incrementally over time improves not only their ability to complete it on schedule but also their thinking about it— their ability to explore and develop their ideas. Students, of course, need to learn to manage their time—it's one of the skills that college requirements make obligatory. But we can help them by staggering elements of the writing assignments we give them, by requiring submission of work in steps or stages, and by providing them with opportunities to expand, explain further, and revise.

Final Suggestions

Design assignments backwards. Begin with the desired writing product. Know what you want students to produce, and then decide on the kind of assignment or project to best realize that result.

Characterize the desired product. Break down the student project or assignment into its constituent parts and its elemental characteristics, as well as the particular skills required to produce it. What kinds of connections must students make? What kinds of evidence must they provide? What conventions of the assigned form or genre (essay, lab report, literature review) must they know? What is the proper tone, expected length, and so on, in the assigned genre of academic or professional writing?

Target particular skills in shorter assignments. Give students the opportunity to practice what the final desired product demands. Design short assignments that ask students to perform discrete tasks, such as summarizing texts, describing experiments and surveys, making connections between readings, analyzing and selecting evidence, or linking case studies to general principles.

Applications

1. Design a major writing assignment for one of your courses. Scaffold the assignment with appropriate small-scale exercises.
2. Select a text, image, scene, case, scenario, or other object you want your students to analyze in writing. Develop short assignments that require them to annotate and ask questions of the text.
3. Have students free-write about a passage or image, and then fill out a double-column notebook. Ask them to discuss whether and how their observations and thinking changed in the process.
4. Have students revise a short piece of writing they have already drafted. Ask them to explain what changes they made and why.

Interdisciplinary Teaching and Learning

For many reasons, learning theorists laud the concept of interdisciplinary teaching and learning. The real world, they point out, is not organized according to the artificial division of academic disciplines; nor does meaningful learning occur without some connection to a real purpose in an actual context. Interdisciplinary teaching and learning are of value because they allow for making connections and discovering relationships between ideas; applying and synthesizing knowledge; developing the imagination; creating coherence; and stimulating intellectual curiosity. These benefits of interdisciplinarity have been linked, David Epstein (2019) suggests, with gains in deep structural reasoning and with breadth of knowledge, which are important for solving complex problems (p. 119).

New ideas often emerge from dialogues between and among different disciplines, dialogues that can spark and fuel creative thinking. In addition, bringing together different disciplinary approaches, models, and investigative techniques can be an aid to problem-solving. The perforation of borders allows ideas to flow freely across them, and this two-way flow of ideas can stimulate imaginations in mutual and reciprocal ways. Interdisciplinary work encourages experimentation and play, which can work together to take thinking in new directions.

These benefits of interdisciplinary teaching and learning obtain for students and teachers alike. Teachers profit from being shaken out of their ordinary ways of doing things, from adapting their teaching to accommodate the approaches of colleagues from other disciplines with different kinds of knowledge and expertise. They learn firsthand that considering questions, subjects, texts, problems, and issues from different disciplinary perspectives can be exciting and productive—and that there is more than one way to approach learning. And in co-teaching scenarios, teachers become excited by the opportunities to learn from one another, while students benefit from seeing their teachers engaged in collaborative teaching, learning, and thinking.

The development of hybrid disciplines reveals thinking that transcends the confines of a single discipline—biochemistry and biochemical engineering, for example, or astrophysics, geophysics, and environmental science, to cite a few more. In the social sciences, such hybrids include social psychology, economic sociology, social geography, and the increasingly influential discipline of behavioral economics.

But there is an even more important reason to think across the curriculum: disciplinary tools from one discipline can be applied to and used in another. For example, the tools of mathematics, including geometry, statistics, calculus, set theory, Boolean algebra, and topology, can be used in the social sciences, natural sciences, and computer science. In *The Mathematics of Life* (2013), Ian Stewart explains that mathematics is important to biology today in ways analogous to the importance of mathematics in the past as the partner and handmaid of physics. Mathematics assists biology in the Human Genome Project, in analyses of the structure of viruses and the organization of the cell, and in the study of ecosystems, to cite just a few examples. As Stewart notes, mathematical applications for biological research include probability and chaos theory, dynamics and mechanics, knot theory and game theory, and differential equations and symmetry groups.

Stewart, moreover, claims that mathematics serves not only as a set of tools to analyze data but also as a method for understanding living organisms. He suggests that mathematics is now used "not just to help biologists manage their data, or improve their instruments, but . . . to provide significant insights into the science itself, to help explain how life works" (p. 11). In fact, mathematicians are adjusting their thinking to accommodate biologists' questions, and adapting their techniques to answer those questions.

Much of cross-disciplinary thinking is directed toward thinking critically—doing analysis with the tools of two or more disciplines. But there is also a creative thinking benefit. Among the values of crossing disciplines with one another is the resulting cross-fertilization—a metaphor that comes from the life sciences of biology and agronomy. In the narrow sense, agronomists cross-breed different plants and seeds to obtain hardier strains that, for example, are especially resistant to heat. Bioengineers do something similar microscopically at the cellular and the molecular levels.

Crossing disciplines has a number of benefits. Among them are the fresh angles of approach supplied by each discipline's methodology and the new and differing perspectives each has on the other (Klein 1991). For example, considering literature from the perspective of sociology and psychology can foreground aspects of literary works otherwise unnoticed. These approaches can highlight a novel's psychological elements, for example, or its socioeconomic dimensions, helping us understand the internal motivations of literary characters, or how their relationships are shaped by issues of status, class, and power. In turn, we can examine the novel as evidence or illustration of the social structures in place when and where it was written. We can conduct such analyses across disciplines, of course, only if we have at least some familiarity with a number of disciplines.

Perhaps the most important benefit of cross-disciplinary teaching and learning emerges in the context of facing complex, "wicked" problems involving uncertainty and ambiguity. Epstein (2019) references a number of studies that highlight the benefits of breadth of knowledge and experience in those situations (p. 213). Something else entirely is offered by the academy's hyper-specialization, which is remarkably efficient and useful for solving "kind" problems—clearly and narrowly defined problems that lack the uncertainties and ambiguities of wicked problems.

Chapter Ten

Critical Thinking

Critical thinking is a type of thinking in which we reflect, consider, and analyze when making decisions and solving problems. Based on careful reasoning, critical thinking is purposeful thinking guided by logic and supported by evidence. Critical thinking involves defining problems, identifying arguments, evaluating data, raising questions, and using information to make sound judgments. The derivation of the word "critical" from the Greek word *kritikos*, which means "judge," highlights the evaluative dimension of critical thinking.

Critical thinking does not necessarily involve criticizing ideas (although being "critical" in this way is sometimes one element of thinking critically). Nor do we bring critical thinking only to serious subjects or important issues. We can think critically about what kind of popcorn to buy or what hat to wear, as well as whether to marry or remain single, attend graduate school, or move to a foreign country. The topics we can think critically about are endless.

Someone engaged in critical thinking is typically making perceptive observations, establishing careful connections, asking probing questions, and making meaningful distinctions. Critical thinking involves analyzing, interpreting, and evaluating evidence; applying knowledge; and thinking both independently and interdependently.

Certain tendencies, or dispositions, are essential to critical thinking: open-mindedness, honesty, and flexibility; perseverance; and reasonableness, diligence, and focus. Critical thinkers reconsider ideas and sometimes change their minds. They recognize the legitimacy of alternative views, embrace ambiguity, and remain open to continued learning.

Critical thinking competencies include self-direction—the self-awareness and self-regulation to manage our thinking and our motivation for thinking—and the ability to ask productive questions; in fact, asking the essential significant questions is as important as answering them. For example:

- What do you know about *x*?
- What don't you know that you need to know?

- What have you assumed and why?
- What is the evidence for and against *x*?
- What are the criteria for evaluating *x*?
- What questions can you ask about *x*?

Underlying these questions is the fundamental critical thinking question: "How do I know what I think I know?" And, "What evidence do I have for what I think I know?" And further, "What relevant evidence (or kinds of evidence) is missing?"

Critical thinkers constantly challenge their thinking and the thinking of others. They exhibit a stance of deliberate skepticism, refusing to accept assertions without evidence to support them. They also try to consider their own ideas from the perspective of others who might see things differently. As Ann Berthoff (1981) points out, teaching critical thinking is teaching "how judgments and opinions, generalizations and interpretations, are related to context and perspective" (p. 114). It's helping students develop a "capacity to see relationships methodically" (p. 114), whether these relationships are causal or temporal or spatial, synchronic or diachronic, and whether they appear as ends and means, beginnings and endings, or parts and wholes. Understanding relationships is essential.

Critical Thinking in Practice

One way to induce critical thinking in your students is to provide them with brief scenarios that highlight assumptions and implications, two essential features of critical thinking. Here is one such scenario, taken from "The Ethicist" column of the *New York Times Sunday Magazine*. In these weekly columns, ethicist Randy Cohen (and later Kwame Anthony Appiah) presents two or three short letters he has received that focus on a situation with ethical implications. We will consider one such letter from a woman whose husband and son had attended a Boston Red Sox baseball game. Here's the situation:

During the game, her 11-year-old son "coaxed" a player into tossing him a ball. A fan seated nearby offered the boy $30 for the ball to give to his own son. The boy's father told him to ask for $50. They agreed on $40, and both parties seemed pleased with the transaction. The wife reported that her husband said it was a good lesson for his son in "supply and demand." She, however, was uncomfortable with the transaction. She concluded her letter by asking the ethicist what he thought.

What do you think? The first consideration about this scenario is whether there is an ethical issue at stake here at all. The second is whether you agree with the boy's father that a lesson was taught and learned regarding "supply and demand." Were any other "lessons" being taught and learned in this little scenario? If so, what are they?

A third consideration is to look closely at the facts of the situation and think about the assumptions we make based on the details provided. We ask students the following questions: Do you assume that it was a foul ball that was tossed into the stands? What do you assume from the word "coaxed"? What did the eleven-year-old boy do to get the Red Sox player (or was it a player from the opposing team?) to toss him the ball? And what might we infer about the player as he tossed the ball to the boy in the stands? To what extent do your assumptions and inferences affect your judgment about the father's and boy's actions in selling the ball? Does it make any difference what price they sold the ball for? Why or why not?

In addition to these questions regarding what happened at the ball game, we move to another set of questions about how the various parties conceived of the associated issues: What arguments would you make in support of the father's (and son's) actions? What arguments might support the mother's feelings of uneasiness at the transaction? Considering these questions requires students to evaluate the scenario from multiple perspectives—that of the ballplayer who tossed the ball to the boy; that of the father, the son, and the mother who wrote the letter to Cohen (and that of the father who bought the ball for his son, whose mother is absent from this scenario).

Thinking Critically about an Image

Images can also make effective critical thinking prompts. One we've had repeated success with is a political cartoon by Christopher Vorlet that appeared on April 23, 2005, in the *New York Times*—on the op-ed page, as an accompaniment to an article entitled "War Isn't Fought in the Headlines." It pictures two figures in silhouette holding weapons—one wears a turban and holds an assault rifle and a sword in the air; the other wears a helmet and holds an assault rifle pointed downwards. Where speech or thought bubbles would normally appear, a profusion of curving, circular lines appears above the one, and of squarish, angular lines above the other. But even these minimal observations border on speculation, given the figures are entirely filled in.

We begin with making observations, move quickly to making connections and inferences, and then form an interpretive conclusion. It's a good idea to remind students of this analytical framework—observing, connecting, inferring—when they engage in analytical work. And it's important to have them begin by making observations about the image before jumping to inferences and judgments about it. This requires repeated emphasis, as there is a strong tendency to hurry to interpretation and judgment. In working with this and any image, it is crucial to slow down the process of analysis by expanding and enriching the initial stage of noticing and perceiving. Doing so will pay dividends with the quality of the inferences and interpretations produced.

Here is an exercise you can use to walk students through their analysis and interpretation of the image:

Exercise—Observation/Evaluation/Interpretation

1. Jot down at least five details you notice about the image. Begin with some observations. (Remind students that observations are statements that can be verified.)
2. Make some connections among your observations. Try to focus on relationships—mostly comparative and contrasting connections. Focus on similar and contrasting details.
3. Proceed to a few inferences. (Remind students that an inference is a statement about the unknown based on something observed.)

   - What, for example, do you call the weapons that each figure holds?
   - What do you make of the way in which those weapons are being held?
   - What about the attire of the figures? Their postures and gestures?
   - What do you notice about the patterns of the lines that appear above their heads in the "bubble" that conventionally indicates speech or thought in a cartoon?
   - What kind of speaking or thinking is represented by those lines?

With provisional answers to these questions, students should be ready to develop an interpretation—a tentative conclusion about how they understand and interpret the image, how they explain it to themselves and to others. Ask them to write a paragraph of seven to ten sentences that offers an interpretation of the image and its accompanying caption.

Commentary

Here are some of our observations about the process of interpreting a political cartoon and its caption.

We know a good deal about the image because we have taken time to observe each of its elements. And we have asked a number of questions about the details of the image, including its relationship to the underlying caption. What might we infer from what we have noted and queried so far? We might infer, for example, that the two soldiers are foes, one a US Army infantryman (or perhaps a Marine, or even an allied soldier) and the other an Iraqi or Afghan insurgent (or perhaps a foreign Taliban mercenary insurgent). We might infer that the figure on the left is about to attack the one on the right—or we might infer that he is defending himself from the other figure, a trespassing invader of his homeland.

About the lines drawn above each figure we might infer that they represent radically different kinds of language and thinking. This inference could lead to another: that these adversaries not only do not understand each other or think like each other but that they speak mutually incomprehensible languages, possess diametrically opposed values, and have radically different understandings of the world.

About the caption beneath the figures we might infer that war is fought, on the one hand, on the ground of a particular country and, on the other, in the heads of the enemy combatants. This last possibility is suggested by considering the last word of the caption, "headlines." If we break that word into its component parts, we get a literal rendering of what is pictured above the figures—"lines" that reflect what is going on in the "head" of each. The more angular lines above the American, or Western, soldier could be seen as reflecting an orderly, logical, analytical mode of thinking and operating. The less patterned, seemingly less orderly lines above the head of the insurgent could be understood to reflect a more emotional and chaotic kind of thinking and acting. That's often how students and workshop participants have characterized them.

And yet, with a shift of perspective, the lines above the head of the non-Western soldier might be described as swirling curls, something reminiscent of various Middle Eastern scripts, including Arabic script.

Armed with these inferences, we are now ready to push toward an interpretation. Arriving at an interpretive conclusion about such a suggestive image isn't easy. But our conclusion, remember, does not have to be final; it can remain tentative and provisional—and probably should. How might we formulate our understanding of this political cartoon as a conclusion, however provisional?

We might conclude that it suggests the mutual incomprehension at the heart of the cultures and worldviews of the soldier-figures depicted. The minds of these soldier-figures, like the worlds they inhabit, are dramatically different. We might conclude that there does not appear to be much hope for dialogue between them, that any kind of real understanding is impossible. We might conclude, at least provisionally, that Vorlet's drawing, with its accompanying caption, suggests that wars are fought by those whose languages, ways of thinking, values, and conceptions of right and wrong differ so dramatically that the conflict between them has little likelihood of ever being resolved.

This, of course, is only one interpretation of the image and caption. As you made your observations, connections, and inferences, you were probably developing your own perhaps different interpretation—though there may be some overlapping elements as well. It is interesting to consider how someone from another culture would interpret this image—someone from the Middle East, perhaps someone from Iraq or Afghanistan, or someone who is living through the war in those places. During a workshop on this exercise offered in Europe shortly after the war in Iraq, a number of participants considered the Western solider the intruder. For them, the non-Western figure was a freedom fighter defending his country against invasion by a Western power.

Alternatively, in arriving at an overall interpretation of the image, one might emphasize the ways the thought/language lines above the heads of the military figures overlap slightly. Coupling that observation with the fact that actual combat is not shown might lead to a somewhat more positive interpretation: that communication and understanding between these figures and what they represent might indeed be possible. Without question, there is more than one way to "see" this image, more than one way to understand and interpret it.

Thinking Critically about a Poem

A different kind of challenge is involved in thinking critically about literary works, especially poems, which often work by implication more than they do by direct statement. A poem tends to suggest much more than it says outright. Poems afford rich opportunities for critical thinking in part because they provoke us to think deeply about language and its uses. They also require readers to pay close attention to their structure and tone. Through analyzing those and other poetic elements, readers come to a provisional understanding of what a poem says and suggests, what it implies about its subject and situation. The poem that follows, Emily Dickinson's "Much Madness is divinest Sense," prompts readers to consider the nature and power of majority thinking.

> Much Madness is divinest Sense—
> To a discerning Eye—
> Much Sense—the starkest Madness—
> 'Tis the Majority
> In this, as All, prevail—
> Assent—and you are sane—
> Demur—you're straightway dangerous—
> And handled with a Chain—

A reader's goal in reading a poem is to interpret it, and the first step in the interpretive process is observation. After we make a number of observations about it, we make connections among our observations. An exercise like the one that follows induces students to make observations and connections that can lead them to draw inferences toward making an interpretation. In the process, students need to slow down and pay attention to the text—to its words and lines and sentences. They need to attend to its images and sounds and rhythms. From those and other elements of language and form in the poem, they will arrive at an idea regarding sense and madness that Dickinson has provoked them to think about.

To see how we direct students toward that end, we invite you to join them in doing the following exercise.

Exercise—Observation

Make five observations about Dickinson's poem. Consider its words, especially the repeated words. Look at its sentences and how they are punctuated. Listen to the poem's sounds and rhyme. What structural patterns do you notice? What parallels and contrasts do you see and hear? If you were to divide the lines into stanzas, where would you make the breaks and why?

When we ask ourselves questions about what the poem's details suggest or imply, we find ourselves thinking about its significance or meaning. To show you this process, let's begin with observations about the poem's language and structure.

Notice how "Sense" and "Madness," the poem's key terms, are repeated and capitalized. Notice, too, how these words appear on the same line—twice, in reverse order the second time: "Madness and "Sense" and then "Sense" and "Madness." Imagine a letter X drawn between the repetition of "Madness" and "Sense." The Greek letter "chi," or "X," provides the name of this inversion: "chiasmus."

Much Madness is divinest Sense—

Much Sense—the starkest Madness—

Observe how all but one line ends with a dash rather than a period or comma, and how three of its eight lines also include a dash within the line. What effect do these interlinear marks of punctuation achieve—both those at the ends of lines and those within lines? They create an effect of interruption, of fragmentation, of stopping and then going again. They create emphasis.

Observe, as well, that other words besides "Sense" and "Madness" are capitalized—"Majority," "All," "Chain"—as are the first words of each line. Which of those first words in each line do you find most emphatic, and why? The dashes immediately before and after the words "Assent" and "Demur" emphasize them. Commas are used instead in one other place in the poem with a caesura (an interruption within a line): "In this, as All, prevail—."

Being opposites in meaning, "Assent" (to agree) and "Demur" (to disagree) balance and parallel each other, as do "sane" and "dangerous," "this" and "All," and "Sense" and "Madness."

In terms of sounds, we might notice that the only full or true rhyme in the poem comes at the end, on the words "sane" and "Chain." We can hear off-rhymes, or slant rhymes, in "Sense" and "Madness," "Madness" and "dangerous," and "Eye" and "Majority."

Our work so far has been to attend to the poem carefully, observing and making connections among our observations, but mostly observing. The following exercise will push you to begin thinking about some of what you have noticed and about the assertions of the poem's speaker. The exercise will prod you a bit further in the direction of interpreting the poem, making inferences based on the implications of what it says (its language) and what it suggests (through its details).

Exercise—Interpretation

What does the speaker of the poem imply about madness? What does the speaker say directly about madness, and what can you infer from what the speaker says? How are sense and madness determined? Who decides, that is, what is sane and what is not sane, or "insane"? What is the significance of being handled with a chain? What is implied by its inclusion in the poem—and by its use on particular individuals?

These questions will help you move toward a provisional conclusion—an interpretation. One way to follow the logic of the poem is to divide it into three segments—lines 1–3, 4–5, and 6–8. Sense and madness—opposites—are the dominant issues. Dickinson ascribes the condition of each to the other; madness, the speaker says, is actually "Sense," and sense is "Madness"—at least some of the time.

To perceive the sense in madness and the madness in sense, however, we need to have a "discerning Eye." Not everyone can see the reversible nature of these opposites—the sense in madness and the madness in sense, in the manner of a yin-yang pairing. Not everyone can see that something that appears mad or crazy might be sensible, and conversely, that something that appears sane and sensible can reveal, on closer inspection, or from another perspective, a kind of madness.

The poem's opening lines do not assert that madness is always sane or that sensibleness is always crazy. The lines don't insist that what appears to be madness is never really madness, or that what appears to be sensible never is. What the poem does say is that when "Madness" is "Sense," it is "divinest Sense"—a special, extraordinary kind of sense that requires seeing things from a different (perhaps spiritual?) perspective. Note the superlative form in both "divinest Sense" and "starkest Madness." When something is fundamentally mad that appears sane, that madness is stark, mad to the core—fundamentally and intensely insane.

The poem's concluding lines (lines 6–8) suggest that if you agree with the majority, if you "Assent" to what the majority believes, then you are considered "sane" and sensible. If, however, you "Demur" from or disagree with the majority, you are considered "dangerous"—perhaps even insane—and thus need to be "handled with a Chain." Why? Because those who "Demur" threaten the status quo; they are a danger to the majority view. And that dangerous threat, or threatening danger, cannot be tolerated by the majority because it challenges the majority's authority and could undermine its power.

In the last three lines of the poem, as in the first three lines, Dickinson employs a pair of contrasting terms ("Assent" and "Demur") to accentuate the contradictory responses. We might infer from this a suggestion by Dickinson—or her speaker—that it is dangerous to disagree with and diverge from conventional ways of seeing and doing things. At the same time, the poem seems to question the validity of such a view by also suggesting that it is more often the majority, in their apparent sensibleness, who are mad and the seemingly eccentric mad individuals who are right and sane.

Emily Dickinson invites us, provokes us, to think critically about the issue of sanity and madness. She does this with taut, crisp language that is simultaneously humorous and serious, and she does it through paradox.

How we interpret poems depends largely on the values we detect in them and on our own values, on what matters most to us and why. We appraise any text we read according to our own cultural, social, moral, and aesthetic values. Our understanding is affected by how the poem's values relate to our own.

Dickinson's poem raises many questions regarding values:

1. Which values seem to be endorsed and which are criticized by the speaker—and by extension by the poem itself and its author—in Dickinson's "Much Madness is divinest Sense"?
2. Is her speaker correct about the prevalence of majority views? To what extent does the majority always, often, or sometimes prevail?
3. Is it a good thing, a bad thing, or some of both when the majority view prevails? Under what circumstances is this the case?
4. What do you think about those who "Demur"—who don't assent to the majority view and who may suffer the consequences of not assenting and being different?
5. What are the dangers and virtues of going against the grain of conventional wisdom, behavior, and attitudes?
6. To what extent is Dickinson (or her poem's speaker) sympathetic to the minority? To what extent does the poem invite us to think about how the majority responds to minority views?
7. How important is it for you to be or not to be in the majority? How important for you are alternative perspectives, minority perspectives, or other ways of seeing, doing, and being? Why do you value—or why do you not value—alternative perspectives?

Dialectical Thinking

One way to approach this openness to alternative perspectives is to consider dialectical reasoning, which psychologist Richard Nisbett (2015) has described as more typical of Eastern, as opposed to Western, modes of thought. Unlike linear logical thinking, which, according to Nisbett, characterizes much Western thinking, dialectical reasoning does not prioritize propositional truth or logical validity. Instead, it embraces contradiction and conflict, change and uncertainty. Often, its goal is to understand how conflicting propositions might somehow both be true. Western thought, by contrast, adheres to the principle of identity, in which $A = A$; A is itself and nothing else. Two additional essential logical propositions, Nisbett notes, typify Western thought:

1. **Noncontradiction:** A and not A cannot both be true.
2. **Excluded middle:** Something must either be or not be, with nothing in between.

Dialectical reasoning operates differently. Its essential principle is that things do not stay as they are. Reality is always in process; things change as a matter of course. Being is always becoming. Dialectical reasoning, argues Nisbett, includes two additional related principles:

1. **The principle of contradiction:** Contradiction underlies change. Change and contradiction are both constantly occurring.
2. **The principle of relationships (holism):** The whole is more than the sum of its parts. Parts are only meaningful in relation to the whole.

One benefit of dialectical thinking is its capacity to generate a "middle way" when exploring an issue or problem. A may be right, but not A is not necessarily wrong. Instead of choosing between dialectical oppositions, we embrace them both: Look before you leap *and* he who hesitates is lost. Plan for the future *and* live each day as if it's your last. Light is both particle *and* wave.

Dialectical thinking attends to contexts and relations. It opposes separating form and content. It is holistic, emphasizing how opposites complement rather than contradict each other. It understands events as moments, as elements of a continuously evolving process. It recognizes the uncertainty and provisional nature of knowledge. David Epstein (2019) describes the value of "ambidextrous thought" (p. 257), which resists conformity and which seeks and creates "cross-pressures" (p. 258) to avoid forms of cognitive entrenchment. Dialectical thinking can be used as a way to generate different kinds of oppositional thinking to avoid cognitive lockdown.

Students need to be encouraged to develop the habit of dialectical thinking—as do their instructors. Questions like the following can direct them toward the goals of thinking dialectically:

Questions for Dialectical Reasoning in Relation to Answers/ Solutions

1. Does the answer avoid rigid application of a rule?
2. Does it account for differing perspectives?
3. Does it recognize the possibility of change?
4. Does it identify possible compromise positions or outcomes?
5. Does it express uncertainty rather than dogmatic confidence?

Challenges to Critical Thinking: Biases and Bad Habits

Our students face many challenges in learning to think critically. Among these are a set of biases to which they (and we along with most people) are prone. The best-known and perhaps most common and intractable is *confirmation bias*, a tendency to seek and find evidence supporting what we believe while ignoring or dismissing evidence that contradicts our beliefs. Confirmation bias is amply evident in discussions of politics and religion, as well as in conversations about things that happen in the workplace and in arguments over disputes where blame and fault are in question.

An equally powerful bias is our *tendency to overestimate ourselves*—our abilities and talents as well as our chances of success in any enterprise. We overestimate the likelihood of good things happening to us and underestimate unfortunate events in our future. This bias derives in part from a sense that we deserve good fortune, and in part from a sense of our superiority over others. Both of these biases, of course, reflect either an ignorance of chance events and probabilities or an unwillingness to see ourselves as subject to large-scale statistical data patterns, or both. We may understand how these patterns apply in the abstract and how they affect others, even people we know. But we are reluctant to see how they apply to ourselves.

Research has repeatedly shown that almost all of us possess *unconscious biases*—factors that shape our behavior and our attitudes below the level of conscious awareness. We often deny this possibility, as we consider ourselves somehow immune to unconscious bias and conscious of any biases we may possess. And so, as a first step toward helping our students to think critically about their ideas, attitudes, and beliefs, we should alert them to these cognitive distortions to which we are all susceptible.

Other kinds of bias that interfere with clear and critical thinking include survival bias, local bias, status quo bias, and blind-spot bias. *Survival bias* may be present when someone argues for the strong possibility of success—for a new business enterprise, in achieving literary or athletic recognition at a high level, in becoming wealthy or an acknowledged leader in a particular field. Discounted in popular success stories across many domains is the large number of those who failed to become highly successful. How many high school athletes think they will excel at the most competitive college sports level? How many college players go on to professional careers? Or should we ask, how few of these athletes make it through the ever more stringent winnowing process? Critical thinking accounts for this bias toward survivorship, recognizing that the odds are greatly against the vast majority of aspiring athletes and celebrities and other hopefuls.

Another common bias that critical thinkers can avoid is *local bias*, a tendency to favor the local over the global, us over them, what we bring to the table versus what others contribute. We prefer and give preference to events, activities, people, and places closer to home and add value to local products and processes.

There are two additional common biases that critical thinkers should avoid. A bias toward the *status quo* is shown by anyone who prefers to leave well enough alone and stay with what is currently in place, even when there is strong evidence that something else, perhaps a significant change, is needed. A related bias, *blind-spot bias*, prevents us from seeing our own weaknesses even as we easily detect them in others.

We are subject to many other kinds of biases and illogical patterns of thinking, but we will conclude with two biases that behavioral economists frequently mention: anchoring and availability. How many times have you entered a department store to see high prices on the first merchandise you encounter there? Those prices are placed so that when you find a product you want to purchase you will be likely to spend more than you originally intended. The initial high prices you encountered have "primed" you, *anchored* you to high prices, such that the next prices you see, even though higher than you'd like, seem not so bad in comparison.

The *availability bias*, the tendency to consider things we recently heard about or experienced as more common than they actually are, was first described by Daniel Kahneman, author of *Thinking, Fast and Slow* (2011). We need to help students understand that, for example, front-page headlines reporting terrorist attacks and beach closures due to shark attacks are no indication that these are frequent occurrences. After an aviation disaster, people tend to avoid air travel, preferring to drive to their destinations rather than fly, although statistically the likelihood of dying in a car crash far exceeds a person's chances of dying in a plane crash.

In *The Coddling of the American Mind* (2018), Greg Lukianoff and Jonathan Haidt identify other dangerous tendencies toward uncritical thinking. Among them are catastrophizing, or seeing the worst possible outcome as the most likely one; overgeneralizing; perceiving large patterns (usually of negative outcomes) from a small sample of incidents; and dichotomizing, a form of all-or-nothing, black-and-white binary thinking. They also mention mind reading, or thinking you know what others are thinking without evidence for it; discounting positives and negative filtering, which are flip sides of simple-minded interpretations of people and events; and refusing to take responsibility for one's actions and their outcomes. Each of these cognitive distortions is a form of fallacious thinking; they represent just a few of the many kinds of logical fallacies that critical thinkers should avoid.

Although Kahneman argues that there is little we can do about many of our inherent biases, Nisbett suggests that learning to recognize our tendencies toward particular kinds of biases is a first step toward minimizing their influence over us. All these forms of uncritical thinking can be ameliorated by recognizing one's tendency toward them; by cultivating intellectual virtues, such as asking questions, seeking understanding, and being open to and respectful of others and their views; and by practicing self-reflection and self-awareness. Such positive thinking habits provide a foundation for critical thinking.

Applications

1. Which of the elements of, or approaches to, critical thinking resonate most for you? Which elements or approaches might you use with your students?

2. How valuable do you find Richard Nisbett's ideas about dialectical thinking? How might you use them in your teaching?
3. To what extent are you subject to the various biases described in the final section of this chapter? Do you agree more with Daniel Kahneman or with Richard Nisbett about your ability (and people's ability generally) to overcome those biases?
4. How might you encourage students to avoid the biases and cognitive distortions identified by Kahneman, Nisbett, and Lukianoff and Haidt?

The Last Day of Class

What should you do on the final day of the semester—your last day with your students? If that day has been designated for an exam, course evaluation, or activity across multiple sections of a course, this question has been decided for you. But when you have the option of deciding for yourself what you might do for your last class meeting, there are other possibilities.

One, of course, is to give a final exam or test. A second is to offer a review session in preparation for a final exam given during an official exam period. A third is to use the time to review the key course concepts with your students. This gives you a final chance to check their understanding of the main takeaways of the course and to calibrate, modulate, and otherwise adjust this understanding to better achieve your course goals.

Just as your first day of class was your chance to make an important "first impression" on your students—to present yourself to them and to give them an idea of your teaching persona—so too the last day offers an analogous opportunity to leave your students with a "final impression" of you and your course. It's a chance to impress upon them important lessons for learning, not only regarding your course and its concepts and principles, but for larger-scale, long-lasting learning beyond your course and beyond their college years.

How might you take advantage of such an opportunity? What might you do to leave some kind of lasting impression on your still impressionable students? It's not an easy question to answer.

One option is to debrief with them about what they learned, what they wish could have been included to increase their learning, and what they would recommend be added or subtracted in future iterations of the course for the next groups of students. Another more elaborate possibility we've found rewarding is to have students present a group project (low stakes, high interest) that encapsulates key elements of the course. For example, in a course on critical (and creative) thinking RD has taught, groups of three students present a ten- to twelve-minute exercise-activity for the class that involves doing some kind of critical and/or creative thinking. Anything goes. And it often does.

The element of surprise with these presentations is critical. Nobody knows what any group is preparing for their final coup de grâce. (Groups will have worked together for half an hour in two prior classes, with each group keeping its preparations secret.)

Students are not evaluated on a high-stakes critical standard (though that is a possibility). Instead, they decide whether each presenting group engaged the rest of the class in some form of critical or creative thinking. If the answer is yes, that's enough—grades are no longer important. The applause after each presentation, however, is a pretty clear indicator of which groups wowed their classmates.

In this final session, evaluation is less important than consolidating the knowledge and skills that students have gained in the course. Equally important is students' positive attitude toward learning. Are these students now more confident about their capacity for critical and creative thinking? Do they believe that they can continue to improve and develop their knowledge and skills? Those are the questions that matter.

Chapter Eleven

Assessment and Grading

Assessment is not grading, and grading is not assessment—though the two are often conflated and sometimes confused. Instead of seeing these two forms of evaluation as the same, we need to distinguish between them, related though they may be. When we grade students' work, we evaluate their performance against a standard that can be clarified and explained with a rubric, or evaluative tool. When we assess a student's work, we evaluate its level of proficiency as a work in progress. Grades are final in a way that assessments are not.

Assessment

We use the term "assessment" in this chapter to mean an evaluation of a student's proficiency in and progress toward completing a task—whether an exercise, an in-class assignment, or an online or take-home assignment, and whether low- or high-stakes, simple or complex. For simple tasks, a binary yes-or-no assessment is likely to tell us whether students "get it" or not. For more complex tasks that are part of a longer project, such as a research paper, assessment more often takes the form of checking to see that students are on track—that they are following assignment guidelines for each stage of the accruing work. Assessment also measures the extent to which students are succeeding at various performance levels: Are they analyzing texts or simply summarizing them? Are they applying concepts they have learned or simply explaining them? Are they synthesizing a complex of materials or simply cataloging them? How well are they doing these things?

In *Classroom Assessment Techniques* (2009), Thomas Angelo and Patricia Cross emphasize in-class assessments: brief exercises that students do individually and together in pairs and small groups to test their understanding of concepts, principles, and processes. We explained some of these in-class assessment techniques in chapter 3. We believe that classroom assessment techniques illustrate par excellence the concept of active, participatory learning.

First, and most important, classroom assessment is student-centered, focusing on the learner rather than the teacher. The goal always is to improve learners' understanding.

Second, it is teacher-directed. Each teacher decides what to assess, and when and how to do it. Moreover, each teacher decides what to do in response to information gleaned from classroom assessment techniques.

Third, assessment can be mutually beneficial for students and instructors alike. Students strengthen their understanding and learn the limits of that understanding, while assessment prompts instructors to devise strategies to enhance and improve student learning and comprehension.

Fourth, assessment is formative rather than summative. Its purpose is less to grade student performances with supporting evidence than to gain an understanding of how much and how well students are learning what we expect them to learn.

Fifth, assessment is context-specific. Instructors select each technique to meet the needs of students at particular junctures of a course and particular moments in a class session.

Sixth, classroom assessment is ongoing rather than occasional and sporadic. It becomes part of the course's modus operandi—the planned regular work of teaching and learning.

Here are a few additional active learning techniques that Angelo and Cross suggest are useful for assessing students' understanding. They are designed for in-class learning immediately upon the introduction of new concepts and skills, rather than for more formal testing and grading later in the term (when it is often too late to make the necessary teaching adjustments).

Pro-Con Grids

Have students make a table of pros and cons for a given issue, problem, or value consideration. A cost-benefit analysis is one type; another is a "yellow hat"–"black hat" analysis, which compares the upside, positive, optimistic, best-case-scenario outcomes with the downside, negative, pessimistic, worst-case-scenario possibilities. It is important for students to fill out both sides of the grid—that is, to fully engage in alternative thinking, regardless of which side they may personally favor. And it's also important to push students to explain why particular prospects are pro or con, yellow or black hat, in their boxes. It's the thinking behind their judgment that matters.

Characteristics Matrices

Have students create a table of items to be compared and contrasted based on characteristic features. For example, in identifying differences between mammals and reptiles, they could include features such as having scales or fur, being cold- or warm-blooded, and birthing live young or laying eggs. This kind of simple informational grid could be supplemented by more complex grids that chart interpretive or analytical categories, such as characteristic differences between what sociologists call *Gemeinschaft* and *Gesellschaft* societies according to the nature, level, and quality of their social bonds, and what those differences imply for the political, social, and cultural life of each kind of society.

Problem Recognition and Problem Solution Tasks

In many disciplines, but especially in mathematics or social or natural science courses, problem identification and problem solution exercises, assignments, and challenges are central, even critical, to successful learning. One of the most important discoveries of recent learning theory is the importance of students identifying the kind of problem they are attempting to solve. It is much easier for them to solve a set of problems of the same type than a mixed set of problems. (See chapter 4 for more on the idea of interleaving problem types.)

When students solve problems, alone or with others in pairs or small groups, have them explain their process. Whatever the discipline and type of problem, the critical element of teaching and learning resides in students comprehending and being able to explain how they arrived at their solution. As teachers, we need to understand how students reason so that we can intervene when their reasoning makes partial sense but has gone off track owing to misinformation, insufficient understanding of key concepts, or faulty logic. We can then provide appropriate corrective feedback.

Angelo and Cross (2009) present many more examples of classroom assessment techniques, which they divide into categories: assessments related to course knowledge and skills; assessments of analysis and critical thinking; assessments of synthesis and creative thinking; assessments of application and performance; assessments of learner attitudes, values, and self-awareness; and assessments of learners' responses to class activities, materials, and assignments.

In analyzing the assessment data you collect from your students, you might ask yourself these questions:

- What proportion of your students are learning satisfactorily?
- Which students are learning well, and which are not? Why might this be the case?
- What do successful learners do that less successful learners might emulate?
- Which elements or aspects of the course are students struggling with? Why?
- What changes in assignments, intervention, presentation, and the like might you make in your teaching practice to improve your students' learning?

We have been considering various classroom assessment techniques as low-stakes, informal ways of gauging students' understanding—as formative interventions with opportunities for immediate feedback—but these techniques can also be used as summative evaluations in higher-stakes, end-of-unit or end-of-course examinations.

Assessment as Meaningful Feedback

Just as feedback in personal and professional situations can be both confusing and helpful, so too can feedback we offer students on their class and coursework. We need to be clear about what kinds of feedback we give students at different intervention points, and why we are providing it.

In *Thanks for the Feedback* (2015), Douglas Stone and Sheila Heen describe three types of feedback typically provided in both academic and professional work contexts: positive reinforcement, coaching, and evaluation. As a form of encouragement during the stages of their work on a project, we can offer students *positive reinforcement feedback*, a kind of appreciation for the effort they are making. This appreciation feedback may be useful in motivating students, but it is rarely of value in helping them understand the relative success of any particular task they have completed—whether a report, paper, exam, project, presentation, or something else. For that, students need two other kinds of feedback: coaching and evaluation.

Coaching feedback is typically offered during the early and middle stages of an assignment, production, or performance; *evaluative feedback* is more often provided when the assignment, production, or performance has been completed. Evaluative feedback is more formal and final than coaching feedback, which offers ways for students to improve their performance on an assignment. Coaching feedback assesses and guides; evaluative feedback grades—with or without a number or letter attached.

Evaluation is useful as feedback because it lets students know where they stand in relation to one another, or in relation to an established standard. The evaluative feedback offered can be binary—a student does or does not meet the standard; he or she can move on to the next step, stage, or level, or not, until the standard is achieved. Evaluation may also be presented as a range of performance achievement levels, from adequate to superlative, from barely meets the standard to exceeds the standard, with various performance stages in between, as exemplified by the traditional span of grades from F to A.

Students want to know where they stand, and evaluative feedback can give them that information. Students also want to know how they can improve and reach a higher level of performance (often so that they can get a better grade). Coaching feedback offers them that kind of assistance, whether or not they eventually reach the higher performance standard and grade.

All three forms of feedback can be helpful to students. We need to decide which type of feedback we want to give them, when to provide it, and how. And we need to be clear about which type of feedback is being provided, and why. In addition, we need to help students understand how each type of feedback can be useful for them.

Grading—Preliminary Considerations

Students, not surprisingly, are very concerned about their grades—grades on assignments, grades for individual courses, and their overall cumulative grade point average. And they are concerned for good reason. We don't need to go into detail here about why grades matter to students. But the fact that they do matter a great deal can put pressure on us as teachers who are required to evaluate their performance relative to department and school standards, as well as our own.

Grading by letter or number may well be one of the least pleasurable of our responsibilities as educators. Most teachers are far more interested in the work of teaching and learning than they are in assigning grades. Most of us are happy to develop formative assessments with varying feedback mechanisms to assist students in their academic progress. It's when we have to come up with a letter or number that fixes students in one or another grading category that anxiety sets in—for both teachers and students. Knowing how important grades are to students for admission to competitive graduate and professional programs and to competitive internship and employment opportunities, we may struggle with giving them a C or even a B, grades that surely place them in lower sectors than some of their better prepared and academically more successful classmates. And yet we need to do just this.

We may need to use grading from time to time as a way to let students know that they are not meeting an acceptable standard and are performing at a subpar level, a C– or a D. And if students are not attending class, fail to submit assignments, or are performing woefully below an acceptable standard, we may well have to give them the failing grade they deserve.

We have found it effective to tell students that we are not so much "giving" them a grade as awarding them the grade they have earned. We award them credit for what they have done, for how well they have performed, based on our course performance expectations and grading standards. And while we are certainly judging our students according to how well they have met these expectations and standards, shifting the language of grading this way puts the responsibility directly on students. The work they do and the manner in which they do it determines their grade. We add up their points, apply a grading rubric, and see where each student winds up.

Why We Grade

Grades serve a number of purposes. In *Effective Grading: A Tool for Learning and Assessment* (1998), Barbara Walvoord and Virginia Anderson suggest that we use grades to do the following:

1. To evaluate student work
2. To organize lessons, units, and other segments of academic work to mark transitions and bring closure (such as a final course grade)

3. To motivate students to continue and to improve their learning
4. To communicate to students and parents, as well as graduate
    and professional schools and potential employers, a student's
    academic performance and future potential

Grades also serve as feedback about students' level of success in learning. Without a clear explanation of the meaning of a grade on a test, paper, or project, the grade's feedback is limited to a performance evaluation—fair, good, solid, or outstanding—but conveys no sense of why the student's performance has earned a particular grade.

Grades sometimes also function to sort students. Some programs, for example, set a quota, usually in set percentages, for how many students (or what percentage of them) can be awarded an A or A–. In such instances, grades distinguish top performers from the rest. Grades are more often used this way in science and engineering courses, especially in the courses that serve as gateways to professional degrees in medicine and engineering.

How We Grade

The process of grading is not limited to a single approach or set of actions. You might use a different grading process for different kinds of assignments. Informal, low-stakes assignments may be graded simply with a check, minus, or plus and allocated a small percentage of a student's overall course grade. Conversely, a major exam, paper, report, or project may be graded according to a detailed rubric and account for a significant portion of a student's final course grade. The time you spend evaluating student performances on different kinds of assignments will, accordingly, differ, as will student effort (and anxiety) on those assignments.

Here are some questions to consider when planning your grading system:

- What is most important for the assignment—content, structure, reasoning, accuracy, the final answer, the process by which the answer(s) and explanation(s) are developed?
- What percentage of the grade will be allocated to these important parts of students' efforts?
- Will you award partial credit or points on a sliding scale? Or will you be grading on an all-or-nothing basis?

- Will there be a penalty for late assignments? If so, how heavy will it be?
- If you assign letter grades, will you add + or –?
- If you assign number grades, what do the numbers mean, and how do they scale?
- Will you employ different grading scales for different assignments?
- Will you be grading on a curve?
- Will you assign split grades—for example, a grade for content and/or reasoning along with a grade for clarity, organization, style, format, and other similar features?
- To what extent will you comment on the assignments that you grade? What will be the nature of these comments?

Considering these questions carefully and thoroughly—and conveying your thinking to your students about them—is essential for achieving the purposes your grades are designed to serve. Grading your students consistently will also help them better understand what is expected of them, especially for the highest levels of performance, and why you have established the criteria upon which you evaluate them. Being transparent about your process of grading lets your students know that you are not keeping secrets from them, or springing surprises on them, but rather that you want them to understand that you take this part of your responsibility seriously and that you are devoting care and thought to the process and want them to succeed.

Whatever comments you provide with your grades should be limited to ones that can be clearly understood by students and are useful for subsequent learning. In commenting on final drafts of papers, for example, your comments can be brief, pointing to each paper's strengths and weaknesses simply and directly. The time for more elaborate explanatory comments on papers is on intermediate drafts, or during earlier stages of multi-stage projects, so that students can take your suggestions into consideration as they work to complete the project or revise the paper productively.

Another suggestion is to grade selectively. Not every assignment needs to be graded. For low-stakes assignments especially, provide brief but specific feedback—and not too much. Where possible, use the digital shortcut of copying and pasting responses that you commonly offer to many students, whether encouragement, general advice, or a type of correction needed by many students.

Grading Challenges

Among a number of challenges that arise with grading and assessment are fairness, bias, and consistency.

Students expect to be treated fairly, especially in the arena of grading. How can we ensure that our grading process and our grading system are fair, that we are treating students equitably, rewarding them for their successes and downgrading them for their errors and inadequacies on tests and papers, projects and presentations? Does being fair to students mean that you should treat every student exactly the same way? Or is there room to treat each student according to his or her needs, acknowledging that some need more and different kinds of attention and intervention than others? If you believe that fairness allows for such differentiation, how do you ensure that your grading of students' performances—your evaluations, formative assessments, and summative grades—is fair? And what does that actually mean in practice? These questions do not admit of a single or simple answer.

Bias can easily creep into our grading, particularly when we work closely with students in small classes, when we see how hard some of them work, how many drafts of a paper they produce, how much time they devote to a project, and the like. We can easily lean toward giving a student a better grade than is warranted for a particular performance or product. Bias can also affect our grading through how appealing (or unappealing) we find particular students. We will like some students more than others; we will enjoy teaching some students more than others. And so we need to be careful when it comes to grading their work to avoid being influenced by those feelings.

Consistency in grading presents challenges both within our grading for any particular assignment and across our grading for the suite of assignments for a course. If we change our grading standards from one assignment to the next, students will become confused about what we value, what we want from them, and what constitutes excellence. If we are inconsistent in applying our grading standard within a particular assignment, students will see that one student has received a higher (or lower) grade for the same level of work as another.

Grading Criteria

Other factors that complicate grading include how well prepared students are for a course, whether they have completed prerequisites, whether the course is open to first-year students as well as students nearing graduation, and whether your school has highly selective admissions criteria, open enrollment, or, more likely, something in between. These considerations play into the development of our grading criteria. A further complication is the extent to which evaluating student performance in a course is based on their relative standing to one another only, or whether the grading standard reflects criteria by which students are evaluated across multiple sections or iterations of a course.

Determining and disseminating clear grading criteria can help both teachers and students in a number of ways. Clear criteria can make the entire grading process easier for instructors by making it more consistent and efficient. Efficiency in grading saves teachers time, and consistency in grading ensures that students are treated equitably and fairly.

Clear grading criteria help students understand what you consider important, and why. They convey your expectations to students about what particular performance levels on tests and papers, on reports and projects, look like. These criteria also help students understand how they will be evaluated.

Two other pieces of advice: Avoid or at least minimize discussion of grades during class time. And try not to change your grading policies, including your policy for grading late work, once you have established those policies and discussed them with students.

Grading Rubrics

One way to communicate the criteria by which you will evaluate student work is through a rubric. Besides conveying to students what is important for their work in your course, a rubric can help you as well. A well-designed rubric can save you time in grading student work. Instead of repeating the same or similar comments over and over, you can let the rubric do that work for you and devote any new comments to more targeted and personalized feedback. Grading rubrics also cut down dramatically on students' questions about their grades on exams and papers and reduce complaints about grades as well. When a student does challenge or otherwise question a grade, you can review his or her paper against the rubric; the burden of proof is on the student to show why the exam or paper fits the rubric description for one grade rather than another.

How detailed should you make your rubrics? As detailed as necessary to help students understand how you are evaluating them. As detailed as necessary to convey what matters most, and no more.

To reduce student questions and complaints about grades, be sure to include your grading policies, standards, and procedures on your syllabus—and be sure to review them with your students just before and after work is due. Reminding students of your grading criteria helps them focus on what you value most as they study for exams or prepare graded assignments.

Rubric scales illustrate ways to identify performance evaluation measures with three, four, five, and six levels of descriptive terms. Here are a few examples:

Developing	Competent	Exemplary	
Weak	Satisfactory	Strong	

Beginning	Developing	Accomplished	Exemplary
Poor	Fair	Good	Excellent

The language you use for your rubric categories matters, as it does for the more detailed explanations you provide for each performance level. As you can see from the examples of three- and four-stage rubrics here, the language of the first example in each category may be a bit more encouraging than that of the second example. Which kind of language you decide to use will reflect your teaching persona, as well as your attitude toward your students and their learning.

Designing Rubrics

The first decision to make when designing a grading rubric is whether you will use a holistic or analytic rubric. *Holistic rubrics* evaluate a performance as a whole, as a gestalt, without breaking down the assignment to be graded into discrete small parts. *Analytic rubrics*, on the other hand, identify specific elements and aspects of the assignment to be evaluated—for example, content, organization, grammar, style, presentation, format, and so on.

Each type of rubric has advantages and disadvantages. From the students' perspective, holistic rubrics emphasize what they can do rather than what they cannot do. From the instructor's perspective, holistic rubrics save time in grading by minimizing the number of evaluative decisions he or she must make. The disadvantages of holistic rubrics include their lack of specific targeted areas for student improvement and growth. Holistic rubrics can also be difficult to apply when a student's work varies considerably across evaluative criteria.

Analytic rubrics, by contrast, account for specific areas of strength and weakness in student performances. The particular areas can be easily weighted, which is difficult, if not impossible, with holistic rubrics. A disadvantage, however, is that analytic rubrics are more time-consuming to create and apply, as there are more judgments to make about each student's performance.

You must satisfy a number of requirements no matter which type of rubric you design. First, you need to be sure to align the grading criteria in your rubric with your course goals and objectives. Second, the criteria you establish and the performance levels you identify must be readily observable and measurable. Third, you need to ensure that the performance levels are distinct from one another and described in clear, precise language. Fourth, you need to decide how you will weight your criteria.

In the descriptions you need to write for each level of your rating scale, try to describe observable, measurable performance qualities. Be sure to use parallel language across your descriptive categories. And indicate the degree to which each standard must be met—minimally, partially, adequately, completely—or set some other set of evaluative terms. (See the appendix for two sample grading rubrics.)

A Note on Grade Appeals

One of the most important benefits of well-written and carefully crafted rubrics is their use in any grade appeal process. When a student wants to challenge a course grade or a grade for an assignment, having a clearly written rubric available makes it easier for the person deciding whether or not a grade adjustment is warranted. In evaluating the validity of a request for a grade adjustment, the decision-maker can go to the rubric descriptions for each level of performance to assess a student paper, report, project, or other production or performance. Some wiggle room remains, however, as the rubric's evaluation standards need to be interpreted and applied. But the more clearly written those standards are, the easier they are to apply and the better they can be understood.

Alternatives to Grading

In "The Case against Grades" (2011), Alfie Kohn argues that giving students grades for academic performance is destructive of authentic learning. Grades, he claims, function as a disincentive to learn. According to Kohn, grades diminish students' interest in learning, lead them to prefer easier rather than difficult challenges, and diminish the quality of their thinking. Kohn has done his own research and examined decades of previous research on grading. He concludes that no recent research has contradicted his observations.

When students are motivated by grades rather than by an intrinsic interest in and desire to learn, their learning suffers in two ways: they learn less, and what they learn they learn less well than when they learn things for their own sake, for the pleasure of learning. When motivated by grades and performance, students generally don't retain what they learn, even superficially, for long.

What can we do to avoid, or at least minimize, grading's pitfalls and deleterious consequences? There are at least places to start. One is not to grade everything that students do. Avoid grading students for every facet of a project, for each little bit of work they submit. Instead, offer them feedback in the form of comments on that work. Let them know what they are doing right, what they might consider doing next, what questions they might think about, and how they might develop their thinking further. Let them know whether they are on track or not, and whether their work reflects superficial or deeper responses to the assignment.

The second tack is to intervene less often to evaluate student work and more often to demonstrate an interest in it. Respond as a serious reader. Encourage students to take themselves and their work seriously by letting them know that you are an interested reader, not merely someone hovering over them with a red pencil, ready to pounce on every error and criticize every false move. Include in this approach ways to acknowledge what students are doing right and to direct them toward doing more and doing better—not to please you but to please themselves. Engage students' ideas, not just the limited ways in which they might be expressing them. Help them develop their thinking, improve their explanations, and deepen their understanding through thoughtful and interested responses to their work well before you need to evaluate it for a grade.

Applications

1. Which of the classroom assessment techniques discussed here do you look forward to using in your classes?
2. What kinds of feedback do you plan to give students on their assignments for one of your courses?

3. What is your biggest grading challenge? How do you plan to address that challenge?
4. Identify the grading criteria for an assignment for one of your courses and the weight you will assign to each criterion.
5. Write an analytic rubric and a holistic rubric for an exam, paper, report, project, or other significant assignment in one of your courses.

Teaching as Creative Problem-Solving

Teaching requires and exemplifies creative problem-solving. Designing a course and syllabus, aligning exams and assignments with course goals and objectives, planning lectures and class discussions, motivating students, developing grading rubrics and assessment tools, using technology—these and other aspects of teaching require problem definition and problem-solving.

How might we implement problem-solving approaches not just in the design and construction of our courses but also in how we teach them? How might we cultivate our students' ability to experiment, imagine, and reflect? How can we help them identify problems worth solving, and how do we model the problem-solving process for them? How can we support their critical and creative thinking as they engage in problem-solving activities and projects?

Problem-Solving Processes

Problem-solving, like learning, is a process; it's a method that requires not only latitude, versatility, and improvisation, but also a thoughtful, analytical approach. In *Learn Better* (2017), Ulrich Boser explains the four phases of Hungarian mathematician George Pólya's approach to problem-solving:

> In the first phase, *understanding*, we attempt to identify the core or nature of the problem. We ask what we know and what we don't know; we try to get our minds around the problem.
> In the second phase, *planning*, we devise a plan; we map out an approach to the problem. We try to find a connection between what we know (any data or other information we possess) and the unknown element(s) of the problem.
> In the third phase, *doing*, we implement our plan; we act on the plan we devise in phase 2. In this phase, we essentially attempt to prove that our plan to solve the problem is viable. If we discover that it's not, we return to phase 1.

If our phase 3 work is successful, we go on to *reviewing* in phase 4;
we look back to learn from our success (and missteps). We
reexamine the path that led to the problem's solution and see
what we can learn from it for solving future problems.

Problem-solving requires asking ourselves questions—about evidence,
about alternative explanations and approaches, about counterarguments,
about bias. We also need to set goals and break complex challenges down
into simpler, more accessible parts. Problem-solving requires that we develop background knowledge, do research, test ideas, get feedback from
others, and more.

We can adopt any number of approaches to developing our pedagogical problem-solving. Here is one process you can try:

- Plan—act—evaluate—reflect—revise. Plan—act—evaluate . . .

Once you complete the cycle from planning to enacting, you repeat it,
as often as necessary. We might ask several questions during this reitera-
tive process: What percentage of our time should we devote to planning
and acting? What percentage to evaluating and reflecting? How many revisions will it take to be satisfied with what we are creating?

A related and alternative problem-solving approach is what some have
described as "observe and envision." This approach is also iterative and
recursive.

- Observe and reflect
- Envision and express
- Stretch and explore

This approach to problem-solving comes out of studio work, specifically studio art and design. Grounded in skills and dispositions, it requires an alertness to opportunities for creating and critiquing our work
and helping students create and critique their reports, papers, projects,
and presentations. In the process of working through problem definition
and iterative solutions, we develop our craft, hone our skills, and deepen
our understanding not only of what we do but of how we do it. This approach, like the first one, requires continued engagement, patience, and
persistence.

A third approach to problem-solving is used specifically for design
thinking—the kind of workshop approach common to places like the

Stanford d.school. Both a discipline and a method, the design-thinking model looks like this:

1. Define the problem
2. Ideate
3. Prototype
4. Test
5. Refocus
6. Redefine
7. Re-ideate
8. Re-prototype
9. Retest
10. Continue the process

There are some key questions to ask in working through this design process: Is the project (solution) feasible? Is it viable? Is it desirable? Like the first two approaches, design thinking is a process and not a template, a flexible method and not a rigid system. It too is iterative and recursive rather than linear.

In her book *Mastermind: How to Think Like Sherlock Holmes* (2013), Maria Konnikova provides an overview of a Holmesian approach to problem-solving in a series of questions that hew to the famous detective's case-solving practices: (1) Are you using all available information and evidence and not just what's readily available? (2) Are you weighing the evidence carefully, sifting the incidental from the essential, the relevant from the irrelevant? (3) Are you analyzing the problem in terms of logical sequence, with each step inexorably linked to what comes before and after? (4) Are you considering all logical possibilities, even those that seem far-fetched? (5) Are you focused on the problem, without being distracted by side issues?

Finally, remember that, as we engage in the work of teaching and learning, we are also, to some extent, makers. We produce things—syllabi, assignments, rubrics and assessment tools, case studies, and more. Like artists in particular and like all of us generally as human agents, we are, as Amy Whitaker notes in *Art Thinking* (2016), "deeply engaged in the creation of value and in the act of making a contribution, by presence or work or kindness or talent or collective effort on projects that are smaller or larger than ourselves" (p. 300). As teachers, we give of ourselves to our disciplines and to our students. We are always figuring things out, and always engaged in a lifelong experiment of educating ourselves while teaching our students.

Applications

Whichever problem-solving models we adopt and adapt, a number of questions can help us negotiate our creative and critical teaching tasks:

1. What processes do you value in your own problem-solving practice? How can you cultivate problem-solving strategies in your pedagogical practice?
2. What can you learn from artists, athletes, musicians, engineers, scientists, advertisers, and businesspeople?
3. What models and procedures from the artist's studio or the scientist's lab might you adapt in developing your pedagogy and implementing it in your classroom?
4. How can you use the models of the sketchbook, notebook, workbook, practice room, or artist's space to explore and experiment and enable your students to do likewise?

Problem-solving presents an ongoing set of challenges for us as teachers. Every chapter of this book, along with the prologue and each of its interludes, provides opportunities for us to engage in one or another form of creative problem-solving. This kind of work never really ends.

We wouldn't want it any other way.

Appendix

A College Teaching Survival Kit

This appendix contains a teaching survival kit: critical resources you can use to jump-start various facets of your teaching. It includes five discrete tools for your teaching:

1. An inventory of the book's **checklists** that itemize what you need to do, for example, to manage class discussion or to promote critical thinking
2. A series of **templates** you can use and adapt for preparing a syllabus and lesson plan that will promote active learning, manage group work, and much more
3. A pair of sample **grading rubrics** keyed to textual analysis and critical thinking
4. A list of key **teaching and learning centers** with extensive pedagogical resources
5. A brief list of **periodicals**, both print and digital, about teaching and learning

Following the "College Teaching Survival Kit" is a list of references we found useful in writing *The Craft of College Teaching*.

A Checklist Inventory

Throughout *The Craft of College Teaching*, you will find a number of bulleted checklists. Use these checklists as a quick reference for teaching strategies you can implement.

1. Motivating student learning, p. 11
2. Stimulating students' curiosity, p. 18
3. Questioning—KWHLAQ, p. 19
4. Course design goals, p. 27
5. Syllabus purposes, p. 32
6. Active learning and agency, p. 47
7. Active learning questions, p. 54

8. Principles of active learning, p. 68
9. Teaching and learning strategies, p. 72
10. Improving explanations, p. 76
11. Principles of successful discussions, p. 82
12. Discussion practices, p. 84
13. Student participation in discussions, p. 87
14. Slide design tips, p. 121
15. Planning group work, p. 125
16. Teaching with technology, p. 141
17. Analyzing information, p. 143
18. Conditions for experiential learning, p. 152
19. Effective mentoring, p. 159
20. Writing and revising, p. 176
21. Critical thinking questions, p. 183 and p. 193
22. Assessment questions, p. 202
23. Grading questions, p. 205
24. Problem-solving, p. 214

Templates

Syllabus

- Your name and title, office location and hours, and contact email (office phone number is optional)
- URL for course website (if applicable)
- Prerequisites (if any)
- Texts, materials, and supplies
- Course description
- Course goals
- Course and school policies on class participation, plagiarism, technical support, students with disabilities, and the like
- Course methods
- Course schedule (of class meetings, assignments, exams, and so on)
- Grading policy, including grading standards, criteria, and scale
- Assignment and exam information
- Course policies on attendance, lateness, late work, missed exams, requests for extensions, incompletes, and expectations for student conduct and behavior in the class, laboratory, or studio
- Student resources (writing and learning centers, for example)

- Supplementary and recommended material, such as readings, films, and websites
- Caveats—for example, how the syllabus can change and ways to inform students of revisions to the syllabus
- Teacher assistant information (if applicable)

Lesson Plan

Objectives (or goals): These are typically written in behavioral terms. For example: "Students will explain clearly while using technical terminology, the major parts of the brain and their corresponding functions." Or, "Students will be able to analyze the claims made in an argument and evaluate the evidence offered in its support."

Hook (or bridge): This is a strategy to engage students' attention and interest—for example, bringing a 3D model of the brain into class and holding it up for students to see, or starting a class by projecting an image of the brain onto a screen with all (or none) of its parts labeled.

Content: The information and concepts you will teach that help students understand what is being taught.

Activities: What you and the students will do during the class period—usually broken up into two, three, or more segments, depending on the length of the class, the nature of the material, and the level of the students' knowledge and preparation. These might include, for example, writing responses to a question, summarizing part of a reading or a lecture, or solving problems.

Assessment: A way of evaluating what students are learning during the session, either while they are engaged in that learning or afterwards.

Timeline: How much time you devote to each element of your class lesson plan. How will you "chunk," or otherwise divide, the time allotted for your class sessions?

Active Learning

- Activities need not be long to be effective. When starting out with active learning, or during sessions in which time is at a premium, aim for no more than three to five minutes, ten minutes maximum.

- If you assign multiple exercises during a session, don't require students to report their results to the class after every exercise.
- When an activity is wildly successful, it may take more time than you envisioned. Have a plan B for the class—and for the class that follows.
- Avoid using the same techniques too often. Vary the type of active learning activities you implement, and do not always require that students turn in the results of their work in some form.
- When using pair-share activities, pair students up with different partners—sometimes with a student sitting next to or behind them, other times with a partner across the room.
- Develop some longer, more important (and graded) assignments based on an in-class active learning exercise. Think/pair/share exercises are particularly appropriate for this kind of work.
- Announce how much time is being allotted for the activity, and let students know when there is a minute or two of class time remaining.
- Debrief by asking some pairs and small groups to explain what they discussed and learned. In small classes, all pairs or groups can respond; in large lectures, ask for a few volunteers or cold-call a few.

Cornell Note-Taking for Students

1. **Record:** During the lecture, use the note-taking column to record the lecture using telegraphic sentences.
2. **Question:** As soon after class as possible, formulate questions based on the notes in the right-hand column. Writing questions helps to clarify meanings, reveal relationships, establish continuity, and strengthen memory. Also, the writing of questions sets up a perfect stage for exam-studying later.
3. **Recite:** Cover the note-taking column with a sheet of paper. Then, looking at the questions or cue words in the question and cue column only, say aloud, in your own words, the answers to the questions, facts, or ideas indicated by the cue words.
4. **Reflect:** Reflect on the material by asking yourself questions, for example: "What's the significance of these facts? What

principle are they based on? How can I apply them? How do they fit in with what I already know? What's beyond them?"

5. **Review:** Spend at least ten minutes every week reviewing all your previous notes in order to retain a great deal for current use and also for the exam later.

6. **Summarize:** After class, use the space at the bottom of each page to summarize the notes on that page (see table 4.1).

Explanations

- Pitch language at the level of the learner. Good explanations are understandable. Disciplinary language may be expeditious, but it's not always comprehensible to students.
- Pace language at the speed of the learner. Speak slowly enough to be followed by your students, yet fast enough to remain interesting.
- Provide malleable explanations capable of being reshaped, reformed, reconstituted, and reconfigured. Find alternative ways to explain key concepts.
- Repeat as often as needed—perhaps in the format of a theme with variations.
- Illustrate with relevant, time-sensitive, and culture-sensitive examples that are meaningful for your students.
- Offer multi-sourced explanations—not just from the teacher, but from students as well.

Discussion

1. Ask students to identify one concrete image, scene, or moment from an assignment they read or viewed. They don't have to analyze or interpret their choice, but they do need to describe it so that their classmates know what they are referring to. You can follow up by asking why they selected what they did for this description exercise.

2. Have students write down two questions they have about the day's assignment.

3. Ask students to pair off and decide together on the primary value of a reading due for the day's class and its connection to the goals of the course.

4. Have students identify one passage from a reading assignment that resonated for them because they found it interesting, provocative, important, confusing—give them a range of options.

5. Ask students to find a second passage that relates in some way to the first passage they selected. Have them write a sentence or two explaining the connection. Ask for volunteers to share their thinking after first reading their selected passages.

6. Present students with a brief scenario to think about, with one or two guiding questions. Give them two or three minutes to think and jot a few notes; then pair them or group them in threes to discuss their thinking. Have each pair or group contribute to the class discussion overall.

Group Work

1. What is the learning goal of the exercise?
2. How is the activity connected to the class session and to the course overall?
3. How can you ensure that students understand the purpose and goal of the activity, as well as its alignment with the course goals?
4. What product will you require the groups to produce? What will they do at the end of the group work time allotted?
5. What time limit will you put on the overall group activity? Will you divide it into parts and provide time limits for each part? How will the timing be enforced? By you, by a group member, or in some other way?
6. What will be your role while the groups are on task?
7. How will you frame the group assignment? How much guidance will you provide? Will you provide this guidance orally or in writing (on the board, with an instruction sheet)?
8. How will you assess the group activity and provide feedback on it?
9. How will you connect the group activity to what came before it during the class session, to what may follow it during that session, and to what precedes and succeeds it in the course overall?

Analyzing Information

1. Where did this information come from?
2. What is the evidence for it?
3. Why is this information important to know?
4. What's missing from this information?

Daniel Willingham (2012) suggests a related process for evaluating information:

1. **Strip it:** Boil it down to its key claim. Identify its essential supporting evidence.
2. **Trace it:** Identify who is providing the information and what others may have said about it and about the provider.
3. **Analyze it:** Consider how trustworthy the information is.
4. **Accept or reject it:** Decide whether the information and associated claims are sufficiently well supported to warrant acceptance.

Mentoring

- Assess prior knowledge at the beginning of the mentoring relationship: draw this information out through low-stakes writing exercises or activities designed to demonstrate existing knowledge. Asking, "So what do you know about research?" is not enough; students don't know what they don't know.
- Assume nothing about your students.
- Repeat and review key principles.
- Don't immediately provide all the answers; know when to let students struggle; give them space to wonder, think, and question before you give them the answer (unless they reach it themselves).
- Assess student learning as you proceed: What do they remember from last week? What's still unclear? What's their takeaway from today? Reflective writing, unlike point-blank questions, can be effective in eliciting this information.
- Encourage students. Let them know that failure and learning are part of the process of learning and discovery.
- Demystify the practice of research by explaining how you do research. What kinds of successes and failures have you had?

Share with students your personal experience as a professional practitioner to let them know that research is a human endeavor.

- Ask open-ended questions. Listen and ask follow-up questions.
- Guide students to think for themselves, and engage them in inquiry and exploration. Avoid telling them what to think about their discoveries.
- Break large projects down into parts and stages; design smaller assignments to build up to the larger project.
- Teach the student, not the topic.
- Meet your students where they are: some may need guidance in developing their skills in critical reading, writing, conducting research, and giving presentations.

Critical Thinking—General

- What do you know? (And what don't you know that you need to know?)
- What have you assumed?
- What does it mean?
- What is the evidence?
- What are the criteria?
- What questions can you ask?

Critical Thinking—Dialectical

- Does the answer avoid rigid application of a rule?
- Does it account for differing perspectives?
- Does it recognize the possibility of change?
- Does it identify possible compromise positions or outcomes?
- Does it express uncertainty rather than dogmatic confidence?

Grading

- What is most important for the assignment—content, structure, reasoning, accuracy, the final answer, the process by which answers and explanations are developed?
- What percentage of the grade will be allocated to these important parts?

- Will you award partial credit or points on a sliding scale? Or will you be grading on an all-or-nothing basis?
- Will there be a penalty for late assignments? If so, how heavy will it be?
- If you assign letter grades, will you add + or –?
- If you assign number grades, what do the numbers mean? How do they scale?
- Will you employ different grading scales for different assignments?
- Will you be grading on a curve?
- Will you assign split grades—for example, a grade for content and reasoning along with a grade for clarity, organization, style, format, and like features?
- To what extent will you comment on the assignments that you grade? What will be the nature of these comments?

Sample Grading Rubrics

This first sample rubric is for analysis of an advertisement that includes both image and text. Student performances on the assignment are graded on a letter grade scale.

Grading Rubric for Advertisement Analysis

A: Accurate and thorough consideration of *all* elements of the advertisement. Images analyzed with care. Implications and appeals of the images explained persuasively. Text of the ad analyzed thoroughly. Thoughtful explanations for the inclusion of various segments of the ad's language; consideration of the implications of the ad's words and phrases, including tone.

B: Reasonably accurate and moderately complete consideration of *most* elements of the advertisement. Images analyzed with some thoughtfulness. Implications and appeals of the images explained to a moderate extent. Text of the ad analyzed but not completely. Explanations for the inclusion of various segments of the ad's language; consideration of the implications of the ad's words and phrases, excluding tone.

C: Somewhat accurate and incomplete consideration of the elements of the advertisement. Images explained but not fully. Appeals suggested but not fully explained. Text of the ad summarized rather than analyzed. Little in the way of analysis of the ad's language, including why various segments were included and what their implications are. Little, if any, recognition of various parts of the ad.

D: Inaccurate presentation of what the ad is and does. Incomplete attention to the ad's images, language, and appeals. Substandard explanation. No analysis.

F: Incorrect, incompetent response to the question. Disorganized, confused thinking and writing. No analysis. Erroneous inferences and suppositions.

This next sample rubric is designed for students analyzing a magazine article. The assignment is provided first, then the rubric, which is graded on a scale of 0–20 points. The students' grade on this assignment constitutes 20 percent of the course grade.

Read "The Operator" by Michael Specter, an article published in *The New Yorker* on February 4, 2013. You can search for the piece online by typing in "The Operator Dr. Oz." You can also find it at www.newyorker.com/magazine/2013/02/04/the-operator. The article asks whether Dr. Oz, the most trusted doctor in America, is "doing more harm than good."

Your assignment is to read the article carefully and critically. I suggest that you read it twice—once just to get a sense of what it is about and what ground it covers, and then again, taking careful notes. Pay attention to the author's language and to how he selects and presents information about Dr. Oz.

Apply what you have learned in the course so far; give evidence that you are using what you have learned from the assignments, resources, lessons, and forums, especially those on **connotation** and on **reports**, **inferences**, and **judgments**.

Identify the **assumptions** and examine the **evidence** that Michael Specter uses to support his point of view—his perspective, or "take"—on Dr. Oz, which you will have to infer and interpret from what you observe about his language choices, selection of detail, and structuring of his article. Support your view of Dr. Oz, as well as your understanding and interpretation of the article, with evidence from the text, including brief quotations.

Grading Rubric for Dr. Oz Article Analysis

18–20: Accurate and thorough consideration of *all* elements of the article. The writer's language and selection of detail analyzed with care. Implications of the writer's word choices and selection of detail explained persuasively. Thoughtful explanations for the inclusion of various parts of the article, including quotations from and references to other people; consideration of the tone of the article. Author's point of view considered and evidence for and against it provided. Assumptions and the author's perspective identified and evaluated.

16–17: Reasonably accurate and moderately complete consideration of *most* elements of the article. Partial analysis of author's language and selection of detail. Implications of the writer's word choices and selection of detail considered. Reasonable explanations for including quotations and references from the article. Minimal consideration of the tone of the article. Questions raised about the author's point of view.

14–15: Somewhat accurate but incomplete consideration of the elements of the article. Minimal, if any, analysis of the writer's language and selection of detail. Modest but not necessarily persuasive explanation of the article's point and purpose. Some consideration of quotations from the article and references to other people. Minimal, if any, consideration of the tone of the article, its assumptions, and the author's perspective.

11–13: Inaccurate presentation of what the article is, says, and does. Incomplete attention to the article's language and selection of detail. Substandard explanation. No analysis.

10: Incorrect, incompetent response to the question. Disorganized, confused thinking and writing. Erroneous inferences and suppositions. No analysis.

Teaching and Learning Centers

Centers for teaching and learning go by various names and designations. More important than what they call themselves is what they do: provide support services for faculty members and graduate students to improve their teaching and advance and deepen their students' learning. A number of teaching centers, such as those at Harvard and Stanford, offer a wide menu of pedagogical options for you to explore. And we encourage you to do just that—click your way around a few of these centers' websites, drilling down on topics of particular interest.

Assumption College, D'Amour Center for Teaching Excellence, https://www
     .assumption.edu/people-and-departments/organization-listing/center
     -teaching-excellence
Brown University, Harriet W. Sheridan Center for Teaching and Learning,
     https://www.brown.edu/sheridan/sheridan-center
Columbia University, Center for Teaching and Learning, https://ctl.columbia
     .edu/
Harvard University, Derek Bok Center for Teaching and Learning, https://
     bokcenter.harvard.edu/
Princeton University, McGraw Center for Teaching and Learning, https://
     mcgraw.princeton.edu/
Purdue University, Center for Instructional Excellence, https://www.purdue
     .edu/cie/
Stanford University, Center for Teaching and Learning, https://ctl.stanford
     .edu/
University of Kansas, Center for Teaching Excellence, https://cte.ku.edu/
University of Michigan, Center for Research on Learning and Teaching,
     http://www.crlt.umich.edu/
University of Tennessee at Knoxville, Teaching and Learning Innovation,
     https://teaching.utk.edu/
University of Washington, Center for Teaching and Learning, https://www
     .washington.edu/teaching/
Vanderbilt University, Center for Teaching, https://cft.vanderbilt.edu/
Washington State University, Center for Teaching and Learning, https://news
     .wsu.edu/tag/center-for-teaching-and-learning/
Washington University in St. Louis, The Teaching Center, https://
     teachingcenter.wustl.edu/

Print and Digital Periodical Resources

Although periodicals, both print and digital, come and go with regularity, it's worth seeking out the more stable ones and regularly following their articles, blogs, columns, and the like. Find a couple of these resources that resonate for you because they touch on matters of teaching theory and practice that matter most to you. Perhaps the articles are consistently brief and get to the point quickly. Perhaps they are written in a clear, direct style. Find those that contribute to productive conversations about teaching—and at some point, consider contributing yourself to this important ongoing conversation.

Association of American Colleges and Universities (AAC&U): *Diversity and Democracy, Liberal Education, Peer Review*

Carnegie Foundation for the Advancement of Teaching: *Carnegie Commons Blog*: "Thinking about Improvement," "Thinking about Networks," "Improvement in Action," "Networks in Action"

Chronicle of Higher Education: *Chronicle Review, Chronicle Focus, Faculty Focus, The Teaching Professor*

Inside Higher Education

Journal of Engineering Education

National Teaching and Learning Forum

References

Alexander, B., et al. (2019). *EDUCAUSE horizon report: 2019 higher education edition*. EDUCAUSE, April 23. https://library.educause.edu/resources /2019/4/2019-horizon-report.

Ambrose, S., Bridges, M. W., and DiPietro, M. L. (2010). *How learning works*. San Francisco: Jossey-Bass.

Angelo, T., and Cross, K. P. (2009). *Classroom assessment techniques: A Handbook for college teachers*, 2nd ed. San Francisco: Jossey-Bass.

Ariely, D. (2010). *Predictably irrational*. New York: HarperCollins.

Aristotle. (1931/2004). *Rhetoric*. Translated by W. R. Roberts. Mineola, NY: Dover.

Atkinson, C. (2011). *Beyond bullet points*. Redmond, WA: Microsoft Press.

Baenninger, M. A. (2018). "Learning everywhere: The end of 'extracurricular.'" *Liberal Education*.

Bain, K. (2004). *What the best college teachers do*. Cambridge, MA: Harvard University Press.

Barell, J. (2003). *Developing more curious minds*. Alexandria, VA: Association for Supervision and Curriculum Development.

Barkley, E. F., and Major, C. H. (2016). *Learning assessment techniques*. San Francisco: Jossey-Bass.

Bean, J. C. (2011). *Engaging ideas*. San Francisco: Jossey-Bass.

Berthoff, A. E. (1981). *The Making of meaning*. Montclair, NJ: Boynton/Cook.

Bok, D. (2017). *The Struggle to reform our colleges*. Princeton, NJ: Princeton University Press.

Boser, U. (2017). *Learn better*. New York: Rodale.

Botstein, L. (2018). "Redeeming the liberal arts." *Liberal Education* 104:4. www .aacu.org/liberaleducation/2018/fall/botstein.

Boyer, E. (1990). *Scholarship reconsidered*. Princeton, NJ: Carnegie Foundation for the Advancement of Teaching.

Brint, S. (2018). *Two cheers for higher education*. Princeton, NJ: Princeton University Press.

Brookfield, S. (1999). *Discussion as a way of teaching: Tools and techniques for democratic classrooms*. San Francisco: Jossey-Bass.

Brooks, D. (2019). "Students learn from people they love." *New York Times*, December 24, A23.

Brown, P. C., Roediger, H. L., III, and McDaniel, M. A. (2014). *Make it stick: The Science of successful learning.* Cambridge, MA: Harvard University Press.

Burke, K. (1968). *The Philosophy of literary form.* Berkeley: University of California Press.

Carlin, W. (2016). PowerPoint presentation at New York University Wagner Graduate School of Public Service, October.

Carson, A. (1986/2016). *Eros the bittersweet.* Princeton, NJ.: Princeton University Press.

Cherches, T. (2019). "Experiential learning and the 5 core competencies of an effective instructor." Unpublished paper, January 21.

Chi, M. T. H. (2000). "Self-explaining expository texts." *Advances in Instructional Psychology* 5, 161–238.

Christensen, C. R., et al., eds. (1991). *Education for judgment: The Artistry of discussion leadership.* Boston: Harvard Business School.

Clark, R. C., and Mayer, R. E. (2011). *E-learning and the science of instruction.* San Francisco: Pfeiffer.

Crouch, C. H., and Mazur, E. (2001). "Peer instruction: Ten years of experience and results." *American Journal of Physics* 29:9, 970–77.

Deutsch, D. (2012). *The Beginning of infinity.* New York: Penguin.

Dickinson, E. (1998). "Much Madness is divinest Sense." In R. W. Franklin, ed., *The Poems of Emily Dickinson: Reading edition.* Cambridge, MA: Harvard University Press.

Dikker, S., et al. (2017). "Brain-to-brain synchrony tracks real-world dynamic group interactions in the classroom." *Current Biology* 27:9, 1375–80.

DiYanni, R. (2015). *The Pearson guide to critical and creative thinking.* Upper Saddle River, NJ: Pearson Education.

DiYanni, R. (2016). *Critical and creative thinking: A Brief guide for teachers.* New York: Wiley Blackwell.

Duarte, N. (2008). *Slide:ology.* Sebastopol, CA: O'Reilly Media.

Duncan, D., and Southon, A. S. (1976). "Six ways to discourage learning." American Astronomical Society Education Office. https://aas.org/education/Six_Ways_to_Discourage_Learning.

Dweck, C. (2007). *Mindset.* New York: Random House.

Ehrlich, G. (1985). *The Solace of open spaces.* New York: Viking Penguin.

Ehrlich, T. (2005). "Service learning in undergraduate education: Where is it going?" *Carnegie Perspectives,* July. https://eric.ed.gov/?id=ED498997.

Epstein, D. (2019). *Range: Why generalists triumph in a specialized world.* New York: Riverhead.

Eyler, J. (1993). "Comparing the impact of two internship experiences on student learning." *Journal of Cooperative Education* 29:1, 41–53.

Eyler, J. (2009). "The Power of experiential education." *Liberal Education* 95:4. https://www.aacu.org/publications-research/periodicals/power-experiential-education.

Eyler, J., and Giles, D. (1999). *Where's the service in service learning?* San Francisco: Jossey-Bass.

Felder, R. M., and Brent, R. (2003). "Learning by doing." *Chemical Engineering Education* 37:4, 282–83.

Felder, R. M., and Brent, R. (2016). *Teaching and learning STEM*. San Francisco: Jossey-Bass.

Feynman, R. (2005). *The Pleasure of finding things out*. New York: Basic Books.

Firestein, S. (2012). *Ignorance*. Oxford and New York: Oxford University Press.

Firestein, S. (2015). *Failure*. Oxford and New York: Oxford University Press.

Frederick, P. (1981/2012). "The Dreaded discussion: Ten ways to start." *Improving College and University Teaching* 29:3, 109–14. https://doi.org/10.1080/00193089.1981.10533690.

Freeman, S., Eddy, S. L., McDonough, M., Smith, M. K., Okoroafor, N., Jordt, H., and Wenderoth, M. P. (2014). "Active learning increases student performance in science, engineering, and mathematics." *PNAS* 111:23, 8410–15.

Frost, R. (1995). *Collected poems and prose*. New York: Library of America.

Gannon, K. (2018). "How to create a syllabus: Advice guide." *Chronicle of Higher Education*, September 12. www.chronicle.co,m/interactives/advice-syllabus.

Godin, S. (2007). "Really bad PowerPoint," *Seth's Blog*, January 29. https://seths.blog/2007/01/really_bad_powe/.

Goodblar, D. (2018). "I'm not ready to quit grading." *Chronicle of Higher Education*, March 21.

Goulish, M. (2000). *39 Microlectures*. New York and London: Routledge.

Grazer, B. (2016). *A Curious mind*. New York: Simon & Schuster.

Haak, D. C., Hille Ris Lambers, J., Pitre, E., and Freeman, S. (2011). "Increased structure and active learning reduce the achievement gap in introductory biology." *Science* 332:6034 (June), 1213–16.

Hamlin, A. (2017). "Approaching intellectual emancipation: Critical reading in art, art history, and Wikipedia." In R. DiYanni and A. Borst, eds., *Critical reading across the curriculum*, vol. 1, *Humanities*, pp. 104–22. Hoboken, NJ: Wiley Blackwell.

Hand, D. J. (2015). *The Improbability principle*. New York: Farrar, Straus and Giroux.

Handelsman, J., et al. (2004). "Policy forum: Scientific teaching." *Science* 304:5670, 521–22.

Harvard University Derek Bok Center for Teaching and Learning. (n.d.). "Syllabus Design." https://bokcenter.harvard.edu/syllabus-design.

Hetland, L., and Winner, E. (2007). *Studio thinking*. New York: Teachers College Press.

Holmes, J. (2016). *Nonsense*. New York: Broadway Books.

Howard, J. (2019). "How to hold a better class discussion: Advice guide." *Chronicle of Higher Education*. https://www.chronicle.com/interactives/20190523-ClassDiscussion.

Johnston, P. H. (2004). *Choice words*. Portland, ME: Stenhouse Publishers.

Johnston, P. H. (2012). *Opening minds*. Portland, ME: Stenhouse Publishers.

Kahneman, D. (2011). *Thinking, fast and slow*. New York: Farrar, Straus and Giroux.

Klein, J. (1991). *Interdisciplinarity*. Detroit: Wayne State University Press.

Kohn, A. (2011). "The Case against grades." *Educational Leadership*, November.

Kohn, A. (2018). "Science confirms it: People are not pets." *New York Times Sunday Review*, October 28, 10.

Kolb, D. A. (1984). *Experiential learning*. Englewood Cliffs, NJ: Prentice-Hall.

Kolb, D. A. (2015). *Experiential learning*, 2nd ed. Upper Saddle River, NJ: Pearson Education.

Konnikova, M. (2013). *Mastermind: How to think like Sherlock Holmes*. New York: Viking.

Kovach, B., and Rosenstiel, T. (2011). *Blur*. New York: Bloomsbury USA.

Kuhl, P., et al. (2016). "Neuroimaging of the bilingual brain: Structural brain correlates of listening and speaking in a second language." *Brain and Language* 162, 1–9.

Lang, J. (2008). *On course*. San Francisco: Jossey-Bass.

Lang, J. (2016). *Small teaching*. San Francisco: Jossey-Bass.

Levenson, M. (2018). *The Humanities and everyday life*. New York: Oxford University Press.

Lorenzo, M., Crouch, C. H., and Mazur, E. (2006). "Reducing the gender gap in the physics classroom." *American Journal of Physics* 74:2, 118–22.

Lukianoff, G., and Haidt, J. (2018). *The Coddling of the American mind*. New York: Penguin Press.

Macaulay Honors College. (n.d.). "People of New York City." https://macaulay .cuny.edu/academics/nyc-seminars/people-of-new-york-city/.

Manguel, A. (2015). *Curiosity*. New Haven, CT: Yale University Press.

Mazur, E. (1997). *Peer instruction*. Englewood Cliffs, NJ: Prentice-Hall.

McKeachie, W. J., and Svinicki, M. D. (2014). *McKeachie's teaching tips*. Belmont, CA: Wadsworth.

McKinney, M. (2006). "Learning your students' names." *Tomorrow's Professor* 752.

Milkova, S. (n.d.). "Strategies for effective lesson planning," in *University of Michigan GSI Guidebook*. University of Michigan, Center for Research on Learning and Teaching. http://www.crlt.umich.edu/sites/default/files /instructor_resources/strategies_for_effective_lesson_planning.pdf.

Moon, J. A. (2004). *A Handbook of reflective and experiential learning*. New York: Routledge Falmer.

Newkirk, T. (2017). *Embarrassment and the emotional underlife of learning*. Portsmouth, NH: Heinemann.

Newkirk, T., and Miller, C., eds. (2009). *The Essential Don Murray*. Portsmouth, NH: Boynton/Cook/Heinemann.

Nisbett, R. (2015). *Mindware*. New York: Farrar, Straus and Giroux.

O'Neil, C. (2016). *Weapons of math destruction: How big data increases inequality and threatens democracy*. New York: Broadway Books.

Paff, L. (2015). "Coaching strategies to enhance online discussions." *Faculty Focus*, March 23. https://www.facultyfocus.com/articles/online-education /coaching-strategies-to-enhance-online-discussions/.

Patel, V. (2018). "One way to be a better mentor to grad students? Try an advising statement." *Chronicle of Higher Education*, October 10.

Pauk, W. (2001). *How to study in college*, 7th ed. Boston: Houghton Mifflin.

Pink, D. (2011). *Drive*. New York: Riverhead.

Postman, N. (1996). *The End of education*. New York: Random House.

Prince, M. J. (2004). "Does active learning work? A Review of the research." *Journal of Engineering Education* 93:3, 223–31.

Ramirez-Esparza, N., Garcia-Sierra, A., and Kuhl, P. K. (2017). "Look who's talking now! Parentese speech, social context, and language development across time." *Frontiers in Psychology* 8: article 1008.

Reynolds, G. (2011). *Presentation Zen*, 2nd ed. Berkeley, CA: New Riders, 2011.

Ritchhart, R., Church, M., and Morrison, K. (2011). *Making thinking visible*. San Francisco: Jossey-Bass.

Savarese, R. J. (2018). *See it feelingly*. Durham, NC: Duke University Press.

Scholes, R. (1989). *Protocols of reading*. New Haven, CT: Yale University Press.

Schwabish, J. (2017). *Better presentations*. New York: Columbia University Press.

Schwartz, M. (n.d.). "Best practices in experiential learning." Ryerson University, Learning and Teaching Office. https://www.ryerson.ca/content/dam /lt/resources/handouts/ExperientialLearningReport.pdf.

Sexton, J. (2019). *Standing for reason*. New Haven, CT: Yale University Press.

Sigmon, R. L. (1979). "Service-learning: Three principles." *Synergist* 8:1(Spring), 9–11.

Sigmon, R. L. (1994). *Serving to learn, learning to serve: Linking service with learning*. Washington, DC: Council of Independent Colleges.

Smith, G. A. (2008). "First-day questions for the learner-centered classroom." *National Teaching and Learning Forum* 17(5), 1–4.

Smith, G. A. (2014). "Student resistance to active learning? Connect your approach to what learners value."

Stewart, I. (2013.) *The Mathematics of life*. New York: Basic Books.

Stone, D., and Heen, S. (2015). *Thanks for the feedback: The Science and art of receiving feedback well*. New York: Penguin.

Thoreau, H. D. (1854/1989). *A Week on the Concord and Merrimack Rivers / Walden: Or Life in the woods / The Maine woods / Cape Cod*. New York: Library of America.

University of Tennessee at Knoxville, Teaching and Learning Innovation. (n.d.). "Experience Learning: The Twelve Types of Experiential Learning." experiencelearning.utk.edu/types.

Vanderbilt University, Center for Teaching. (n.d.). "Discussions." https://cft
.vanderbilt.edu//cft/guides-sub-pages/discussions/.

Wachter-Boettcher, S. (2017). *Technically wrong: Sexist apps, biased algorithms, and other threats of toxic tech*. New York: W. W. Norton & Co.

Wagner, T. (2012). *Creating innovators*. New York: Scribner.

Walvoord, B., and Anderson, V. (1998). *Effective grading: A Tool for learning and assessment*. San Francisco: Jossey-Bass.

Weiman, C. E. (2014). "Large-scale comparison of science teaching methods sends a clear message." *Proceedings of the National Academy of Sciences (PNAS)*, 111:23, 819–32.

Weimer, M. (1999). *Improving your classroom teaching*. Newbury Park, CA: Sage Publications.

Weimer, M. (2015a). "Nine ways to improve class discussions." *The Teaching Professor*, September 30. https://www.teachingprofessor.com/topics/for -those-who-teach/nine-ways-to-improve-class-discussions/.

Weimer, M. (2015b). "Are we clear? Tips for crafting better explanations." *The Teaching Professor*, November 18. https://www.teachingprofessor.com /topics/for-those-who-teach/are-we-clear-tips-for-crafting-better -explanations/.

Whitaker, A. (2016). *Art thinking*. New York: Harper Business.

White, E. B. (1977). *Essays of E. B. White*. New York: Harper & Row.

White, E. B., and Strunk, W. (2000). *The Elements of style*, 4th ed. New York: Penguin.

Wiggins, G., and McTighe, J. (2007). *Understanding by design*. Danvers, MA: ASCD.

Willingham, D. (2009). *Why don't students like school? A Cognitive scientist answers questions about how the mind works and what it means for the classroom*. San Francisco: Jossey-Bass.

Willingham, D. T. (2012). *When can you trust the experts?* San Francisco: Jossey-Bass.

Wolf, M. (2018). *Reader, come home*. New York: HarperCollins.

Wurdinger, S. D. (2005). *Using experiential learning in the classroom*. Lanham, MD: Scarecrow Education.

Wurdinger, S. D., and Priest, S. (1999). "Integrating theory and education in experiential learning." In J. C. Miles and S. Priest, eds., *Adventure programming*, 187–92. State College, PA: Venture.

Index

abstract conceptualization abilities, 146

active experimentation abilities, 146

active learning: agency and, 46–47; applications of, 57; benefits of, 43–44; challenges of, 44–45; definition of, 42; employing, 16–17; getting student buy-in for, 45–46; key principles of, 68–71; in productive study habits, 65; relevance and, 55–57; with scientific teaching, 58–60; suggestions for using, 54–55; techniques for, 42–43, 47–54; template for, 219–20; visualization in, 137. *See also* experiential learning; service learning

activities: classroom, 151; experiential, 150–51; external, 151; kinds of, 155; of lessons, 37–38; pre-writing, 171–72

advertisement analysis, grading rubric for, 225–26

agency, active learning and, 46–47

Alexander, B., 137–38

alignment, 28–29

Ambrose, Susan, 15

analytic rubrics, 209, 210

analyzing, 81, 182, 188, 223; in explanations, 75; template for, 223; text, 123, 199, 226

anchoring, 194–95

Anderson, Virginia, 204–5

Angelo, Thomas, 48, 199–200, 201–2

annotating, 161–63, 165

Annotation Studio (MIT), 135

Appiah, Kwame Anthony, 183

application, 2, 17

apprenticeships, 153

argument metaphor, 41

Ariely, Dan, 95

Aristotle, 99, 146

Art Thinking (Whitaker), 215

assessment, 199–200; aligning with course goals, 29; applications for, 211;

characteristics matrices in, 201; characteristics of, 200; definition of, 199; of lessons, 38; as meaningful feedback, 202–3; pro-con grids in, 200–201; problem recognition and problem solution tasks in, 201–2; of syllabus, 32–33, 35–36

assignments, 124, 161; creating for audience, 135–36; grading, 204–7; with real-world applications, 14; scaffolded, 141. *See also* writing assignments

Atkinson, Cliff, 111

attitudinal change, 148

autonomy, in motivation, 9–10

availability bias, 195

background knowledge, 48, 67, 101–2, 214

backward design, 26, 104, 177–78; for lessons, 37–38; three-point approach to, 26–29

bad habits, 193–95

Barell, John, 19

Barkley, E. F., 109

Bean, John, 124

Beckett, Samuel, 72

The Beginning of Infinity (Deutsch), 77

Berthoff, Ann E., 2, 183

Better Presentations (Schwabish), 112

Beyond Bullet Points (Atkinson), 111

biases, 193–95; in grading, 207; unconscious, 194

binary thinking, 93, 195

black hat analysis, 200

blaming, 195

blind-spot bias, 194

blogging platforms, 131

blogs, 90

Blur (Kovach, Rosenstiel), 143

Bok, Derek, 1–2, 3

Boser, Ulrich, 213–14

Botstein, Leon, 2, 18

CPSIA information can be obtained
at www.ICGtesting.com
Printed in the USA
LVHW111929221222
735793LV00008B/1127